THE VATICAN
MOSCOW
WASHINGTON
ALLIANCE

BOOKS BY AVRO MANHATTAN

(All are currently out of print)

The Catholic Church in the 20th Century
The Vatican in World Politics
Spain and the Vatican
Latin American and the Vatican
Catholic Power Today
The Vatican and the U.S.A.
The Dollar and the Vatican
The Vatican Billions
Religion in Russia
Religious Terror in Ireland
The Vatican in Asia
Terror Over Europe
Terror Over Yugoslavia
Vatican Imperialism in the Twentieth Century

THE VATICAN MOSCOW WASHINGTON ALLIANCE

AVRO MANHATTAN

Published by Chick Publications
P.O. Box 662, Chino, CA 91710
Printed in the United States of America

I.S.B.N.: 0-937958-12-3

Contents

Preface

1. Guns in St. Peter's Square, Rome   17

2. Birth of the Vatican-Washington Alliance   20

3. Mysterious Death of Two Popes.   26

4 Plots in the Conclave   31

5. A Pope of the People   36

6. The Bishop Who Knew Too Much   40

7. Murders in the Vatican   46

8. First Joint Vatican-Washington Operation   53

9. Papal Master-Plan for a Catholic Counter Revolution   58

10. The Pope-U.S. Presidential Hot Line   63

11. The Vatican and the Cold War   71

12. The Swastika and the Triple Tiara   81

13. The Missing Testament of a Dying Pope   88

14. De Gaulle and the Envoy "Extraordinaire"   100

15. The Vatican-Washington Axis   109

16. Stalin's Plan for a Red Papacy   119

17. The Pontiff Who "Opened the Window"   134

18. *Red Flag Over the Vatican*   146

19. *Election of a Pink Pope*   161

20. *The Countermine That Failed*   171

21. *Red Hat vs. Red Tiara*   180

22. *Soviet Spies and Vatican ''Observers''*   190

23. *The Vatican's Watch on Israel*   209

24. *Russian Dossier on Three Popes*   223

25. *The First Historical Compromise*   235

26. *Cardinals and Commissars*   246

27. *From Christ the King to Christ the Worker*   260

28. *A Marxist Pope?*   271

29. *Castros in Cassocks*   283

30. *A Red Jesus for Black Africa*   300

31. *The Cross, the Hammer and Sickle, and the Latin American Revolution*   316

32. *The Threat to America*   327

33. *The Future Wars of Religions and Armageddon*   347

Pope Pius XII · Pope John Paul II · Pope John XXIII

Preface

As the White House in Washington is the symbol of the U.S., and the Kremlin in Moscow of the Soviet Union, so the Vatican in Rome is that of the Catholic Church. While the first is identified with the economic dynamism of the West, and the second with the revolutionary dogmas of Marxism, the third is the political facet of a religion claiming to be the only repository of truth. Because of that, the Vatican will side with one or the other, or indeed with anybody else, as long as it can further its own influence.

The pattern has been one of historical consistency. Early in this century, for instance, it sided with the Empires of Monarchical Europe; after World War I, it sustained the Fascist Dictatorships; following World War II, it fanned the Cold War by supporting the U.S. against Soviet Russia; after the Vietnam War, it sided with Soviet Russia against the U.S. In the eighties it has struck another working partnership with the U.S.

The creation of the last two major partnerships became identified, one as the Vatican-Moscow alliance, and the other as the Vatican-Washington alliance. While to each superpower the alliance was an individual partnership with the Vatican, to the Vatican, both alliances were but the organic components of a far wider pattern in which they were considered as one single unit, as far as their long term grand strategy was concerned.

The obvious ambiguity of the Vatican-Moscow-Washington alliance, therefore, although a political contradiction, nevertheless was a political reality, with the capacity to further the interests of the Catholic Church, within and outside the two superpowers.

When seen in this light, consequently, the Vatican-Moscow alliance of yesterday, no less than Vatican-Washington alliance of today, can be assessed for what they really are; partnerships meant to benefit not Moscow or Washington, but the Catholic Church. Nowadays the latter is manipulating left-wing ideologies as skillfully as she did right-wing movements prior to and during World War II.

What prompts her to employ the former, just now? The sober

fact that almost half of mankind is already under communist rule. In her opinion, it is only a matter of time before the rest of the world will follow suit.

To meet the challenge of the forthcoming communist take-over of pre- and post-World War III, she has already formulated a long term strategy of her own: the creation of a peculiar new brand of Catholicised Communism. Its launching was done under the protective wings of the Vatican-Washington alliance itself. It has since been mainly identified with the grand scale implantation of Catholic Marxism in the very back yard of the U.S., namely in Latin America.

Liberation Theology is not an abstraction. It is a most devastatingly novel doctrine. Currently it is subverting most of the South American Continent with the most successful experiment ever undertaken by the new Catholic Marxian revolution.

Its potential for total socio-economic disintegration is comparable with the Bolshevik cataclysm of 1917 in Russia. The most striking difference between the two is that whereas the latter had been inspired by Lenin preaching Karl Marx, the former is being carried out under the aegis of Christ, holding the hammer and the sickle.

The injection of Marxist tenets into Roman Catholicism is meant to undermine the economic and social structures of the lands where it is preached. The election of a pope, John Paul II, hailing from a Communist Catholic country like Poland, is the clearest indication of the course along which the Catholic Church now has so decisively embarked.

Catholic Marxism, although theologically conservative, is a sure formula for world revolution. It is the most dangerous ideological imponderable to emerge in the Western World in recent years. Its ultimate objective is the partial overthrow of the current world order, as a preparatory step for the advent of a Catholicised world communism. In a society doomed to collapse, Marxist Catholicism would thus turn the Vatican into a global, super-religious, ideological imperative whose capacity to withstand both the U.S. and Soviet Russia would be second to none.

The potential outbreak of World War III, far from hampering, would help to further its expansionistic dreams. Wars in our times have invariably begotten communism. World War I produced Communist Russia. World War II produced Communist China. Regional wars since then have produced communist regimes in Africa and in Asia. World War III will produce a communist world. When that happens the Catholic Church will have produced a communist Christianity of her own. This she will use as the most suitable ideology with which to force herself, not only upon Catholic countries, but also upon those which are not.

What will be the role of the Catholic Church in a world where the hammer and the sickle has replaced the cross, where Lenin has supplanted Christ, where Bolshevism has taken the place of Christianity, and where God has been substituted by contemporary Man? The role she will play will be simplicity itself; the Leninisation of Christ, and the Catholicisation of Lenin.

"Ubi Lenin, ibi Jerusalem" (Where Lenin is, there is Jerusalem) is her newest motto. For today, and even more for tomorrow. The motto is ominous, for Protestantism, for the Orthodox Church, for the Evangelical Churches, for the whole of Christianity; also for any nations like the U.S.; indeed for the Western World itself, and beyond.

By adopting a Catholicised Marxism, the Catholic Church has launched into the contemporary world the most insidiously destructive religio-ideological imponderable the like of which has never been seen since the emergence of either Bolshevism or Fascism. Its contribution to the near future will be not only the destabilisation of the balance of power between the U.S. and the Soviet Union, but equally the mounting exacerbation of the conflict.

The ever widening gulf between the two will spell the emergence of the Catholic church as a global superpower in her own right.

The maximisation of such paramountcy will lead to the minimisation of any opposition to her. Hence individual and collective coercion will emerge against anyone, men, movements or nations not conforming with her.

The objectives at stake are immense, encompassing as they do the society of today and the world of tomorrow. Her current alliances, first with Moscow and then with Washington, are the clearest indication that she is still using both to prepare for her own forthcoming imperium.

To ensure its establishment, she will stop at nothing. Machiavellian manipulations and international intrigues are as justifiable to her as the rigging of papal elections, the "elimination" of ecclesiastics, and indeed, the accelerated physical demise of contemporary popes. Witness that of Pope John Paul I, who died a mysterious death after only thirty three days of reign; or the election of a Polish pope, whose elevation to the papacy has been reckoned to have been no less mysterious.

The whole background of secretive operations, activated by the Soviet and U.S. intelligence machineries currently operating behind the Vatican's most recent political partnership, the Vatican-Washington alliance, in the twilight world of global ideological warfare, could hardly be credible had they not been substantiated by hard factual evidence.

This book should help to elucidate the objectives and nature of their most recent activities, now in full swing.

Avro Manhattan

PUBLISHER'S NOTE

We prayerfully chose the works of Avro Manhattan to shed light on Bible prophecy in history and to strengthen our publications which expose the great whore of Revelation, chapters 17 and 18. The works of Avro Manhattan appear on the index of forbidden books in the Vatican. Even his life has been in jeopardy.

It was not by accident that we were to publish the works of Avro Manhattan. The Lord placed Dr. Rivera in London in 1967 to meet with this distinguished historian. Mr. Manhattan attended a meeting of brave and faithful Christians who knew that Dr. Rivera had been a Jesuit priest working in Vatican intelligence. There Dr. Rivera gave his testimony for the first time after he was saved.

Dr. Rivera confirms the information printed in this book as being factual. He also knew some of the sources. He was also aware of the Jesuits' slander and fabrications concerning liberalism and atheism made against Avro Manhattan to discredit his works.

The Lord gave us this book along with others to witness to the truth that we have printed about the "mother of abominations." We must alert Christians to the need to reach the lost Roman Catholics. We must show them that they must turn to Jesus Christ as their own Savior by grace through faith.

J. T. C.

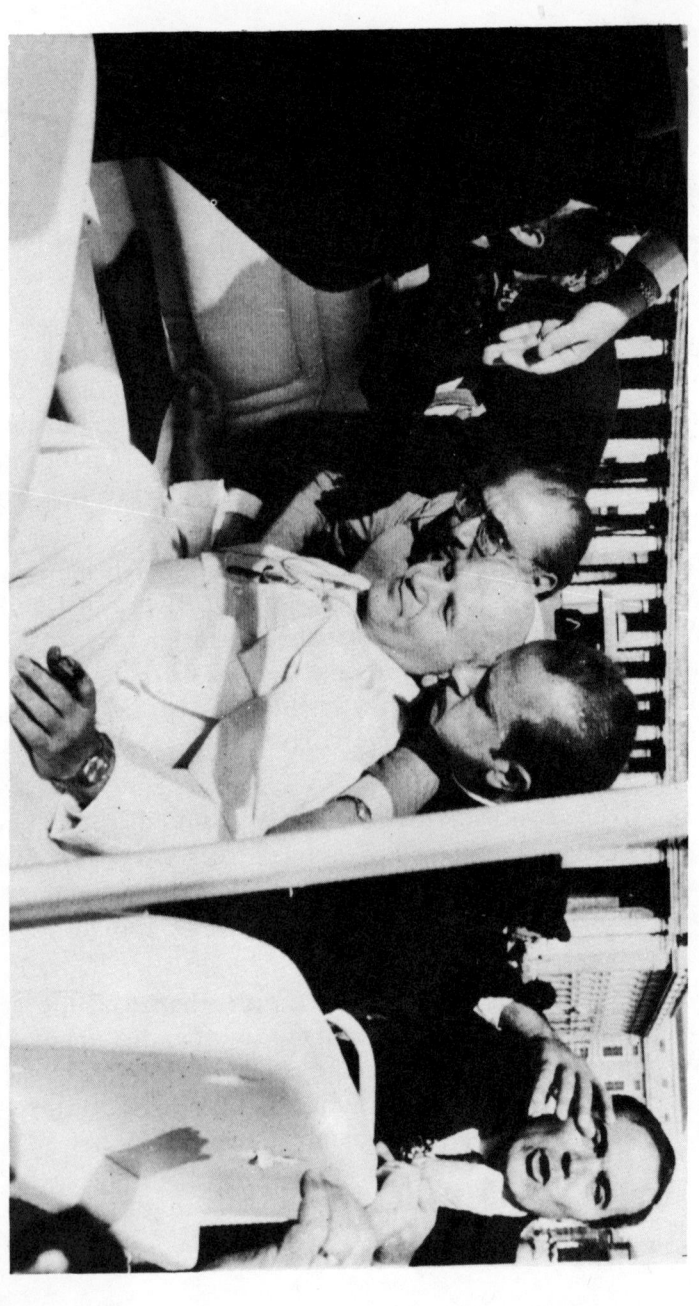

Blood on his hands, Pope John Paul II is assisted by aides in St. Peter's Square moments after he was shot May 13, 1981.

CHAPTER 1

Guns In St. Peter's Square, Rome

One sunny day, May 1981, as Pope John Paul II was blessing the crowds in St. Peter's Square, Rome, gun shots were heard. "Why did they do it?" he asked, before collapsing, seemingly mortally wounded.

This question was repeated at once by millions, all over the world.

A few weeks before, on March 30th, U.S. President Reagan also had been shot and badly wounded. Yet the deed was viewed almost universally as a sine qua non of the presidential office.

Why the contrast?

Because, whereas the power of the American President derives from the economic and military might of the U.S., that of the Pope stems from a great intangible: religion.

In the eyes of hundreds of millions of believers, the Pope is the Vicar of Christ on earth, the visible head of the Catholic Church, also their supreme spiritual leader. Because of that, he claims that he cannot remain neutral in conflicts which deal with the rights and the wrongs of modern man. Hence he supports or opposes certain contemporary ideologies, purporting to champion or to suppress the most basic human aspirations.

The imponderability of such a religious stance gives him an influence transcending that of any nation or group of nations. And since the earth is split into two belligerent cultures, one polarised, mostly in the western and the other mainly in the communist world, it follows that the pope becomes a political leader of the first magnitude, on a par with those of the U.S. and Soviet Russia.

Therefore, by exerting an influence equal to that of Washington and Moscow, he can easily help to sway the balance of power between the two even when acting merely as a seemingly impartial arbiter. Thanks to this, he can affect the gravest issues on local and global levels, his intervention being potentially capable of modifying the political fortunes of Europe, the Americas or the Socialist countries, not to mention those of the Third World.

The more so, since in addition to his religious authority, numerically he can outnumber both the U.S.A. and Soviet Russia, with their 240 and 275 millions respectively. His catholic adherents are nearing the 800 millions, most of them scattered in the key nations of the two most influential continents of the world. Hence the importance of the right pope being elected at the right moment, for the right objective, for the right ideology, and thus, for the right superpower.

Seen in this light, therefore, the answer to the wounded John Paul II, could not have been clearer. A superpower had attempted to eliminate a pope whom they had considered as the political ally of their ideological opponent.

The Conclave which had elected him after having assessed the ideological stance of the two hostile rivals, had found one of them wanting. That is, the one he had either offended or opposed.

The Cardinals who had chosen Pope John Paul I, his predecessor, had also made their choice in accordance with such criteria. As a result John Paul I's elections appeased one superpower by championing a current world ideology, and automatically thwarted the interests of the other. It could not be otherwise. Since the two papal elections, by contributing to the creation of an ever widening gulf between two opposite cultures, that of the U.S.A. and Europe, and that of Soviet Russia and her Marxist satellites, had provoked an unprecedented reaction in both, each having seen in the two popes either a potential ally, or a perilous foe.

In either case the magnitude of the objectives at stake, and the pressure of world events had made it imperative for the rival superpowers to act with the utmost ruthlessness to tip the papal balance in their favor.

Because of the above, the target of their activities became the same: the elimination of one pontiff, who, by having supported one given ideology, had incurred the hostility of the other. That spelled not only the ideological identification with any particular pontificate, but equally the necessity of the physical elimination of the pope who had embodied it, as the necessary corollary of a papal strategy with which he had identified himself.

Thus, while Pope John Paul I, the herald of a seemingly non-political compromise pontificate, died a "sudden" and unexplained death soon after his elevation, his successor Pope John Paul II, the initiator of an uncharted ideological campaign, was gunned down by a superpower he had set to oppose. The lethal drug used in the "liquidation" of the first pope, like the bullets fired during the attempted assassination of the second, being but the tip of the iceberg beneath which the hostile religio-political counter-currents were operating within the secretive walls of the Vatican.

CHAPTER 2

Birth Of The Vatican-Washington Alliance

Following a very active day during which Pope John Paul I dealt
cheerfully with papal business, some of which included appointments and replacements in the hierarchy of the Church, he gave a
final brisk order to Cardinal Baggio for the removal from his See of
Cardinal Cody of Chicago, and then he retired to his bedroom at
about 10:30 as usual.

"He was tremendously alert and in a wonderful frame of
mind," declared Patriarch Maxim Hakim, another prelate who had
been with the Pope that same afternoon, "The very picture of
health."

At 3:30 in the morning a taxi driver noticed a light in the papal
chamber. At 4:30 his nun housekeeper left a cup of coffee outside

The body of Pope John Paul I is carried across St. Peter's Square as thousands gather to see him. After an outdoor funeral, he was buried October 4, 1978.

the door. When at 5:30 the Pope failed to appear and his secretary called on him, he was dead.

"His face was serene, his smile still visible," it was announced. "He died peacefully, holding in his hands a devotional book, 'The Imitation of Christ.'"

Almost simultaneously another Vatican source disclosed that Pope John Paul I had retired carrying "sensitive" documents. One of these, it was confirmed, was a paper dealing with the impending removal of controversial Archbishop Cody of Chicago.

Soon afterwards, however, it was asserted that far from holding "The Imitation of Christ", the Pope's hands, like his body, were level with the floor. Someone had even tried to massage his heart. The papal doctor's verdict was unequivocally blunt: "John Paul I perished between 10:30 and 11:00 the previous evening of a "massive heart attack."

The news stunned the world.

His rule had lasted only 33 days.

"Murdered," was the almost unanimous reaction. When immediately afterwards pressing demand for an official investigation and even an "autopsy" were inexplicably refused, the suspicion became a certainty.

"Why and by whom?" it was asked.

The manner of his death had the hallmark of an "intelligence" operation. Its timing that of a political motivation.

The latter was reckoned at once to have been the most likely. It was assumed that pressing ideological consideration had been responsible for the Pope's sudden demise. Probably, it was said, because his pontificate had been assessed as a disestablishing political factor by certain interested parties inside and outside the Vatican. The speculation was not as farfetched as it sounded. It had a solid base of reality.

After the death of Paul VI (6th August 1978), a pope who had pursued a policy of cooperation with Russia, the choice of his successor became of supreme importance for both the supporters and the opponents of his policy. Whereas Paul VI's followers began a vigorous lobby for the election of a pro-Russian pope, their rivals wanted the opposite, a pro-American, or at least a "non-committed'' pope.

At the conclave which followed, the two parties were soon locked into two immovable solid blocks. The stalemate was finally broken by the Cardinal Suenens of Belgium who suggested a compromise. That envisaged the nomination of a politically naive candidate, Cardinal Luciani, the Patriarch of Venice.

The candidature, which surprised everybody beginning with the candidate himself, following the dexterous manipulation of lobbying and votes, carried the day. Luciani was elected Pope John Paul I. When immediately afterwards, Cardinal Suenens, his sponsor, asked Luciani whether he would accept the papacy or whether he would refuse it, Luciani still in a bewildered daze, said yes. ''Holy Father,'' replied Cardinal Suenens, ''Thank you for saying yes.''

''Perhaps it would have been better if I had said no,'' the new Pope had answered, a most prophetic comment soon to be proved right.

The election of John Paul I as a compromise pope was interpreted at once on political terms as a stunning defeat for those who had opposed the pro-Russian policies of the deceased Paul VI. The latter, a powerful group of ecclesiastic and lay interests, had emerged before Paul's death as an active opposition within the Curia itself, tacitly supported by the U.S.

The Curia-CIA coalition

Cardinals in Rome and elsewhere, having formulated a policy of opposition to Paul VI, jointly with high prelates in key positions in Europe and the Americas, had formed a kind of secretive but effective alliance with the most influential intelligence agencies of the U.S. Amongst these were the Directorate of the CIA, the Central Security Agency, the special strategic wing of the Pentagon, and other policy formulators of the American Administration.

The Curia-CIA Coalition had come into existence with the precise objective of neutralising the pro-communist policies of Paul VI commonly known as the Vatican-Moscow alliance.

The U.S., which had followed the alliance for years, had grown seriously alarmed at its progress, not only because of its accommodating attitude to an expanding world communism but because it had identified the Catholic Church with an offensively orientated Soviet Union determined to acquire the capacity to project its ideological and military presence around the world.

The Curia-CIA Coalition gave themselves a dual task:

a. The discreet sabotage of Paul VI's Vatican-Moscow alliance while he was still alive, and,

b. The promotion of the election of the next pope, following his death.

They began with an insidious campaign of denigration against Paul VI, a campaign which culminated in a persistent demand for his "resignation" as a pope. The world press, including a good portion of the Catholic press, followed suit. They were "providentially" helped by the "sudden" deterioration of the already frail health of the Pope. The deterioration was so unusual that ugly rumors concerning the "acceleration of his demise" circulated for a while after his death. The rumors were never substantiated.

The second Curia-CIA Coalition's objective however, was far the most vital: preliminary moves for the election of a pope who was willing to destroy the Vatican-Moscow alliance. But if the preparation for "their" pope was paramount, the instrument via which "their" new pontiff could destroy the alliance was even more so.

The alliance necessitated a powerful political substitute with which to fill the void once its links between the Vatican and Moscow had been severed. The Curia-CIA think-tank had already formulated one with such religious-ideological plausibility that it made the whole project politically acceptable and pragmatically viable. Their formula was simplicity itself: the rejection of Paul VI's Vatican-Moscow alliance, and its substitution with the sustenance of existing communist systems outside Soviet Russia.

But with two provisos:

a. that such systems became independent from Moscow, and

b. that they be tacitly activated by a dual Vatican-USA sponsorship with their operations inspired jointly by Rome and Washington.

The formula spelled the Vatican-American acceptance for the potential transformation of a vast portion of the socialist world into a Catholic-American sponsored communist condominium. Although, because of its unprecedented nature, it was a dangerous ideological imponderable, assessed from a pragmatic stance it was a political masterstroke.

Thus it effectively encouraged the repressed nationalist aspirations of the satellite regimes within the Soviet zone (such as those in Eastern Europe), it facilitated the strategic commitment of the Pentagon, while simultaneously debilitating those of Soviet Russia. Last but not least, it counter-matched the messianic objectives of a menacingly expanding Soviet imperialism.

The first operation inspired by the newly born Vatican-Washington alliance was launched almost immediately after the election of a Curia-CIA sponsored Pope, John Paul II, as we shall see presently.

CHAPTER 3

Mysterious Death Of Two Popes

When the pro-Russian Cardinals inside the Conclave of August 1978, outsmarted the Curia-CIA Coalition with the election of a "non-political" pope, John Paul I, the Coalition set in earnest to "neutralise" his pontificate. The task appeared insurmountable. The "wrong" pontiff was firmly upon Peter's throne. A new papal reign, manipulated by pro-Soviet cardinals, had already been set in motion. As for its duration, that depended upon the length (or the shortness) of the life of the new pope.

Since the conventional policy of patient opposition was useless, the urgency of the ultimate objective necessitated the prompt formulation of a most ruthless policy. This was considered, seconded and set in motion within days of John Paul I's election.

Its linchpin rested upon the termination of the rule of John Paul I. But since that depended upon either the "resignation", or the problematic event of his death (two unlikely occurrences) its promoters decided upon a daring operation: John Paul I's physical demise.

In less turbulent times the project would have been unacceptable. And even today it sounds unjustifiably dramatic. Yet when colossal political interests are at stake, they make such a proposition plausible; indeed, a dire necessity.

That this is not idle speculation was proved by the suspicious death of another Pope, Pius XI, before World War II. Then, like now, the stakes were immense. The dilemma similar. The only difference was that, instead of a menacing Soviet Russia, the world was faced by an aggressive Nazi Germany.

The support or opposition of the Catholic Church was vital. At the beginning Pius XI had welcomed Fascism as the most effective opponent of communism and called Mussolini the man sent by Divine Providence. Afterwards, however, realising how he and Hitler were heading for war, he warned the Church against the two dictators.

Concerned about the effect of the papal warning, Mussolini, at the instigation of Hitler, sought to prevent it from becoming public. The Pope who had already written, and indeed printed, his message, suddenly got ill. He died soon afterwards. (See Chapter 13, The Missing Testament of a Dying Pope.)

The rumors that Pius XI had been poisoned were never substantiated. Yet, the credence was firmly held by some of Pius XI's closest friends, one, a prelate second only to the Pope himself, Cardinal Tisserant, Dean of the Sacred College of Cardinals.

Cardinal Tisserant kept a secret diary about the events of those fateful days. The diary was so compromising, that he gave strict instructions it should be taken away from the Vatican immediately after his death. He feared that, had it fallen into the hands of the Church, they would have been "doctored" or even destroyed.

Cardinal Tisserant held that one of Mussolini's physicians (the father of one of his mistresses), a familiar figure at the Vatican, had administered poisoned "injections" to the harassed Pius XI on direct order from Mussolini.

The doctor had had access to the papal bedchamber immediately after the death of Pius XI because he was in charge of the "embalming". The embalming factor, Cardinal Tisserant asserted, was the most plausible excuse to destroy any trace of the poisoning to avoid the possibility that an "autopsy" might reveal the true cause of death.

Notwithstanding it, the face of the deceased Pius XI showed bluish marks, unusual in death by natural causes. The same type of marks were also detected upon that of Pope Paul John I in 1978 and whose autopsy had been so inexplicably refused.

Another no less telling fact was that Cardinal Tisserant was told the Pope had been in a "grave condition" 49 minutes after he had actually been dead. (February 10th, 1939).

When Cardinal Tisserant died, February 21, 1972, his secret diaries were still considered so damning that they were transferred from France into a Swiss bank.

The death of Pius XI proved providential for the Nazis, since his successor Pope Pius XII, a former Nuncio to Germany who had helped Hitler into power, pursued such an ambivalent policy that he sided with Germany, even if tacitly, during the most delicate periods of World War II.

The accelerated demise of Pius XI, in short, had become a necessity for the pursuance of the interest of the superpower of his time. The "demise" had been carried out to permit the attainment of two objectives:

a. The riddance of a hostile pope.

b. The election of a new cooperative pope as his successor.

Two other popes were made to die in similar circumstances during the 18th century for having gone against the establishment of their times. One was by the very Jesuits who necessitated "the right pope" the better to carry out their political objectives, as we shall see in another chapter. Which goes to prove that the unnatural demise of a pontiff was not the prerogative of the twentieth century.

The silent murder of Pope John Paul I

As with Pope Pius XI, who had to be removed for having become an obstacle to the prosecution of the aggressive policies of Nazi Germany on 1939, so also with Pope John Paul I, for having become an impediment to the prosecution of an anti-Russian policy in 1978.

The smooth prosecution needed the removal of its main obstacle, the reigning pope. Hence the necessity for the anti-Russian coalition, and behind them, of the superpower for which they operated, to reach a radical decision: the "neutralisation" of the new pontificate, in other words, the "liquidation" of John Paul I.

Assessed in such light, therefore, their operation was neither unprecedented or even less exceptional. Indeed, in the eyes of the superpower which was operating behind them, the feat had become a dire, urgent necessity. An assessment, which only less than three years later in 1981, the other rival superpower had also reached when it tried to assassinate Pope John Paul II, whom they had come to consider as inimical to their policies.

Although the operation against John Paul I was a risky one, since it could have provoked serious reverberation had it failed, yet it was certainly not anything beyond the capability of the "intelligence" apparatus of any committed comtemporary superpower.

"Sensitive" liquidation of embarassing people, nowadays, are factual facets of almost any administration. Intelligence apparati are part and parcel of small and large nations and it is an unpalatable truth that they are used more often than admitted.

To most of them, crude violence and firearms are taboo. Chemical formulae are more efficient and silent. Many leave no trace in the organism, allowing the conclusion that death is a natural one. The most sophisticated are disguised as heart attacks.

A typical case occurred in London, England, shortly before Pope John Paul I's death. Georgi Markov, a Bulgarian defector and a BBC broadcaster, one day was "accidentally" pricked by the umbrella of a stranger at a bus-stop. The umbrella had a poison-pellet no bigger than a pinhead. The combined work of detectives, metallurgists, pathologists and toxicologists discovered that the poison which had killed Markov was "ricin". This is one of the five most toxic materials known; the others being tetanus, botulinus, diptheria and gramicidin.

One grain of ricin is enough to kill about 36,000 people. It can be fatally injected, swallowed, or just inhaled. It has the ability to cause very strong agglutination of the red cells. Since ricin is almost impossible to detect in the body, it makes the ideal weapon for any "accelerated" demised.

Devices more impossible to detect even than ricin nowadays are to be found in the silent arsenals of most countries of the world. Political targets can be liquidated via a "seemingly" natural prolonged heart ailment, or via sudden "natural" heart failure. When prepared in advance, not only are they undetectable, death is attributed to ordinary disease.

Once those who had planned to remove Pope John Paul I had decided to do so, they set the twilight world of the "accelerated" natural demise technique into motion. The result was seen soon afterwards when the newly elected Pope, following a day of cheerful activities, was found unexpectedly dead after only 33 days of pontificate, one of the shortest in almost 2000 years of Church history.

The spontaneous reaction "they have murdered him" was never confirmed. The agency which caused his death was never discovered.

Yet the political reality was a stark one. The Church now needed a papal successor, and that's precisely what the formulators of the alternative new Vatican idelogical strategy had wanted.

From then onwards what they had to do was simplicity itself: "rig" the election, and with the support of the superpower for which they were operating, nominate "their" pope.

CHAPTER 4

Plots In The Conclave

After John Paul I's death, the Conclave reconvened to elect a new pope, the second within two months. This time, however, unlike before, the name of the papal candidate was already on the lips of some of the leading members of the Curia-CIA Coalition: Karol Wojtyla of Krakow, Poland, a communist satellite of Soviet Russia.

Their vigorous lobbying, which made of the new Conclave one of the shortest in recent times, yielded startling results almost at once. In contrast to its shortness, it might not be amiss here to mention the longest. This occured in 1268 after the death of another "foreign" pope, Clement IV, when the Cardinals, after retiring in the Conclave in Viterbo, could not make up their minds whether to elect an Italian or another "foreign" candidate.

The excess of political intrigues made the Cardinals so dilatory that finally the city's authorities, prompted by Saint Bonaventure, locked up all the members of the Sacred College inside a recently erected papal palace, put them on short commons, and removed the roof.

The result was so swift that they elected a new pope so admirable that afterwards he was beatified as St. Gregory X.

In the Conclave of October 1978, the Cardinals behaved almost with the same exemplary swiftness, not because of the removal of the roof but because a secret cabala had already masterminded the election of "their candidate."

Considering the difficulties of the previous Conclave, the election appeared almost as a miracle. From the initial five votes with which they started, in favor of a "seemingly" non-candidate the Cardinal of Krakow, they got a dozen. And then from there in ever quicker succession to 90, well over the 75 required for the election. That evening, October 16, 1978, Karol Wojtyla became Pope John Paul II, the first non-Italian since 1532.

The Curia-CIA coalition exulted in a triumph whose magnitude not even they had expected. The victory had exceeded their hopes. And they thanked not only the Holy Spirit, but also the memory of another pope, Pope John XXIII, who only 20 years before had also made a radical break with the past.

If their reverence for Pope John XXIII was due to his revolutionary pontificate, however, it was due no less to the mechanics of his successful election, mechanics which the sponsors of Wojtyla had diligently studied.

The difficulties had been uncunningly similar, a massive conservative opposition determined to block the election of a "progressive."

During the Conclave which followed the death of arch right-wing Pope Pius XII, the Cardinals had split into two irremovable blocks: the conservatives who wanted to carry on the pro-U.S., anti-Russian policy of Pius XII, and the "progressives" who wanted its total abandonment.

The conservatives were headed by arch right-winger Cardinal

Ottaviani: the progressives by a group of "moderates." Two of the candidates of the latter were Cardinal Agagianian, born in Russia, and Cardinal Roncalli, the easygoing Patriarch of Venice.

Agagianian was so immensely popular that the Romans had already been calling him Pope Agagianian long before even the Conclave had met. He was supported by the Communists of Italy, and even more ominously by the Kremlin. (See Chapter 16, "Stalin's Plan For a Red Papacy.")

His candidature scared the moderates, and strengthened the conservatives. The Conclave became locked into an insoluble impasse. At this, a coalition of French Cardinals which had been working secretly for the promotion of "their" candidate, sprang unexpectedly into action by casting the necessary first five votes for Roncalli.

Agagianian at the next ballot lost a dozen votes almost at once. The conservatives, however, voted massively for reactionary Ottaviani, having considered Roncalli "uneligible." Soon a group of moderates joined the solid French block. By the fourth ballot, Roncalli gained again, the parties polarized, and were running neck and neck. On the fifth, non-candidate Roncalli had overtaken archreactionary Ottaviani, who lost by one single vote.

The election of Pope John XXIII, in short, had been due to a coalition of French Cardinals who had masterminded a determined anti-Pius XII, anti-American, and left-wing campaign, secretly briefed by anti-U.S., pro-Soviet Russia, General de Gaulle.

The mechanics had been simplicity itself: a purposeful block of votes as a starter, and the rest of the Cardinals, the majority of them traditionally undecided, will follow.

The formula had worked not only in 1958 with the election of Pope John XXIII, but also in 1978 with that of Pope John Paul I. Here again the two opposing blocks, pro-Russian and anti, had become so immovable that one of the leading members, Cardinal Suenens, in despair suggested the election of not one, but four popes simultaneously, one for each part of the world.

The suggestion was rejected for its unprecedented absurdity. Cardinal Suenens then formed a determined inner group, and copying the French tactics, suggested non-committed Luciani. Luciani's candidature was accepted, for reasons we shall see, and became Pope John Paul I.

In the Conclave which followed, the Curia-CIA Coalition imitated both the French precedent and Suenens. Having already selected "their candidate" they began their campaign with a determined blockbuster of five votes. The group, a vigorous anti-Russian cabala, soon attracted a wider group of Cardinals, mostly American, German, and Latin-American left-wingers, with a sprinkle of Italian.

One of the leading spirits was a notorious ideological wheeler-dealer, Cardinal Koenig of Vienna, a veteran of East European communism, seconded by Cardinal Suenens, John Paul I's godfather, supported by Polish born Jon Kroll of Philadelphia, Cardinal Stefan Wyszynski, Primate of Poland and Cody of Chicago, whose diocese had the largest and richest Polish community of the U.S., about 800,000.

Immediately after Wojtyla became Pope, Cody announced that John Paul II had been a very good friend of his, that he had spent 10 days as his guest in Poland, and even more telling, that he had had lunch with him "before" the Conclave. (The following year Cody was under Federal investigation, accused of having diverted about one million dollars of tax-exempt church funds to a woman friend. In early 1982 he declared he would resign in December, but died on April 25 instead.)

The five vote starter block, like its French precedent, set in motion a voting avalanche. A sizeable number of Germans joined at once with the result that in the second ballot Wojtyla got from 10 to 15 more votes. Soon afterwards, besides the Americans, the Cardinals of the Third World, an important section, came on their side, almost to a man.

The latter did so on several grounds: they wanted a pope who favored the Third World, without any Moscow tutelage, they supported the Liberation Theology, most of them being anti-western, and last, but not least, they depended financially on Germany and the U.S.

The lure of vast sums of money to come for the underdeveloped countries of Asia, Africa and the Latin Americas, the vigorous lobbying of Wojtyla's secret godfather, and the mechanics of the election did the rest. Wojtyla was elected and became Pope John Paul II.

CHAPTER 5

A Pope Of The People

It has been said that the success of the Curia-CIA Coalition in electing "their" man had been too easy, and that some kind of inner and external pressure must have been used to provoke the electoral stampede which created John Paul II. Also, that certain methods of "persuasion" had been used to force the cardinals who, prior to the five-vote blockbuster were mostly non-committed, to jump so massively upon the Wojtyla band wagon.

Both suggestions seem groundless since the three main voting blocks, already briefed by the Curia-CIA's members, could have carried the majority without any outside interference. Even so, rumors had it that the Conclave had been "bugged," the implication being that "intelligence" instructions had made the round between ballots to influence the various individuals and voting blocks to vote for one given candidate.

The rumors, although improbable, could have been justified, containing, as they did, a certain amount of truth. Fear that the Sistine Chapel and adjacent places might have been bugged had existed for years. Certain sections of the Vatican, in fact, had been bugged for decades by a number of nations anxious to know the Vatican's operation in ecclesiastic and political matters. Heading them are the Soviet Union, the U.S., Britain, France, West Germany, Israel and some unnamed agencies operating mostly for the Arab world.

While the usefulness of such mass detection is doubtful, attempts at "listening in" or at information "transference" have certainly been taking place in the very Conclave itself by individual cardinals. Before the age of the micro-transmitters, the methods employed were innocently primitive, indeed quaint. Witness the one used by one of the most notorious of such practitioners. American Cardinal Cushing never hid the fact that he had been in the habit of leaving each session of the Conclave with the exact totals of every ballot scribbled on the cuffs of his sleeves.

The election of a Polish pope in 1978 was a landmark, not so much because it broke a tradition but because the Church had entered into a political course full of imponderables.

As with Pope John XXIII, whose election started the left-wing stance which was to lead to the formation of the Vatican-Moscow alliance, so the election of Pope John Paul II signaled the initiation of another no less historical, religious ideological direction, which was to lead to the Vatican-Washington alliance.

Both popes, being radically minded, wanted and carried out a left-wing revolution.

Thus whereas John XXIII, a Pope "tailor-made" for the people, opened the door of cooperation with a Russian-orientated world communism, so John Paul II was instrumental in launching a Vatican-orientated world communism depending no longer on Moscow but Rome.

Pope John Paul II, perhaps even more than Pope John XXIII, had the qualifications for playing the role: rough physical frame, a non-intellectual Slavonic face, lack of sophistication in manner and theological matters, total absence of diplomatic skill, and above all, a tendency to play the lower instinct of the masses by the constant use of an istrionic populism that bordered almost on clowning.

Last, but not least, he hailed from Poland, a country noted for its archaic religiosity and national emotionalism, the two surest guarantors of genuine hatred against Russia, whether Czarist or communist.

Added to this he was a "pragmatic Marxist." During the two Conclaves, in fact, he had prided himself about openly reading Marxist publications, to the delight of the Cardinals of the Third World who noted the fact.

His own image as the anti-type of the conventional, theologically trained pontiff, skillfully projected by the mass media, fitted him well. Seminaries, conventional studies, diplomatic training, had been conspicuously alien to Wojtyla from early youth. Pope John Paul II's original ambition, in fact, had been to be, not a religious man, but an actor, something which Wojtyla himself openly confessed when already a Cardinal. "I trained for the stage as a young man," he admitted to J. Michener of the PBS series in 1977: "Yes, I wanted to be an actor."

His ambition had been so strong, that when he finally decided to become a priest and applied to the Carmelite Order, he was promptly rejected on the ground that his zeal was not for religion but for his theatrical profession.

During World War II, between 1939 and 1944, he became identified with many activities never accurately recorded except for the fact that at one time, as already mentioned, he did various jobs, had worked in a chemical factory, associated himself with Marxist guerrillas, and had women companions. Indeed, rumor had it that he had been a married man.

His physical appearance, his personal background, his notorious predilection for Marxism, his wooing of the crowds, in short, made of him the most suitable pope for the launching of the Euro-Catholic-American sponsored communism with which the Curia-CIA Coalition wanted to counter attack the Catholic pro-communist stance of the Vatican-Moscow alliance.

One vital question, which few of the Cardinals who voted for him had dared to ask themselves however, had remained an unanswered puzzle. Did John Paul II have the necessary perspicacity for carrying out policies encompassing global problems and the mighty conflicts of the superpowers? Even more important, did he have the vision about a Universal Church whose parish was the entire world and not the obscure Polish backwater of Krakow from which he had emerged?

But even if these questions had been answered in the affirmative, what about the twin traits which have plagued the Poles throughout their history: their emotional nationalism and their cultural calvinism? When, during the Conclave two Polish prelates were asked about a potential Polish pope they were horrified. "For God's sake," they replied, "We Poles are too nationalistic to be trusted with the papacy."

A few days later these same prelates heard that the papacy had, indeed, been trusted to a Pole.

Wojtyla's election, while acclaimed by his promoters, scared many, beginning with himself. "I became afraid of receiving the nomination," he told the crowd in St. Peters that same evening. "But I did it in the spirit of obedience."

To God, or to those who had helped him in his election? Or even more ominous, in obedience to the superpower who had planned to use him, to use Poland and the Vatican for the promotion of policies directed at stopping the ideological and territorial progress of Soviet Russia and Russian sponsored world Marxism?

Within less than six months, the first Polish pope had already forced the papacy to career towards a future looming with somber incognita and unprecedented perils.

CHAPTER 6

The Bishop Who Knew Too Much

When Polish Bishop Andre Deskur was told about Cardinal Wojtyla of Krakow getting the job of the papacy, the Bishop was horror-struck. "Impossible!" he commented.

The bishop, a man who had known Wojtyla better perhaps than anybody alive, should have known. His friendship with John Paul II stretched back to their early youth when Wojtyla had lived in the palace of the Prince-Archbishop, Cardinal Sapieha, Bishop Andre Deskur's uncle.

While there, Wojtyla had studied for the priesthood, working in a factory by day, performing in the theatre by night, and flirting with the Marxist guerrillas; activities which he carried out while hiding in the Archbishop's palace until 1944.

As his closest classmate, Deskur came to know the most intimate details of Wojtyla's life, character and ambitions. These included certain events which had never been clarified after Wojtyla became Pope. Pressed to disclose the origin of Wojtyla's priestly vocation, for instance, Deskur kept silent. He never gave any hint about what happened in Wojtyla's life during the great gap in John Paul II's career between 1939 to 1944, the war years, Wojtyla's twilight period, not to be found in any public record.

When asked about the rumors that John Paul II at one time had been married and had lost his wife during the war, Deskur said nothing, as he did concerning various other rumors which had been circulated before, during and after the Pope's election. Deskur's discretion was deeply appreciated by all those concerned, beginning with John Paul II himself.

The loyalty of the two men was reciprocal and lasted all their lives. Thanks to such a unique relationship, Bishop Deskur became privy to Wojtyla's ecclesiastical progress, from its inception; John Paul II's only true confidant prior, during, and after the Conclave.

The result was that all the intrigues and operations behind the scenes which brought Pope John Paul II to the papacy had been familiar to him, as they had been to Wojtyla himself. The more so, since Deskur had acted also as his personal and political advisor, the only man who knew all that which had to be known about the clandestine operations, about the candidature of John Paul II. This meant that Deskur was possibly the only man who knew about the identity of those who had selected his friend for the papal election.

Although Deskur kept always discreetly in the background, it is nevertheless known that he participated in several vital semi-secretive moves prior to the Conclave which elected Wojtyla.

One of these took place at the Church of St. Stanislas in Rome, October 8th, 1978, only eight days before Wojtyla was made pope. Rumors by then had circulated in certain quarters to the effect that certain influential cardinals, supporters of the Vatican-Moscow alliance, were prepared to make a ''deal'' with the pope-designate, provided Wojtyla and his supporters accepted certain conditions.

Wojtyla and his closest associates met to discuss the potential ''deal.'' The opposition, he was told, was ready to support his candidacy, provided he accepted "ideological flexibility." The offer came from none other than the fiercest supporter of the Vatican-Moscow alliance, Cardinal Benelli, former right hand of pro-Russian Pope Paul VI.

At the meeting there were present Polish Bishop Rubin, General Secretary of the Synod of Bishops, Cardinal Wojtyla, Bishop Deskur, and the secretary of Cardinal Benelli, the latter having deemed the encounter too compromising for him to attend personally.

Prior even to the meeting it had become obvious that the secret block of five had already made recruits in the ranks of the "progressives." Amongst these, Paulo Arns, Archbishop of Sao Paulo, Brazil, several other Latin American Cardinals, half a dozen of the third world, and one or two from the communist countries beginning with Archbishop Frantisek Tomasek, Primate of communist Czechoslovakia.

Wojtyla's name by then had already been whispered, with the utmost discretion, in preparation for what was to happen at the Conclave. One of the main engineers had been another Pole, Cardinal Stefan Wyazynski, Primate of communist Poland, Wojtyla's mentor.

A formidable opponent of Marxism and Marxist Russia, the primate had fought against both with vigor, a source of continuous irritation not only to Moscow and the polish communist regime, but also to pro-Russian Pope Paul VI. Although initially he had supported Pope John XXIII, he had determinedly opposed the policy of the Vatican-Moscow alliance from the start.

When the Curia-CIA Coalition began to formulate their plans during the pontificate of Paul VI they approached the primate for his support. Their idea of a kind of Catholic communism, sponsored jointly by the Vatican and the U.S., did not appeal to him. He flatly rejected their offer.

When, however, the "resign" campaign against Paul VI was commenced he succumbed to the plans. It was after the Conclave of John Paul I, however, that he decided to join the secret preparation for the election of Wojtyla, having realized by then how John Paul I had been nothing but a decoy for those who were still determined to carry on with Paul VI's Vatican-Moscow alliance.

But if the little meeting at St. Stanilas Church had been dominated by Polish tribalism sponsored by the absent Polish primate, it was supported, even if in "absentia," by highly motivated individuals operating in the ecclesiastic and lay fields.

Prominent amongst these Americans of Polish origin — headed by Msgr. Kroll of Philadelphia, notorious for his Polish flights in a helicopter provided by a rich friend — was Cardinal Cody of Chicago, who, although not a Pole, nevertheless had more vested interest in the election of a Polish pope than perhaps any other high prelate.

Msgr. Cody had been the dominant figure in the largest ethnic minority in the U.S., his diocese nearing 800,000 Poles. He had the richest Catholic administration in America, and one of the most influential political pressure groups at a local and international level at his disposal. Politicians in Chicago and Washington, especially those of Polish origin, behaved like puppets at Archbishop Cody's financial and ecclesiastic nods.

The financial and numerical magnificence of Cody, moreover, could influence also the 12 million Catholic Americans of Polish origin in addition to other ethnic Catholic minorities in the U.S. Furthermore, rumors had it that Cody had helped coffers of the Vatican at "delicate" intervals; and that his contributions to the St. Peter's pence had been the highest for decades. Also, that he had "inspired" a lobby in the U.S. and in Rome, for the election of his "friend" Wojtyla.

After his election, Pope Wojtyla displayed a special favoritism for Cardinal Cody even though the latter was under Federal investigation for the misuse of Church tax free funds, as already mentioned.

Bishop Deskur knew most, if not all of the wheeling-dealing which had been going on since the Curia-CIA promotional campaign had been launched. As the confidant of Wojtyla he had been privy to all the manipulations, intelligence intrigues, political deals, and more. Because he had been unofficially at the center of them all, he had come to know the identity of the Curia-CIA personalities, their origin, sources, and last, but not least, the promoting superpower which was operating behind them.

Although gratified that a Pole had become pope, he, nevertheless, like Polish Cardinal Wyszinsky, had become increasingly perturbed about the fitness of Wojtyla for the papal task; also about the new direction which Wojtyla's hidden sponsors intended him to lead the Church.

Wojtyla's personal "weaknesses" were too deep-rooted not to affect his behavior as a pope: egocentrism, personal vanity, and volubility. "One can tell that Wojtyla studied for the stage," commented a Cardinal, after the election, "He does not miss a trick."

His personal vanity, to be always the principal actor, never left him since his early days. The most striking example occurred in 1981 when he insisted upon visiting Japan. Although advised against it by experienced Vatican officials, he flew there, a country with only 400,000 Catholics out of a total non-Christian population of 135 millions.

The crowd who came to greet him was led by Cardinal Asahive Satawaki. It consisted of fewer than 100 people. Only one of the 12 television stations in Tokyo carried his arrival, and that was only for a few seconds. The visit was shatteringly humiliating for a man used to the rapturous welcome of millions. The more so, since no less than 8000 policemen, paid by a polite but brooding Government, had been assigned to provide for his security.

Pope Wojtyla never recovered from the experience and brooded for weeks when in the Vatican. Like a prima donna, he took the whole experience as an affront to him "personally".

This same thirst for personal adulation emerged only hours after his election as Pope when he brazenly asked a group of American reporters to "be good to me." After which, to ingratiate himself with them he cupped his hands like a megaphone and "shouted" his blessing to the milling crowds. Such behavior was more fit for a "pro-football linebacker, than for a pope, no matter how proletarian-minded" as someone promptly commented.

The description was nearer reality than intended. Prior to his official investiture, in fact, Wojtyla gave personal orders that the inaugural mass, the most solemn ceremony of a new papacy, should be celebrated in the morning. The reason? To permit football fans to watch the soccer games in the afternoon on their TV screen. Also, as somebody commented, probably to turn the TV on in his apartment to watch the soccer game himself. The following year the new Pope took tennis lessons from a 27 year old, Wojtek Fibak, Poland's top tennis pro. More telling, when he visited Poland as a Pope (1979), he dismissed all elderly nuns on his Vatican staff, and chose instead six other young Poles. Heading them was Sister Teodata, only 35, tall, slim, and beautiful, who types and sings. "A dubious choice for a pope who claims asceticism to avoid carnal temptations," as a Vatican old-hand commented, after seeing Sister Teodata.

Such were the priorities of the new Pope.

Perhaps a smoke screen to hide the fact that Wojtyla, after all, was only acting as a dummy for his "masters'" voice? Or, even more ominous, the better to disguise another fact that perhaps he was the appropriate instrument with which to woo the masses with his socialist slogans about freedom for striking workers, something which he preached to millions of his compatriots when he returned as a pope to his native Poland.

CHAPTER 7

Murders In The Vatican

The new Pope had not even had the time to recover from the election ceremony before he had to rush to the Gemelli Clinic in Rome. Bishop Deskur, his closest friend, had suffered a severe heart attack shortly before the papal nomination. He was now seriously ill.

Pope John Paul II knelt by the bedside weeping. When told that Deskur would not recover he wept again, as the Bishop lay there unconscious. When afterwards Deskur, having regained consciousness, was told that his friend Wojtyla had been elected Pope he became horrified. "Who will protect him from them?" he said and tried to get up from the bed. "Now I must recover," then he added, trying to get up, "Yes, I must recover."

John Paul II visited him again soon afterwards, dressed only in black. The Bishop's health deteriorated, however, until finally he was sent to Switzerland. Shortly afterwards, he died, seemingly of a heart attack, but never accurately assessed, leaving heart specialists "baffled."

Bishop Deskur was only 54 years old.

What Bishop Deskur meant by "them" was never explained. Whether he alluded to the elusive sponsors of Wojtyla, or to some other unknown elements connected with the future Vatican-Washington strategy, is difficult to say. The fact that Bishop Deskur became suddenly ill only a few days before the papal election, when Wojtyla perhaps needed advice, might have been a coincidence. Yet, the timing of his demise could justify legitimate suspicions.

A primary dictum of any efficient Intelligence Directorate is that the liquidation of individuals who can become an intelligence embarrassment, is not as rare as the authorities care to admit. Witnesses who know too much are better dead than alive.

One notorious case is that of "Ruby" who killed Lee Oswald, the alleged assassin of President Kennedy. Ruby died while in jail. His death proved "providential" to many involved in the dubious forthcoming trial. Again, whether his convenient demise was a natural one is impossible to say. What was certain, however, was that Ruby, like Bishop Deskur, died a premature death, presumably, although never proved, because he "knew" too much.

Only a few weeks prior to Bishop Deskur's death, during Pope John Paul I's short reign, a similar "coincidence" occured at the Vatican itself. John Paul I had had open negotiations with the Greek Orthodox Church, negotiations originally commenced by Pope Paul VI. These dealt with delicate political and ecclesiastical issues related to the Orthodox Church within and outside the Soviet Union.

Orthodox leader Metropolitan Nicodemus had a formal audience with Pope John Paul I. He collapsed there and then, and died literally almost on the Pope's knees of a "massive heart attack" (September 6, 1978). The Metropolitan had been one of the chief negotiators of the policies under discussion.

Less than a month later Pope John Paul I himself died suddenly of a "massive" heart attack, as already seen.

Pro-Russian Pope Paul VI, who died one month before Metropolitan Nicodemus, had been frail, ill and ailing, since the organized manipulation of public opinion calling for his "resignation" had been mounted against him. The campaign was a total failure. Paul, far from resigning, went on with his pro-Russian policies. That involved the acerbation of the plans formulated by the Curia-CIA operators anxious to launch their own.

The pressure of the growing conflict between Soviet Russia and the U.S. made the promotion of a radical change at the Vatican a dire necessity. But since that depended upon the election of a new pope, the demise of Paul VI would have been a blessing since it would have meant the termination of his pro-Russian stance.

The year of the three popes

On August 6, 1978, Pope Paul VI died of a "heart attack". Probably a natural one. Yet, it was asserted at once that his life could have been saved or at least prolonged. "I must say that the behavior of his doctors is unacceptable," commented a celebrated physician, Professor Christian Barnard, the first man to pioneer heart transplants and foremost world heart expert.

Another no less striking case was that connected with the Jesuits, who since Wojtyla was made pope, became a growing embarrassment to the Vatican-Washington alliance. This was chiefly due to their activities in Central America where they had involved the Church with the left-wing guerrillas whose main guidance had become the "Theology of Liberation" once tacitly encouraged by Paul VI.

As the exponent of the Vatican-Washington alliance, John Paul II advised the Jesuits to curtail their revolutionary operations. The admonition was ignored. When, soon after his election, John Paul II visited Mexico he was shocked at the extent of the Jesuits' involvement in the revolution of Latin America, and urged also by Washington, he told them to stop forthwith their agitations.

The Jesuits stood firm, thereupon the Pope took a drastic step. He imposed his own "personal" papal representative to rule the Order. The step had been unprecedented. "The most shattering thing that has happened to us since a pope suppressed the Order in the 18th Century," commented a horrified Jesuit, October 26, 1981.

The General of the Jesuits, Father Arrupe, was "secretly" dismissed, although the General is elected for life — something which had never happened before. The General pressed a meeting with the Pope twice in early 1981. A compromise, however, proved impossible since Father Arrupe, as the veteran supporter of the policies of the Vatican-Moscow alliance, could not accept the counter-revolutionary, U.S. sponsored policies of the Vatican-Washington alliance.

Pope John Paul II ordered Arrupe to "retire". General Arrupe answered by putting the government of the Order into the hands of one of his four assistants, Father Vincent O'Keefe, an American. The Pope then, sweeping aside the arrangement of Arrupe, took personal control of the whole Jesuit Order. It was a shock that stunned the Jesuits all over the world. (See also Chapter 31 - The Cross, the Hammer and Sickle, and the Latin American Revolution).

The chronology of the events was an interesting one. The General met the Pope first in January, second in April 1981. John Paul II was shot the following month, May 13, 1981. Three months later, August 1981, General Arrupe suffered "a sudden massive heart attack." Although this time the "massive heart attack" failed to provoke an "accelerated demise", nevertheless it left General Arrupe "partially paralyzed" for the rest of his life.

The Pope then castigated the Jesuits, as they never had been before for centuries. He ordered 110 of their top leaders to Rome, to whom he "spoke severely". He became tough with their "operations" in Latin America, where they had been the close advisers of Archbishop Romero, who in 1980 was murdered while saying mass, and where later, 1981-2, the U.S. had been embroiled with financial, economic and military aid to fight the Catholic-Marxist guerrillas.

During an unprecedented eight days meeting in Rome (March 9, 1982) the Jesuits angered the Pope when trying to justify their revolutionary activities in Latin America. John Paul II, however, refused to relent and risk undermining the working of the Vatican-Washington alliance.

The Papal-Jesuits confrontation finally ended with the Jesuits having to "pledge filial obedience" although they were "pained" at his speech to them on March 1st in which he warned them to stay out of politics. (1)

It is obvious that all these "strokes" and "massive heart attacks" within a very exclusive influential circle were anything but accidental. "Perhaps 'providential' might be a better word," was the comment of a garrulous cardinal, on hearing the remark.

Whether such "demises" had been natural or otherwise might never be proved. The fact, however, is that since then the face of the Vatican has radically altered. The year of the three popes (Paul VI, John Paul I, and John Paul II), as 1978 has been called, proved to be the ending of an era, and the beginning of a new revolutionary one more perilous even than that of John XXIII, the previous two decades.

But whereas John XXIII began with the mild reforms of a religious ideological ecumenism, which ended with the Vatican-Moscow alliance of pro-Russian Paul VI, that of Pope John Paul II began with dangerous ideological provocations. Their impact upon the delicate balance of power of Soviet Russia and the U.S. could produce the preliminary disturbances preceding an oncoming conflagration.

The Second Vatican-Washington alliance now in full swing, unlike the first one inspired by anti-communist Pius XII and the U.S. after World War II, was launched upon the wing of a dubious religious-ideological "imponderable" whose operations might engulf sponsors and opponents alike into a nuclear confrontation.

The gloomy remark in St. Peter's Square, Rome, of an unknown American reporter upon hearing of the election of the new Pope

(1) See also Chapter 31, The Cross, the Hammer and Sickle, and the Latin American Revolution.

John Paul II, might have been an extreme one. But it gave the shudders to those who heard it:

"Wojtyla will kick off a third World War," was the comment.

Prejudice or prophecy?

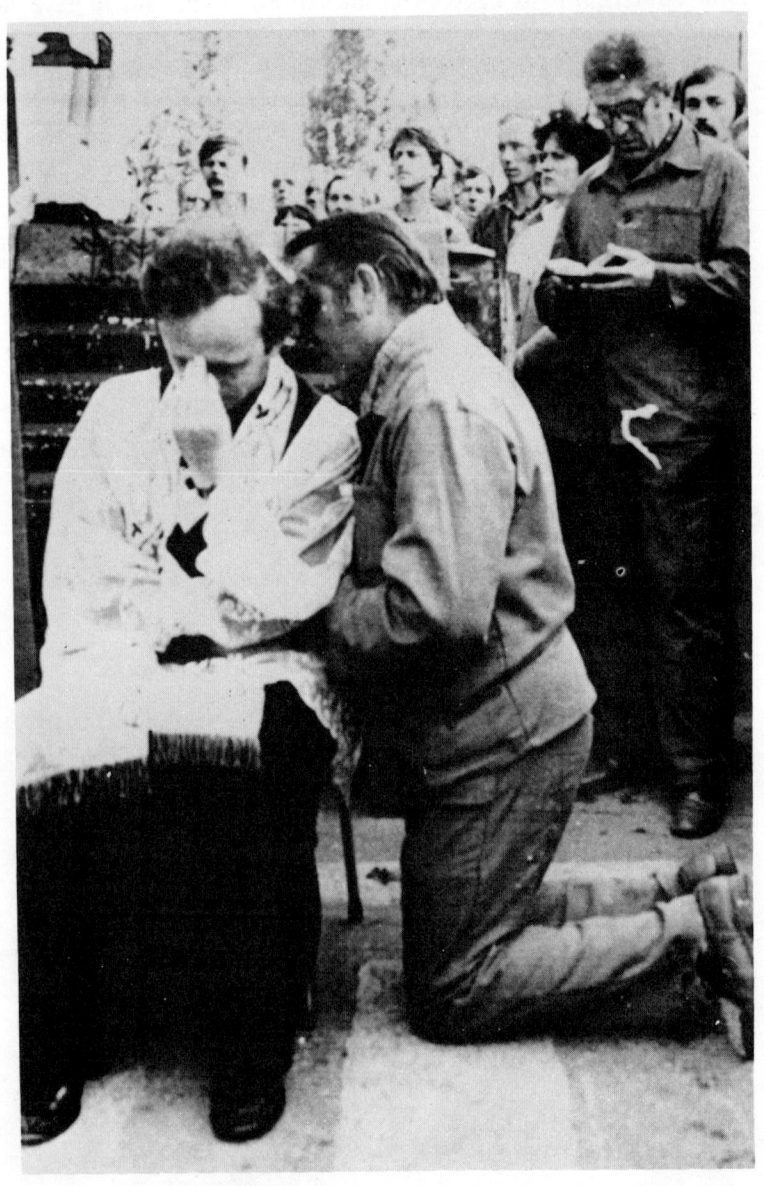

A striking worker confessing during the religious services in the Lenin shipyards in Gdansk, Poland August 24, 1980.

CHAPTER 8

First Joint Vatican-Washington Operation

The reality of the Vatican-Washington alliance became painfully apparent when its papal sponsor was gunned down in St. Peter's Square, Rome, less than three years after his election.

The superpower whose interest he had endangered had acted by attempting to make the alliance collapse via the assassination of one of its main promulgators. The fact that it failed did not nullify the alliance's dangerous nature or even less, slow down the perilous course upon which Pope John Paul II had embarked. On the contrary it had heightened the perils which the novel Vatican-Washington imponderable had brought into the contemporary world.

Within months, Pope Wojtyla, having thrown diplomacy to the

winds, began to act with the rashness of an inexperienced gambler, unaware of the dangerous pitfalls into which he was leading the Church.

In the Spring of 1979, he returned to his native Poland bringing the Vatican into a mine field of immense political complexities. The bewildered communist authorities tottered under the unexpected visit, which they feared could bring an indigenous resurgence of nationalism, encouraged by the religious sponsorship of their papal "guest." Their fear proved correct. After eight days of emotionalism communist Poland was never the same. A papal offspring, disguised as an innocent trade union movement named "Solidarity", emerged soon afterwards fomenting mounting industrial unrest.

From 1980 to 1981 and 1982, with the brassy interference of the Catholic Church, and the secret financial and co-ordinating intelligence machinery of the U.S., "Solidarity" became so arrogantly revolutionary that it exerted growing disruptive power, dictated to the Government, and finally planned even the overthrow of the Regime.

Its main spokesman, one Lech Walesa, a daily mass devotee, sporting the images of the Madonna and of the Pope on his coat, and who used to write with an 18 inch red and white ballpoint adorned with the picture of John Paul II, called at the Vatican where he confabulated in private with His Holiness about the disruptive tactics to use at home.

Simultaneously Walesa conferred with Trotskist Italian trade-union leaders, one of whom was subsequently arrested for suspected links with Red Brigade terrorists (Luigi Scricciolao, February 11, 1982). Following further contacts with the Vatican, Walesa openly averred that his chief advisor was none other than Pope Wojtyla himself.

John Paul II, far from denying it, assured the world that if Soviet Russia invaded Poland to suppress Solidarity's revolution, he, the Pope, would go there in person to oppose them. By the winter of 1981-2, Solidarity — openly encouraged by the Church whose clergy was preaching pro-Solidarity sermons in all its 18,000 churches in a nation which is up to 98 per cent Catholic, and secretly organized by the CIA, — finally made ready for a total take-over.

The attempt became a sure formula for civil war. The authorities banned Solidarity, arrested its leaders, and imposed Martial Law December 13, 1981 to the joint protestation of the Pope and U.S. President (January - February, 1982).

Although taken by surprise, the operators were not. One who knew more than both Pope and President, for instance, was Alexander Haig, U.S. Secretary of State. Almost one year before (March 27, 1981) he had predicted, (quoting the Washington Post February 18, 1982) that "the situation in Poland was grave." Also that "dramatic changes were imminent and internal suppression was coming."

The dual Papal-CIA exercise, which had almost succeeded, imperiled the stability of Poland, and also that of the Soviet Union, internal and external. The creation of a counter-revolutionary Catholic-inspired movement had brazenly tried to topple an established pro-Russian satellite via the use of social agitation masked as a non-political trade union.

The attempt had been an unprecedented set back for Soviet Russia, who by now had come to realize that the new Vatican-Washington alliance had turned into a major political reality; indeed, that it could also be used as a disruptive operation in other Russian satellites.

The implication was an intolerable one. Since the joint Vatican-U.S. sponsored operations, by trespassing from a neutral form of syndicalism into the political arena, could have endangered the military machinery of the Soviet block, namely the Warsaw Pact, in their confrontation with NATO, its European-American military counterpart.

The direct intervention of the Vatican in the Polish counter-revolution created serious concern in the political establishments of the world. The combined influence of the Catholic Church, plus the use of conspiratorial intelligence expertise, could produce political disestablishment in the delicate balance of power between Soviet Russia and the U.S.

The Polish experiment helped to embitter the already tense relationship between Russia and the U.S., already engaged upon the most terrifying armaments race the world had ever seen.

To give one typical example, by early 1982 President Reagan's new budget had included a colossal $215.9 billions in military outlays, plus an enormous $258 billions in spending commitments for 1983, the second instalment of Reagan's five year, $1.7 trillion plan to rebuild the U.S. defense. Soviet expenditure, which matched that of the U.S., is expected to surpass it for the years 1984 and 1985.

But if the novel Vatican-U.S. new religious ideological alliance had been assessed as having been confined mostly to Europe, it soon appeared to have had wider implications. It became crystal clear its field of operation was the world itself. John Paul II, in fact, began to travel from one country, and from one continent to another with an urgency never seen before.

He visited Ireland, England, the U.S., went to Latin America, Brazil, Mexico, switched to the Near East, Pakistan, Turkey and from the African countries, such as Zaire (the former Congo) - where a stampede during the Pope's visit killed nine people with an unknown number of injuries - to the Far East, to the Philippines. There, in 1970, Paul VI had shots fired at him and was even attacked by an assailant armed with a knife and slightly hurt.

His determination in visiting such diverse lands, many of which were not Catholic, and not even Christian, like Pakistan, Turkey or Japan, made his real motivation a matter of worried suspicion amidst politicians and governments alike.

For example, in South America he met the immense crowds with not only the familiar pious homilies, but also with thinly disguised political incitement to civil unrest. During his tours of Mexico, and his 12 day visit to Brazil in 1980 for instance, his stirring allusions to "social justice - the sacred rights of the have nots" and the like were emphasized by dramatic histrionics.

Typical was the theatrical gesture to a small gathering of shanty town dwellers in Brazil, when he took a gold ring from his finger and presented it to them. "The Church wants to be a church of the poor," he said. To another audience he reiterated that, "it is indecent that some should squander that which is missing from the tables of everyone else.''

These seemingly innocent papal gestures and words, were emotional explosives when addressed to the crowds of the Rio slums who lived in tin-and-packing shacks of the hillside Favellas, some of the poorest people in the world. ''Each time we see the Pope's ring,'' commented one of them, ''we shall ask our government, 'This is what the Pope has given us. What have you to offer, and how much longer can we wait?' '' ''The value of the ring is symbolic to help us in our fight for basic human needs,'' said another.

He reiterated the same argument at a mass rally in a stadium which held 150,000 where the crowds, before the Pope's appearance, got out of control killing seven and injuring hundreds.

The papal visitations contributed to a mounting restlessness in a land like Brazil. Although the largest Catholic country in the world, it nevertheless accepted the papal message with apprehension. The stirring of the dormant fires of social unrest, no matter how justified, was a deliberate exercise in popular radicalism when carried out before millions of the poorest of Latin America.

The more so, since John Paul II never indicated how poverty could be reduced, or how the social structure could be changed. By leaving the option open he purposely encouraged a variety of popular remedies, which did not exclude force and even revolution. The fact that many clergy, prior to and after his arrival, participated in demonstrations against the authorities and aligned themselves with strikes and agitations, was not mere coincidence.

It was part and parcel of his travels to Latin America, a preparatory move for the shape of things to come, as they had already occurred in smaller countries like Nicaragua, El Salvador and other central Latin American countries as we shall see presently.

CHAPTER 9

Papal Master-Plan For A Catholic Counter-Revolution

The papal "recommendations" to the dissatisfied crowds of Europe, Latin American, Asia, and Africa made some of the CIA sponsors uneasy. Their partner was creating global waves of social unrest. It had become obvious that the real objectives of the Pope's trips was the muted sponsorship of a novel Catholic-inspired form of communism.

The sponsorship, made robust by religious papal aura, conflicted with the interests of the U.S. The latter backed right-wing administrations, the Church supported Marxist guerrillas.

The doctrine of the "theology of liberation" so consistently encouraged by pro-Russian Paul VI, although officially discarded by John Paul II, continued unabated notwithstanding his deal with the U.S.

The "doctrine" had remained alive and well, like in the past. What the Vatican had done was only a face-lift to appease the U.S. In other words, while autonomous local communism was advised to become independent from Russian ideological hegemony it was also told that if it wanted the Church's cooperation it had to be totally inspired by the Catholic Church at a local level. Politically, however, it had to be coordinated directly by the Vatican.

The equivocal nature of such an arrangement did not pass unnoticed by the U.S., which had taken for granted that the joint U.S.-Catholic operations would be restricted mostly to Europe. The discovery that the Vatican was acting unilaterally made Washington nervous since the potentiality of dangerous subversive ideological commotions had been assessed as increasingly perilous not only for Asia and Africa, but above all, for Latin America.

But if the finding had been a sad eye-opener for the U.S., it became even more so when it was realized that the Vatican had been operating single-handed in the pursuance of religious objectives of its own. Most of these were against religious rivals. Chief amongst these, its millenarian opponent the Orthodox Church, which broke with Rome in 1054, followed by the Protestant and Evangelical communions.

But whereas the U.S. sponsors had tacitly acquiesced by ignoring such ecclesiastical problems, preoccupied as they were by immediate political issues, the Curia had not. Vigorous operations were set descreetly in motion, directed at dissident sections of the Orthodox Church, within and outside Russia.

The ground had already been prepared by Cardinal Rubin, Prefect of the Sacred Congregation of the Oriental Churches, a Pole and a close personal friend of Pope Wojtyla. Although of an ecclesiastical nature, they had far-reaching political implications, the Vatican having commenced them as early as 1970 and before.

In that year, Paul VI had visited Turkey, even although the Turks warned him of death threats on "political grounds." He visited not because Turkey was a Moslem country, but because it was a sensitive strategic pivot in the Russian-U.S. balance of power in the Middle-East. Added to that, it was a no less sensitive center of the Orthodox Church. It housed the historical Orthodox Patriarchate of Constantinople, the bitter rival of the Russian Orthodox Church, the latter headed by the Patriarch of Moscow, under the tutelage of the Soviets.

After his visit to Poland early in 1979, John Paul II forced himself upon an unwilling Moslem Turkey. Once there, he concocted yet another plot. This was not with dissident communist trade unionism like in Poland, but with the Orthodox Patriarchate based in Istanbul, the ancient Constantinople.

The Vatican, the Orthodox Church, and Moscow

The Turkish government wished the Patriarchate to move out of Turkey because of the continuous trouble it gave inside and outside Turkey itself. The trouble was of a highly dangerous political nature since it entailed its neighboring Soviet Russia and thus indirectly the military operations of the U.S. in the Middle East.

John Paul II decided to intervene with the Orthodox Patriarch of Constantinople, by exerting religious and diplomatic pressure against Turkey. The Patriarchate welcomed the help of the Vatican fearing that if the traditional head of the Orthodox Christians had abandoned its 1,500 year old See of Constantinople, it would lose, once and for all, its titular authority upon the 200 million adherents of the Orthodox Church world-wide.

The implication of the move would have far-reaching results. It would have given the excuse for Soviet Russia to take over the honorary primacy of Constantinople for Moscow, whose Patriarch claimed the largest Orthodox following in the world. Had Moscow supplanted Constantinople as the center of world orthodoxy, the religious and political benefits which Moscow would have received would have been immense, since the Orthodox Patriarch of Moscow was under the direct protection of the Soviets.

John Paul II had several "private" meetings with Patriarch Dimitrios with whom he agreed to set up a high level committee aimed at unity. The committee would have had 14 Orthodox prelates from the 14 autonomous orthodox churches within and outside Turkey and Soviet Russia, and 14 Roman Catholics, as "advisors." Because of such papal interference in Turkish affairs, Turkey gave him a frigid formal reception during which, while security was at a maximum, cordiality was at its minimum.

The papal campaign had begun with Pope John XXIII as early as 1958. When, however, from 1978-9 onwards the Vatican-Moscow alliance was replaced by the Vatican-Washington alliance, the nature of the latter assumed an even more critical sensitivity. This was so, not only because of its pro-U.S. orientation, but also because it was directed at the disruption of the Orthodox Church inside and outside Russia, since behind the Vatican-U.S. moves there loomed the Patriarchate of Constantinople, the ideological rival of the Patriarch of Moscow, whose authority would have helped to sap the structures of the Orthodox Church in the Middle-East and also in Eastern Europe, traditionally under Constantinople. Hence Turkey's original reluctance to the visit of John Paul II.

The political motivation of such visits did not go unnoticed by either the Kremlin or Moslem Turkey. Irritation provoked reaction. Reaction triggered ideological responses.

It was while in Ankara, Turkey, in November 1979 in fact, that the Pope was given the first warning of a plot to kill him; a hint of something which was to be finalized in St. Peter's shooting only two years later. The warnings had been frequent whenever he interfered with Islamic affairs. As for instance, when he forced his presence in Islamic Pakistan, a bomb exploded in the National Stadium of Karachi, killing one person minutes before his arrival (February 16, 1981).

Religious and ideological irritation were the hallmarks of his other visits when he met Muslim leaders in July 1980 in Accra, Africa, during his first African tour; or when he insisted on meeting Muslim leaders, even in Davao in the south of the Philippines in 1981. His interference in Moslem affairs finally provoked an open snub when Muslim leaders refused to meet him in Kaduna, Nigeria, during his second African tour in 1982.

The Islamic press assessed him for what he was. "Both Christianity and the papacy," wrote the Nigerian press in February, 1982, "have been transformed into an instrument of European and

American Imperialism.''

Such sentiments expressed the general interpretation of the Muslim world which saw in the papal visitations barely disguised moves directed at creating dissensions.

No wonder therefore, that as early as 1979 during the Pope's first visit to Turkey, a young Turk, having escaped from an Istanbul prison, became determined to kill him to stop him operating as the messenger of an aggressive, American-backed, Catholic expansionism. The result was seen when the escaped Turkish youth, Mehmet Ali Agca, attempted to kill Pope John Paul II May 13, 1981 in St. Peter's Square, Rome.

It is significant that Ali Agca was acting not so much as an instrument of Islamic mysticism, but also as the instrument of a twilight world where Islam, the Orthodox Church, The Vatican, Soviet Russia, and the U.S. all met in their struggle to further their respective interests.

Therefore the papal masterplan for a Vatican counterrevolution, by operating behind the protective shield of the Vatican-Washington alliance, had been turned into a religious imponderable of the utmost importance in the global struggle between the U.S. and the Soviet Union.

CHAPTER 10

The Pope-U.S. Presidential Hot Line

The vital reality of the Vatican-Washington alliance became stunningly evident when U.S. President Reagan picked up the White House telephone on December 14, 1981 and had an eight to ten minute private conversation with his Holiness, Pope John Paul II, at the Vatican.

The casualness of the direct talk between Pope and President revealed not only the operational intimacy of the two leaders, but exposed also the tip of a submerged political iceberg whose massiveness had not as yet been fully assessed by the U.S.

The seriousness of the matter was not that the disclosure had been a startling one, but that it indicated that U.S. policies could be formulated without any direct consultation with either the Senate,

Congress, or any other policy making bodies of the administration. Moreover, that certain fundamental tenets regarding Church and State, and the U.S. Constitution, could be tacitly disregarded, and even bypassed, regardless of the general consensus of the American people.

How often had the Vatican-White House hot line been used in the past, or was used now in the present, or would be used in the future, to shape American policies in accordance with the interests of the Vatican? It was a question full of constitutional uncertainties and political incognita, concerning not only the objectives of the alliance, but also concerning the true nature of the semi-secret relationship that existed between the U.S. and Rome. It also concerned the confidential lobby operating in the higher echelons within the White House itself.

The tradition was not a recent one. It had been practiced, even if unofficially, by several previous Presidents. For instance by President Nixon when he hired the Rev. John McLaughin, a Jesuit, to write his official speeches, during three long years, at a salary of $32,000 per year.

But if the disclosure of the Vatican-Washington hot line had been sensational, the facts discussed by Pope John Paul II and President Reagan were not. It dealt with one of the alliance's offspring, "Solidarity," the Polish Catholic-communist trade union, soon after it had been clubbed down with martial law December 13, 1981 to curtail its Vatican-U.S. inspired manipulations to seize power.

The "Solidarity" operation had been one of the Curia-CIA's joint activities, sponsored by dedicated individuals, and by committed U.S. governmental agencies. Many of the latter, preponderantly staffed by Catholics, exerted an influence out of all proportion to their official duties in a nation still largely inspired by the traditional spirit of Protestantism.

The result was disturbing. It confirmed that the primary formulation of the U.S. policies had become the dominion of highly motivated Roman Catholics, a kind of invisible, but efficient, government within a government. (During recent years the number of lobbyists practicing in Washington doubled from 8000 to 16,000, outnumbering members of Congress by nearly 30 to 1.)

The existence of such an organically orientated Catholic body would have been a matter of concern by itself, but the fact that it enjoyed the patronage of the most eminent individuals of the U.S. political intelligence and military establishments, made their presence one of profound disquiet.

The list, although minimal, was impressive: From General Alexander Haig, Secretary of State, to Mr. Casey, Head of the Central Intelligence Agency; from D. Reagan of the U.S. Treasury, to Mr. Allen of the National Security; from Mrs. Kirkpatrick, UNO, to W. Clark, who replaced Allen in 1982, to W. S. Wilson, the U.S. envoy at the Vatican and convert to Catolicism, and many others in less glamorous but nonetheless very influential posts up and down the administration.

If to the above there are added Catholics in the FBI, the Pentagon and similar bodies, plus the 12 Catholic Governors, and the 129 Catholic seats in Congress (1982-83) (the next largest representation is the Methodists with 85 seats), then the denomination of Catholic power which all these members of the Catholic Church can exert upon the policies of the U.S. can be assessed in all its true significance. But whereas the loyalty of these functionaries can be beyond reproach, it is a fact that, as the committed operators for the Vatican, they can exert an influence out of all proportion to their number.

When to them there can be added the collective vigor of the U.S. Catholic Hierarchy with the denominational, financial, social and political pressure they can exert upon the media, business community, political lobbies on a local, international and national level, then their collective pressure can become so massively influential that it can sway even presidential candidates.

To mention one typical and not unique case, when Ronald Reagan, as a Presidential candidate in October 1980, made a bid for the Catholic vote to help him into the White House, he told Polish-American voters in Philadilphia that he, Reagan, if elected President, was going to fight for the family "in the spirit of John Paul II". "Today," Reagan concluded, "I reaffirm to you my pledge, in the spirit of Pope John Paul II, that I will do all I can to see that common good is once more the true goal of decision making."

At the same electoral meeting, Reagan claimed to share Cardinal Krol's concern (Cardinal Krol was a personal Polish-American friend of Pope John Paul II) about tuition tax to private schools, a paramount objective of the Catholic Church. Reagan's "concern" secured him the backing of the National Catholic Education Association besides dozens more Catholic sponsored bodies, who eventually helped him into the White House.(1)

When assessed against a monolithic block nearing 55 million American Catholics, then the totality of such massive Catholic pressurization is capable of bending the domestic and external policies of the U.S. itself.

The Vatican-Washington alliance has become an integral part of the U.S., not only because it was primarily nurtured by American self-interest, but also, and above all, because of the termite-like penetration of the Catholic presence within the most sensitive structures of American society. Its operations have been identified with those of the U.S. itself. Owing to that, its background must be assessed against its most immediate past.

Birth of the Vatican-Moscow-Washington Alliance

From World War I, or rather from the Bolshevik revolution in 1917, till Pope Pius XII's death in 1958, the Vatican considered Marxism as the greatest evil and combatted it with energy on all fronts. Its support of Fascism was motivated by its determination to destroy it, starting with Soviet Russia.

Following World War II, with the collapse of Fascism, Soviet Russia became enemy number one for the Vatican, and for the U.S. To check Russian ideological and territorial expansion, they formed the first Vatican-Washington alliance as a religious ideological subsidiary of the Cold War.

With Pius XII's death, the Church made a radical turn. To avoid finding herself on the losing side, she decided to embark upon a

(1) Catholic Herald, October 24, 1980

vigorous campaign directed at turning Catholicism into an integrated socio-economic-revolutionary force.

Emphasis on the social aspect of Christianity was given priority, economic justice became acceptable, and the proletarian origin of the gospel brought to the fore. Christ was presented no longer as Christ the King as Pope Pius XII had done, but as Christ the worker, Christ the dispossessed, Christ the proletarian. Indeed, as Christ the revolutionary.

The identification of Christ with workers, peasants and revolutionaries made Christ, and thus the Church, identifiable with the economic and social aspirations of Marxism. From there the gap between a forward looking church and seemingly more tolerant Marxism narrowed, until the Vatican and the Kremlin, having reckoned they had something in common, formed the Vatican-Moscow alliance.

The alliance was supplanted by the Vatican-Washington alliance for reasons we have just seen. The change of lay partners, although a radical one, is a mere tactical device meant to further her interests of the day.

Fundamentally, the Church has not changed one iota in her constant determination to reach her ultimate objective, independently of either Moscow or Washington. In her eyes, the two inimical superpowers are nothing more than two powerful pawns to be used to advance her progress in a corrupt, bankrupt, and doomed contemporary society.

This means that Paul VI, the father of the Vatican-Moscow alliance, and Pope John Paul II, the promoter of the Vatican-Washington alliance, although the initiators of two seemingly inimical alliances, in actual fact, fundamentally are pursuing the same basic objective: namely the total transformation of Christianity into social radicalism encapsulated in the motto of the Latin American Theology of Liberation, "Ubi Lenin, iby Jerusalem: Where Lenin is, there is Jerusalem."

Thanks to the magnitude of such revolution, the Vatican-Moscow, and the Vatican-Washington alliances have become two of the most fateful imponderables of contemporary world politics.

The better to assess them therefore, we must first comprehend the historical events which produced first the Vatican-Moscow alliance, and then the alliance which followed it.

We shall begin with the Vatican and the Cold War.

President Tito of Communist Yugoslavia is received in private audience by Pope Paul VI. (April 1971). The meeting was the culmination of prolonged negotiations between the Vatican and Yugoslavia, which refused at first to coordinate her policies with those of Soviet Russia, but afterward fell into line with the Vatican-Moscow alliance. In the photo, from left to right: Marshal Tito, Pope Paul VI, and a priest-interpreter.

CHAPTER 11

The Vatican and the Cold War

The Third World War has been upon us since the end of the Second. It began as an ideological conflict, euphemistically labeled the "Cold War," and has passed alternately back and forth between a psychological phase, fought on diplomatic fronts and an active phase in the form of localised "hot wars" — the preparatory sparks of mutual mass incineration.

Once Nazism was destroyed, the anti-Hitler allies — the United States and Russia — resumed their respective prewar hostility to each other. Their saber-rattling gave global shivers to a whole generation (from 1945 until 1975, then official end of the war in Vietnam.)

These were the thirty long years when the initial skirmishes of World War III were fought with mounting military terror, before the collective helplessness of the rest of the world.

The Cold War, a universal conflict between two fundamentally opposed ways of life — Russian World Communism on one hand and Christian, libertarian culture of the West on the other — was punctuated by recurrent outbursts of world-gripping menace by both sides.

During this period, the United States staged no fewer than 200 "shows of force, and Soviet Russia 115 official displays Several others were carried out *sub rosa* and are still top secret in both Washington and Moscow.

The seriousness of the frequent flexing of the U.S. and Russian military muscles was not so much the massive display of the latest advances in the technology of warfare: nuclear-powered missiles, long-range bomber squadrons, atomic-powered submarines and the marching battalions of men; it was the ever-present danger that one side or the other might over-react and touch off a nuclear war.

Such a fatal and final crisis confronted the United States during the Korean War in the fifties and again in the Cuban Missile ultimatum to the U.S.S.R. in 1962. The same threat loomed over the Middle East War of 1973.

Those of Soviet Russia are not known, but that they did occur on more than one occasion to counter those of the U.S. is more than a possibility; it is a certainty. Not once, but several times, America was reminded in a not too subtle admonition that the Russian capacity for wholesale nuclear destruction had better not be forgotten.

The super-secret archives of both Kremlin and the Pentagon can testify to this.

These nuclear blackmailing tactics took place not only to impose caution upon each opponent, but equally to further their respective political interests. These were precise, direct and concrete: (1) expansion of their respective global spheres of influence; (2) protection of each power's existing zones of political or economic domination; (3) the "persuasive forcing" of uncommitted states into the camp of one or the other Superpowers; and last, but not least, to infuse respect of the potential enemy for the growing atomic arsenal the foe, thus deterring him from any thought he might have of first-strike capability.

As the Cold War gained momentum, the fear of atomic annihilation spread across the world with ever-increasing rapidity. Within the first ten years, two more nuclear arsenals were made ready for all-out atomic warfare — Britain and France. During the next ten years, four more were added, including Communist China. By the time the thirty-year period — 1945 to 1975 — had ended, an estimated twenty other nations had acquired the ability to manufacture nuclear weapons. At the top of the latter list were Israel and India.

If for this growing doomsday threat be added the mounting size and effectiveness of the weapons and the immense sums being spent on their development (over 300 billion dollars in 1977 and an estimated 400 billion in 1978-79), then it becomes evident that contemporary mankind is still moving on a collision course with Armageddon.

Such an image is not an abstract magnification of fear. It is a concrete, terrifying reality, well understood in the higher echelons of government. The U.S. President, for example, has to remain in a constant state of alertness lest a nuclear sneak attack endanger the U.S. command centre, thus paralysing the whole nation's military capacity.

It was reported on February 11, 1977 that: "President Carter, anxious to test out America's defence for nuclear emergency, travelled in a huge military jumbo jet that would fly him out of Washington at the first warning of nuclear attack." The jet, appropriately called the *Doomsday*, would become the top-ranking command post in a nuclear war. The President's airplane was the only craft that military experts felt was certain to survive a nuclear strike by an enemy. It cost $117 million, and permits the commander-in-chief to control strategic forces on the ground, in the air, and beneath the sea.

"It's the realization of what might occur unless we assure peaceful relations with other countries," said the President, adding that in future he would order emergency nuclear drills without advance warnings.

The white, shining aircraft, almost windowless and crammed with electronic gear, can stay aloft three whole days without refueling. Others are being built for similar operational duty in case of surprise nuclear attacks on the U.S.

Prior to his initial flight, the President tested the system for an emergency getaway from the White House in case of nuclear war. It failed.[2]

A mutual holocaust

In a statement made during the tests and referring to the nuclear capability of both the U.S. and Russia, President Carter gave a chilling estimate of the staggering loss of life that would be sustained by each side in the event of an atomic war.

The U.S. and the Soviet Union, he said, could reduce each other to ashes in a nuclear bombardment, with a loss of life of 50 to 100 million persons *on each side.* An understatement.[3]

There is no doubt that the Russians have conducted similar emergency tests are also in a constant state of alertness.

The other nations of the world must and do share in this continuous state of vigilance, as they following the shifting balance of nuclear capability between the two super-powers. They realise that it would take a simple order from the White House or the Kremlin to release immediate death upon the earth. They know too, that such a disaster could be touched off by accident, miscalculation, or false alarm, despite reassurances of "fail safe" or "positive control" systems.

The show of force by Soviet Russia has not been confined to the mere flexing of military muscles. She has actually carried out brazen territorial occupations. Whole nations have been Sovietised in Eastern Europe. Elsewhere, others have been turned into battlefields, e.g., Korea and Vietnam.

The increasing rivalry between East and West, besides being a source of repeated apprehension among the helpless comity of nations, however, had even more far-reaching results in terms of iseological realignment.

For it was noticed that the display of force on the part of the United States, both as a military deterrent and a political counter-balance against Russia, invariably met with only short-term success.

In political terms, this meant that whenever and wherever such American displays seemed to have achieved anything, her gains were sharply eroded in a short period of time.[4] This inability to maintain an advantage was in sharp contrast to similar victories by the Soviets, who consolidated their gains and went on from there.

It was further noticed that the United States, for all its military posturing, seemed to be less successful whenever Soviet Russia directly opposed its policies or actions anywhere in the world.

In short, throughout this long period, the United States rarely achieved her long-term anti-Communist objectives.

When to all this display of general weakness there was added the formidable expansion of left-wing ideologies, and their continuous emergence within and outside vast areas of the world, to anyone with long-range political vision, a very clear picture of the future began to take shape. Notwithstanding their economic pre-eminence and libertarian ways of life, the United States and her Western allies were on the losing side. In the event of a Third World War, they could be defeated in the military field, as they were currently being defeated daily in the ideological.

By contrast, Russia has successfully and relentlessly pushed forward a programme of territorial and ideological expansion.

Communism, her ideological spearhead, was on the move everywhere. It was becoming increasingly evident that, for large areas of the globe, Communism would become the dominant political force for the rest of the century.

To be sure, such an assessment had not been that of Vatican policymakers when the Church had been dominated by anti-communist crusaders of the calibre of Pope Pius XII and his close U.S. allies — Cardinal Spellman, John Foster and Alan Dulles, and others. It was rather, the cold-eyed assessment of a group of high-ranking prelates who had been active within the darkest corridors of power at the Roman Curia.

From their point of view, nothing it seemed, could stop or even retard the forward march of Communism. Doubts grew as to the wisdom of continued papal support of the U.S. and the West. The Vatican-Washington anti-communist alliance came increasingly under closer scrutiny.

Red pressure appeared to be yielding positive results on all fronts. First, the U.S. had retreated before the Communist advance by allowing the Russian incorporation of Eastern Europe. Then she had retreated in Asia in the 1950s after the Korean War. This was followed by another retreat by failing Hungary after sponsoring the Hungarian counter-revolution in 1956. She had once again retreated before the Soviet-Cuban blackmail in the 60s; and last, but not least, she had retreated after the fiasco of the Vietnam war in the 70s.

The most politically-minded elements within the Church became apprehensive. While Communism was expanding with a rapidity undreamt of in the past, growing legions of Red fifth columnists were occupying more and more positions of influence throughout the West. World organizations had been brazenly transformed into platforms of Marxist subversion.

The United Nations, originally conceived by the United States as a supra-national body for working out world problems, had been turned into an anti-West forum populated by noisy infant Asian and African nations, all babbling revolutionary slogans, *ad nauseam.*

It seemed patent that the Church had chosen the wrong ally. By opposing a potential victor, she was endangering her present stability and her future survival. While Pope Pius XII was alive, these doubts about the wisdom of being allied with the West in an all-out war against Bolshevism remained muted. Upon his death in 1958, however, a swift reversal in policy shook the inner circles of the Vatican.

The new pope, John XXIII (1958-1963) dismantled his predecessor's elaborate anti-communist front while at the same time demolishing, almost at a stroke, the Vatican's ideological alliance with the United States. Thereafter, he looked to Moscow as the prospective new partner.

Washington was abandoned without regrets. As the supreme headquarters of a global cold war, which was being lost on all fronts, the U.S. had become a liability the Church could not afford and an obstacle to the successful prosecution of the new Pontificate.

Pope John, one of the former secret opponents of Pius's close political ties with America, had always contended that the world belonged to the masses of underprivileged individuals and nations. That was a polite way of saying that it belonged to Communism — minus its atheism, of course; but that difficulty could be resolved through dialogue and compromise. John was a "progressive," a "humanitarian" and the leader of a growing group of similarly discontented Catholic radicals active in key positions within and outside the Vatican.

These progressives, who had not previously been overt or vocal, nursing their disapproval in silence while they performed their designated tasks, had nevertheless continued under Pius to expand their coterie. Ultimately, some of them managed to infiltrate the very precincts of the Sacred College of Cardinals, the potential electors of a new pope.

Beginning as early as the end of World War II, they persevered in their belief that the Church's best policy would be an alignment with Communist regimes and with leftists at home and abroad.

The worker priests

Accordingly, while the lower clergy became quickly identified with the Christian proletariat, represented by the emergence of the worker-priests, the higher prelates insinuated themselves into the hierarchy and the career diplomats of the Curia.

The worker-priests and their supporters sympathised with the Communists on sociological and economic grounds. Their fellow-ideologues in the higher ranks did the same for ideological and diplomatic reasons. Certain key prelates, among whom were the Monsignori Roncalli and Montini (respectively the future Popes John XXIII and Paul VI) were active on both levels.

Leftist members of the elite group considered Communism, apart from its most obvious crudities, in harmony with the basic social doctrines of Christianity. They justified their support of Marxism by invoking the ghost of Pope Leo XIII, some passages of whose encyclicals could well be mistaken for the writings of Karl Marx himself.

The two wings, although differing on ways and means by which to turn the Church towards socialism, nevertheless were of one mind about the necessity for the Roman Catholic Church to formulate a radically new policy toward Communism as being the oncoming ideological reality of our times.

In their view, therefore, the Church had better ally herself with the forces of Communism while there was still time to form some kind of working partnership. They would meet Communism's demands half way in the political field, wherever it was making inroads, be it via sundry Marxist parties or via leftist-inspired institutions. The Church would initiate her grand strategy by a diplomatic approach to Russia.

In other words, the Roman hierarchy had decided to implement a policy of detente with the Communist-orientated world
as being the wisest course the Church could follow.

As previously pointed out, in political terms that meant the
abandonment of the Church's alliance with the United States. It
also signified decisively a break with her own past, a bowing
before the seemingly inevitable, and — in theological parlance —
a pact with the Devil, atheistic Communism.

A clamp, wrench, and screwdriver are solemnly blessed by a Catholic bishop for an English worker as part of the Vatican's new policy of interpreting the Gospels in socialistic, if not Marxist, terms.

CHAPTER 12

The Swastika and the Triple Tiara

The acceptance of a world in which Communism, supported by an ever expanding military presence, would become the dominant political philosophy of the century, required considerable logic-chopping by the Vatican leadership.

The ringing words of Pius XII's uncompromising condemnation of Communism still echoed through St. Peter's every corridor and retreat. To his dying day, he had sternly repeated his denunciation of Catholic-Communist "dialogue." "As the Apostle warns," he said, "It is inconsistent to wish to sit at the table of God and at that of His enemies."

Now his successor, John XXIII, was declaring just the opposite: "Meetings between believers and those who do not believe," he said in his encyclical, *Pacem in Terris,* "can be occasion for discovering truth and paying homage to it."

The morality of a detente with Bolshevism, which preached the death of religion, was rationalised on the grounds that Communism had sprung into the 20th century as a result of massive social injustice, not only in Russia, but throughout the world.

Until these worldwide evils and inequities were redressed — so the argument went — Communism would not only expand, but was bound to conquer. Kruschev's famous prophecy ("We'll bury you!) seemed to be coming true. If the Church wanted to prevail in the days to come, the prudent course would be to assist in the levelling of a capitalist-motivated social structure. It was time to think of radical alternatives, to open minds, to promote ideas of social change.

The pro-Marxist elements, inside and outside the Vatican, had no doubts about this. They came to the fore first as the would-be saviours of the Church, and then as advocates of the proposition that Communism, always excepting its atheism, was socially just, politically acceptable, and ideologically in harmony with the spirit of Christianity.

Communism's basic principles, they said, were those of the New Testament, as well as those propounded by the early Fathers of the Church. Had not St. Ambrose said, "The world is given to all, and not only to the rich"? Furthermore, had not several reformist popes advocated socialistic tenets?

Pope Leo XIII, for example, at the height of the Industrial Revolution, had come to the defence of the proletariat with his famous encyclical *Rerum Novarum.* This surely was a papal document which should be interpreted as a socialist manifesto, harmonising Marx's *Das Kapital* with the Christian concept of universal justice. Besides, if it was true that Marx had viewed religion as the opium of the people, Lenin had amended that idea by declaring that religion "must be regarded as a private matter."

If this dictum could be made acceptable to Communists

universally, the Church had nothing to fear from a world dominated by Communism.

According to these progressive churchmen, Communism and Christianity, far from being irreconcilable, were capable of cooperation, of amalgamation even. Indeed, the most radical of them openly envisaged a gradual organic union between the two — a sort of Christian Communism. It would be distinguishably Roman Catholic and vigorously expansionist under the aegis of an official Vatican assertion that Christ and Lenin had preached essentially the same gospels.

While condemning Russia's excesses and geopolitical expansionism, they embraced a Marxist Christianity attired in the specious mantle of Socialism.

Socialism, thus interpreted, permitted them to avoid a direct and too brusque confrontation with the Church's conservative majority.

Flirtation with Lenin

Historically, the Church had begun a flirtation with Lenin and his philosophy immediately following the Bolshevist Revolution in 1917, as we shall have occasion to see presently.

The Catholic progressives who had emerged soon after World War I, set about to implement their leftist aims by various activities. They both initiated and supported proletarian movements, one of the most successful of which was the Young Christian Workers, started in 1924 by a Belgian working-class priest, later to be created a Cardinal by Pope Paul VI (in 1965). These early Catholic radicals aided their Marxist colleagues in the development of a left-leaning press; infiltrated traditional Catholic organizations and then used them to achieve their own social objectives. With their help, Communist-dominated political parties determined to lay siege to the Vatican itself. They enjoyed a certain measure of success, having managed to reach the ear of the Supreme Pontiff, Pope Pius XI.

Pius, a scholar, disciplinarian and authoritarian by nature and training, had at first listened to their rationale, but had then turned against them by setting up the Catholic Party of Italy as his direct answer to the claims of Marxism.

This effort, however, failed. In 1927 he ordered the leaders to dissolve the party in order to favour development of an extreme rightwing movement called Fascism.

In 1929, the Fascist government of Italy and the Vatican signed the Lateran Agreement, and Mussolini granted the Church the extraordinary privileges it had asked. All Italian bishops were required to take an oath of allegiance to Il Duce (Article 20 of the Concordat). The Church had turned its back on Socialism, whether of a Marxist or ostensibly Catholic kind, siding with the anti-Communist political forces of Europe.

The most vigorous and powerful of these was Nazism. The Vatican helped Hitler to gain power and then helped him consolidate his grip on Germany. This was done in party by "advising" the Catholic Party of Germany to vote for Nazi candidates.

The Catholic vote gave Hitler the electoral majority he needed to legally form a government in 1933. Further to this, the Vatican ordered Catholic members of the Reichstag Parliament to support legislation giving Hitler the power to rule by decree. This measure gave Hitler the dictatorial power he needed to destroy the German Communists. After the law had been passed, the Vatican ordered the German Catholic Party to disband, as it had previously commanded its Italian counterpart to do back in 1927.

In response to the Vatican directive, the German Catholic Party demobilised in the summer of 1933.

The whole Vatican-Hitler bargain had been conducted in secret before Hitler became Chancellor of Germany in January 1933. In June of the same year, Hitler and the Vatican signed a Concordat, under terms of which the Church swore allegiance to the Nazi regime. Here are the textual words:

"I swear and promise to honor the legally constituted i.e., Nazi Government. I will endeavour to avoid all detrimental acts which might endanger it." (Article 16 of the Concordat).

Soon afterward, Catholic Franz von Papen, then second in command to Hitler, put the essence of the Hitler-Vatican alliance very succinctly in these words:

"The Third Reich," he said, "is the first power which not only recognises, but puts into practice the high principles of the Papacy." (*Der Volkischer Beobachter,* Jan. 14, 1934).

The Communists of Germany and Italy, followed largely by those of the rest of Europe were thus politically wiped out almost at a stroke. From that time onward, Vatican strategy became anti-Communist in word and deed within the domestic sphere, and anti-Russian in the international.

As a reward, Hitler made von Papen, leader of the dismantled German Catholic Party, second in command to himself. Von Papen was a personal friend of Cardinal Pacelli, lately Nuncio to Germany, then Secretary of State for the Vatican, and the future Pope Pius XII.

The alignment of the Church with the European right-wing powers by Pope Pius XI struck a near-fatal blow to the aspirations of those progressive churchmen who until that time had worked so assiduously for the adoption by the Vatican of a form of Catholic socialism, if not of Christian Communism.

The Vatican's new ideological alliance sent them all scurrying underground, where they were to remain for many long years.

The Church's support of Mussolini and Hitler during almost a decade, however, was marred by constant difficulties. Acrimonious quarrels broke out intermittently between the two dictators and the Church. Finally, Pius XI, while still negotiating with Hitler, condemned Hitlerism in a famous encyclical, *Mit Brennender Sorge,* which created the first serious rift with Germany.

Notwithstanding this deteriorating relationship with authoritarianism, however, Pius XI continued to support it. No doubt this could be explained by the fact that its basic motivation was anti-Communist, anti-Russian, and anti-Marxist.

Lesser of two evils

To Pius XI, the fanatical anti-Communist zeal of the Nazis mitigated their less desirable characteristics. If Nazism was bad, Communism was worse. Bolshevist Russia was out to foment world revolution. To achieve her ends, she was using not only athistic, anti-Christian ideology, but also the might of modern armies.

Since the Church had no armies of her own, she could use those of Germany and Italy. Hitler had become the hammer of the Church.

Seen in such an over-simplified global context, the Vatican was pursuing a policy of obvious self-interest. In the process, it alienated millions of Catholics. Yet the alternative seemed an even grimmer one — a Communist Europe — where the iron heel of the Bolshevists would trample underfoot all the rights of the Church; where alien red dictatorships, controlled by Soviet Russia, would turn the fair European lands into Muscovite colonies. Such a prospect was certainly a thousand times worse than any rightwing dictatorship, no matter how quarrelsome or belligerent.

As history progressed, however, Pius XI began to have second thoughts about his policy of direct support of right-wing extremism. In order to check the rampant charge of the Red Monster, he had unwittingly nursed a black one. Fascism and Nazism had become as dangerous as Bolshevism.

His disenchantment, though slow was steady, until it resulted in a gradual cooling-off of his support for the Fascist-Catholic partnership he had so hopefully fostered since the early thirties.

The Pope's change of heart did not go unnoticed by the sundry left-wing coteries of the Church. The most radical of these hoped against hope that Pius's growing dislike of Nazism ultimately would benefit indigenous European Communism and Soviet Russia. A subtle and relentless campaign aimed at influencing the pope's closest advisers to relent, even if momentarily, papal hostility to both, was promoted with some prospect of limited success.

Not that Pius XI had suddenly become pro-Communist or anything approaching it. He remained opposed to Communism, which he had always regarded as a deadly spiritual plague. His personal experience as a Papal Nuncio in war-torn Catholic Poland during and immediately after World War I had served to confirm and strengthen his view that in practice, Communism was irreconcilable with Christianity.

But now he saw that the Church's free exercise of its power was also impossible under Nazism. He repented having ever helped to consolidate Fascist power. The constant remorse for having killed the Catholic Parties of Italy first and Germany afterwards, gave him no peace.

The prospect of another World War, which now appeared imminent, finally spurred him into action. Early in 1939, he made a dramatic decision. He was going to admit his mistake, openly and to the entire world.

He could not foresee the fateful events that would deny him this final, noble performance.

CHAPTER 13

The Missing Testament of a Dying Pope

It is a fact of history, contemporary and ancient, that during certain tumultous periods, the forceful personality of some individuals can direct and determine the whole course of world events.

The theory that it is the nature of human affairs which will help a given type of leader to emerge, may be justified in many instances; the reverse is no less true in others. The iron will and obsessions of certain personalities may sometimes mould the shape of human affairs.

Lenin, Stalin, Hitler, and Mao-Tze Tung are some of the more obvious examples of our age.

The history of the Church is no less rich in such examples

than the secular one. In recent times, the personality of one man, more than any other, was responsible for determining the policies of the Vatican during one of the most fateful periods of its history. He was Eugenio Pacelli, better known as Pope Pius XII.

Eugenio Pacelli had watched the activities and strategems of the leftist churchmen with the silent alertness of an ideological tiger, ready to strike with feline effectiveness.

As a former Papal Nuncio to Germany during and after World War I, he had seen the rise of both Bolshevism and Nazism. If there was a man who knew the nature and objectives of each, he was that man. He had dealt personally with both systems when these were still young. Indeed, Pacelli at one time (1924-25) had even negotiated with Lenin on behalf of the Pope, with a view of supplanting the Russian Orthodox Church with the Catholic Church.

He had witnessed first-hand the birth and rise of Nazism and, after some doubts as to its ultimate objectives, had helped to bring about its ascendancy in Europe.

To Pacelli, then Secretary of State under Pope Pius XI, the ideological maneuvers of the pro-Russian Catholics within the Vatican were easily suppressed. He smothered them with an ecclesiastical velvet pillow, by displacements, relegation to obscurity, and the promise of advancement.

To the most obstinate, he precluded entry to the Pope's study and made the papal ear unapproachable to their advice, claims or ideas. As Secretary of State, the Vatican had become his domain and the Pope his ideological prisoner, so far as the pro-Communist elements within the Church were concerned.

He was too close to the real seat of power to permit the radical activists to carry on their work. Also, he was an exceptionally subtle politician, a clever career diplomat, ruthlessly determined to promote his own policies, all dedicated to total war against Communism.

At this particular period, he exerted tremendous influence

upon the ideological and diplomatic structure of the Church. This was due chiefly to the fact that he had been the principal formulator of the Vatican grand strategy, at the right hand of the preceeding Pope during the previous ten years – 1929-1939.

Indeed, it was owing chiefly to him that, as previously noted, in January 1933, when Hitler became Chancellor of Germany, the Fuehrer appointed Franz von Papen as his Vice-chancellor.

Cardinal Pacelli saw to it that the leftists' programmes were all de-fused before they could interfere with the continuation of his own personal diplomacy. Pius XI could not, so to speak, free himself from the pro-Nazi straight-jacket into which his Secretary of State had put him.

Notwithstanding this, the pro-Communist Catholics, particularly in France, Czechoslovakia and Italy, continued to work for a change of ideological direction in the Vatican. Even if the Church did not become pro-Communist, at least a policy of active neutrality would have benefitted Soviet Russia, since the withdrawal of Vatican support for Nazism would have profound political effect by influencing millions of Catholics throughout Europe, especially those living in Slavonic countries bordering Russia.

Despite Pacelli's overwhelming influence, the left-wing faction appeared to gain strength as the Pope's attitude towards Nazism continued to worsen. This became apparent when Hitler went to visit Rome.

Instead of receiving him as he had received other heads of State, Pius XI snubbed the Fuehrer and left the Vatican purposely to avoid meeting him. To add insult to injury, he went so far as to call Hitler a modern Nero.

As Nazi Germany was rapidly heading for war, Pius XI prepared to issue a public statement officially condemning Nazi aggression. The move would have had a tremendous political impact, since millions of Catholics, many of whom until then had supported the right-wing regimes because of their Church's approval, would have hesitated to furnish assistance to Hitler, once the pope had spoken against him.

Soviet Russia became greatly interested in the whole business, and certain prelates who were known for their pro-Russian sympathies, were contacted. One of these, an obscure diplomat posted to the Bosphorus, was Msgr. Roncalli, later to become Pope John XXIII.

A very special document

Pius XI prepared a special testament or document in which he denounced both Hitler and Mussolini and their preparations for war. Having done that, he convoked all the bishops of Italy to Rome. The statement was going to be read by the Pope himself on the 12th of February 1939.

Mussolini and Hitler, who had both heard of it, waited with mounting apprehension. Would the millions of Catholics listen to what the Pope was saying? On the eve of the Second World War, this was of immense importance. Upon its outcome there might depend the decision Hitler would make as to whether he would or could begin hostilities.

Pius XI, however, had become very ill. Forty-eight hours before the day he was to make his pronouncement, he was on the brink of death. He begged his doctors to do all in their power to keep him alive until the 12th of February.

I want to warn Catholics everywhere not to support Hitler and Mussolini," he kept repeating. "It might help to stop the outbreak of the war. Let me live another forty-eight hours."

The doctors did their best. Or did they? Ugly rumors that Fascist and Nazi intelligence had a hand in the "timely" death of the Pontiff were never substantiated. The stark fact, however, was that on the morning of the 10th of February 1939, only two days before he could deliver his anti-Nazi, anti-Fascist condemnation, the repentant Pius XI died.

The mere hint that the Pope might have been murdered in

the 20th century sounds absurd. Yet two popes died just as mysteriously less than two hundred years ago. In each instance, their deaths occurred on the eve or immediately after they had issued documents similar in importance to that which would have been announced by Pius XI.

The two pontiffs, like him, had been caught between extreme political interests and revolutionary subversion — in the case of Pius XI, Fasciam and Marxism.

The dominant issue during the 18th century, of course, was not Fascism versus Communism, but between their equivalents, the Monarchists who championed contemporary society of their day and the Jesuits, who were considered the most insidious eroders of the traditional establishment.

The Jesuits had come to be regarded as so dangerous that all the traditional forces were arrayed against them. This not so much because they had been adjudged subversives as that they had managed to infiltrate the infrastructures of European society with the same skill, cunning and efficiency as that of their Marxist counterparts in our day.

The result was predictable. The traditional, conservative governments asked the pope to neutralise the subversive Jesuits or else. In a word, he would have to suppress them or face the consequences. The military occupation of Rome was mentioned more than once during these discussions.

Pope Clement XIII, after endless indecision, postponements, and unconvincing delays, finally decided to do what he had been advised he should do. He capitulated.

He made ready a proclamation announcing the suppression of the Jesuit order. It was said that the document was written and was waiting for the day when it was to be made public. To the surprise of all, however, the Pope was suddenly attacked by a mysterious illness. He died on the 12th of February (a coincidence in dates) 1769 with agonising, unexplained convulsions.

Rumors had it that he had been poisoned. The suddenness of his affliction and the convulsions both pointed to it. The suspicions, however, were never proved. It was suggested by those in the know that the Pope had been made to die before he could publish the announcement of the official suppression of the Jesuit order.

The actual document itself vanished and was never seen again.

His successor, Pope Clement XIV, gave hints to the effect that certain political forces could not be halted. Prior even to his election, he had made some significant comments:

"The time has come," he had said, "for kings to be obeyed, since their arms stretch far beyond their frontiers, and their power can overtop the Alps."

Translated into contemporary terms, if we put right-wing dictators for kings, the historical parallel with the 1939 situation is a striking one.

Again, in July 1773, Pope Clement XIV wrote an order dissolving the Society of Jesus. This bull, *Dominus ac Redemptor*, was published August 16 of that year. After issuing it, however, the Pope relented, in fear of the consequences, and tried to withdraw it. Too late. The Spanish ambassador had already dispatched the document by special courier direct to Madrid.

The papal brief annihilated the Jesuit order throughout the world, closed its schools, cancelled its statutes. Its houses were occupied and its General and other dignitaries were imprisoned.

As soon as Clement had signed the brief, he predicted his own end. "I am lost," he was heard to whisper. Afterward, upon hearing the bells of Rome ring, he made another ominous comment: "They are not ringing for the saints, but for the dead."

A mysterious death

He fell immediately into "a singular state of agonising prostration, sunk under the weight of grief." On October 2, 1774, he died with great, unexplained suffering. His body decomposed so quickly that it was impossible to show his face, as was customary with a deceased pope; and his funeral had to be hastened, omitting the traditional rites.

The Jesuits were universally accused of having had him poisoned. But once more, no proofs were brought to the fore to substantiate such accusations.

The parallel with our times is too striking to be dismissed as mere literary innuendo. Not alone because of the similarity of the untimely deaths of two popes, but because the two pontiffs, squeezed between two irresistible, hostile political forces, had their lives unexplicably shortened after they had written documents having far-reaching political consequences.

To make the parallel more apt with the present century, it must be remembered that all this occurred on the eve of the French Revolution, when the traditional conservative world had begun to disintegrate and was already in a state of near collapse, very much as Western society in the 20th century.

The rising wind of oncoming revolution, was about to become a whirlwind which ended with the fall of the French monarchy and the rise of a new star, Napoleon.

The Church herself was struck by the revolutionary thunder. Churches were closed, her property seized, atheism proclaimed, her cardinals and bishops persecuted. The two papal successors to Clement XIV were sent into humiliating exile, first by the Revolution, then by Napoleon.

Although it is inappropriate to draw too close historical parallels, since history seldom repeats itself exactly, it is instructive nevertheless to cast a glance at the past, to justify our speculation about the present.

In the case of the untimely death of Pope Pius XI, for instance, what becomes evident is that in periods of great political pressures, when momentous historical decisions have to be made, popes can still become subject to personal removal or, in reverse, of personal promotion, as we shall have the opportunity to see presently in the case of another contemporary papal election.

Papal decisions, for or against, certain current ideologies, can still influence great historical events. The present is not only a confirmation of the past, but a clear proof that similar crises may well evoke similar solutions.

In any case, returning to the case of Pope Pius XI and his untimely death: what became of the dramatic Papal Will?

This is not a rhetorical question, or a demand for clarification of what at first sight might appear to be a simple footnote to ecclesiastical history. The very issue of peace or war might have depended to some extent upon its timely disclosure.

That this is no exaggeration is proved by the fact that the dying pope, once he realised how near was his end, had begged the Secretary of State to have his last will and testament published, even after his death.

Before his premature demise, he had had the contents of the will printed at the Vatican's own press, *in secret.* The purpose of the printing and of the secrecy was to have the document ready before anyone hostile to its contents should prevent it from becoming known.

Pius XI's concern about the testament at that particular period, was fully justified. A solemn declaration from the Vatican against the unrestrained belligerence of Hitler would have had an incalculable effect upon the political balance of Europe at that time.

Again, it must be recalled that a word from the Pope could have upset the political support of almost one third of the Germans, who were devout Catholics, to say nothing of the millions of Italians and others in Europe and the Americas. Even in the United States, there were a number of extreme right-wing Catholics, as for example, the energetic Father Coughlin and his supporters.

The uncertainty as to the reaction of German Austria and the many Catholics within the territories occupied by Hitler at that time, might have forced the Fuehrer to reconsider his immediate war plans. This could have compelled him to postpone the date of his attack on Poland — September 1939, the outbreak of World War II.

Another factor of extreme importance at this stage of European history was that of Soviet Russia. Before Hitler's attack on Poland, Russia had been negotiating with England and France in efforts to form a military alliance against Hitler. The negotiations had been elaborate and devious on both sides, but had been especially difficult because of the attitude of a suspicious Stalin.

It is certain that had the Pope's denunciation of Nazism been published the previous February when Pius XI had planned for it to be, the anti-Nazi front would have been greatly strengthened, thus encouraging Russia to sign a pact with the Western powers.

This did not occur. The Soviets suspected the West and with it the Vatican, of playing a double game and of playing for time. It must be remembered that Hitler at this period appeared to hold the mightiest military power of Europe, as in fact the course of events later proved he did. Certain elements within England, France and even the U.S., wanted Hitler to attack Russia, not only to destroy Communism, but equally to divert Hitler's armies away from Europe.

A diabolical pact

Stalin knew this very well; and, fearing a sudden pre-emptive attack from Nazi Germany, much to the chagrin of Communists everywhere, he signed a mutual pact of non-aggression with Hitler. The Berlin-Moscow Axis was born.

That incongruous Axis had a very brief life, it is true. But it suited both partners at the time, each of whom was playing his own game. The Hitler-Stalin Pact upset the balance of power in

Europe, making the outbreak of World War II inevitable.

Hitler and Mussolini, for all their posturing, were well aware of the political influence the Vatican could exert in world affairs. After all, both had been helped to power by this same Vatican. If the Vatican could help their accession, it could also contribute to their downfall.

Vague rumors of Pius XI's intentions had reached the ears of the Fascist, Nazi and Soviet intelligence. It was even said that the Russians, knowing what was afoot, had waited for the Vatican's anti-Hitler pronouncement before formulating their policies vis-a-vis England, France, and Germany. This was never proved, but it could be historically correct. The timing of the unexplained change of Russia towards the Allies and the commencement of the Hitler-Stalin Pact was too sudden to be a mere coincidence.

At any rate, the fact remained that Pius XI died his untimely death. Also, that the very few people near him who knew about the document, kept unaccountably silent. What compelled them to keep their secret? The answer is, they were ordered not to divulge anything whatsoever.

At the same time, *all* the already printed copies of the Pope's anti-Nazi testament vanished from the Vatican's printing plant minutes before the Pontiff expired.

That was not all. The original manuscript, written in the Pope's own hand, mysteriously disappeared from the papal desk.

The enigma was never clarified by any positive disclosures at a later date. But certain deductions could be made, without reaching any specific conclusion.

One of the persons who had individual access to the papal study was the Pope's Secretary of State, Cardinal Pacelli. It must be recalled that he was the same man who had steered the German Catholic Party to an entente with the Nazi Party, thus helping Hitler to power and who, only three months after Hitler had become Chancellor of Germany, had given orders for the

German Catholic Party to dissolve itself, the better to pave Hitler's way to political absolutism.

In the confusion of the interregnum at the Vatican — that is, during the period which has to elapse between the death of one Pope and the election of another — the secret of the missing testament remained well guarded. Rumors leaked out, but were soon forgotten in the rush of important events on the world stage. Hitler was careering ever more rapidly to the verge of war.

Several individuals, however, never forgot the late Pope's fateful will: Count dalla Torre; a young Vatican prelate, Monsignor Montini (later Pope Paul VI); and yet another, a devout Catholic priest and friend of the present author, Dom. Luigi Sturzo.

Dom Sturzo had been the founder and leader of the first Catholic Party of Italy, just after the First World War. Following the Second World War, the party, which was re-named Christian Democratic Party, ruled Italy for 33 consecutive years until 1977, when they had to agree to a "historical compromise" with the Italian Communists, the latter being then the second largest political party in the country.

Dom Sturzo knew the Pope very well indeed. The Catholic Party had been created with the Pontiff's personal help. And eventually it was disbanded by the same Pope's personal command. (1926-7).

This occured when Pius XI, having finally decided to cooperate with Mussolini, began his secret negotiations with him, negotiations which resulted in the signing of a Concordat and the solution of the Roman Question in 1929. The chief negotiator was a brother of Monsignor Pacelli, the future Secretary of State under Pius XI.

The significant thing about all this was that Pius XI, who had been prompted also by his papal nuncio in Germany, after having called Mussolini "the man sent by divine Providence," complied with Mussolini's request to suppress the Catholic Party. Hence, Pius's ordering Dom Sturzo to dissolve the Party two years before completion of the secret Vatican-Mussolini negotiations. Dom Sturzo went immediately into exile.

There was never any bitterness between the two men. Dom Sturzo, who was considered a "progressive" understood the Pope's strategy. He was, however, always hopeful that the Pope would one day see his mistake. That, in fact, was what eventually happened. Because of this mutual understanding, Dom Sturzo remained in close contact with Pius.

When finally Pius XI turned against the Fascist and Nazi dictators, he kept Dom Sturzo informed of the fact; not only of his change of attitude, but also of his forthcoming open condemnation of totalitarianism, giving him the precise date of the papal bombshell.

These facts were revealed to the present author by Dom Sturzo himself on two occasions. The first was when the Italian leader lived in London in the summer of 1939, and the second in the early Spring of 1940, after World War II had begun.

With the exception of a tiny circle in Rome, no one else knew of the anti-Fascist testament of Pope Pius XI.

The reason? A few weeks later, on March 2, 1939, the defunct Pontiff's anti-Communist Secretary of State, Cardinal Pacelli, was elected Pope. He became Pius XII. His immediate order, upon ascending the Chair of Peter: that his papal predecessor's wish concerning an anti-Hitler pronouncement must be totally and permanently forgotten.

And so it was, throughout his long pontificate.

CHAPTER 14

De Gaulle and the Envoy "Extraordinaire"

As soon as he had been crowned, Pius XII gave unequivocal notice that the Catholic Church had embarked upon a policy of total war against World Communism. Thereupon, following word by deed, he commenced a most vigorous anti-Bolshevist crusade.

All the avenues of ecclesiastical and political influence were hermetically closed to all pro-Communist elements within the Church, with the result that within weeks any vestige of power they had had vanished like mist under a meridian sun.

One form of activity in which most of them excelled, however, remained intact: their skill at promotional infiltration, within the infrastructures of the ecclesiastical edifice.

These activities, because of their clandestine nature, drew the support of all the anti-Fascist movements in Italy, Germany, and other countries of a Fascist-orientated Europe. This included the direct, even if subdued cooperation of sundry Communist parties, wherever these were still operating.

Their new strategy forced them underground, rendering their campaign of infiltration and subversion very difficult. When finally World War II broke out, the anti-Communist restriction turned vicious. The Hitler-Stain Pact saw the nadir of their activities. They felt betrayed by both God and man, and many gave up their work in despair.

The Communists, with whom they had consorted — now that Hitler and Stalin had reached a new understanding — refused to fight against Nazism. The rift between the Communists and the Catholic radicals seemed to have widened to the point of irrevocable separation.

Then Hitler's sudden attack on Russia changed everything at a stroke. The situation had been the more unfortunate because by an ironic twist, the Vatican had repeatedly warned Moscow of the impending Hitlerian attack. Stalin, who had always minimised the diplomatic ability of the Vatican, preferring the word of Hitler to that of the Pope, or of someone very close to the Pope, refused to take the warning at its face value, a miscalculation which cost millions of Russian lives, and almost the loss of the Soviet capital.

Now that the U.S.S.R. had been attacked, the Communists throughout Europe became overnight actively anti-Nazi. Their estrangement from the progressive Catholics was immediately amended. Now the Catholic radicals worked closely with the Communist guerillas towards a common objective — the defeat of Nazi Germany and the total victory of Soviet and European Communism.

While the underground fighters were patriots of various political persuasions, the largest and toughest element was composed of Communists. But while the European guerillas wanted only the liberation of their respective countries from Nazi occupation, the Communists regarded the Axis defeat as a stepping stone to two additional objectives: a) help Soviet Russia to achieve a decisive victory; and b) set up Communist regimes in the various European countries after the collapse of Nazism.

Many Catholic leftists were familiar with these goals and lent their cooperation toward achieving them, beginning with the lower clergy, openly encouraged by certain bishops. A few such prelates claimed a privileged influence on the grounds that it was the Vatican which had first given warning to the Soviet Union of the impending Nazi attack.

The mystery of an anti-Communist Vatican's reason for warning the Bolshevist dictator of Russia of the impending attack has never been satisfactorily explained. However, that certain pro-Communist elements within the Vatican itself were at work, there is no doubt, as we shall have occasion to prove presently.

Pope Pius XII meanwhile had become increasingly apprehensive at the obvious Communist practice of setting up Soviet regimes in nominally Catholic countries. Their activity in this sphere encompassed not only those lands bordering Russia, such as Hungary, Czechoslovakia, Poland, and others, but also Western countries like Italy, Belgium and France.

The danger was a real one, since the Red guerillas, with aid given them chiefly by the U.S. and Britain, had become the armed extension of the native Communist parties. These parties commanded the loyalty of hundreds of thousands of urban workers.

Anxiety among the prelates

In addition to their take-over plans, they also talked about retaliation against Catholics who had collaborated with the Axis powers. This created anxiety among the Catholic leadership, since a sizeable number of France's high-ranking clergy had actively supported the Catholic-Nazi puppet government of Catholic General Henri Petain. The Petain regime, in fact, had been one of Pius XII's ideological compromises with a victorious Hitler, following France's defeat by Germany in 1940.

After the fall of France, the Vatican had found itself in a difficult position. It could not openly support the Nazi invaders without risking the bitter resentment of Catholics in occupied France and elsewhere in Europe.

It was a situation which required the utmost skill in world diplomacy. Although the war until then had gone well for Germany, it was far from having been won. The entry of Japan and the U.S. into the conflict even made it possible that it might terminate with the defeat of Hitler.

This prospect became more plausible when the seemingly irresistible march of the German Army was stopped in 1942. By the middle of 1943, Mussolini had already fallen from power. The omen for the future looked dark.

Pope Pius XII had to take careful preparatory steps to insure that he would not find himself — and the Church — on the losing side. He promptly did so, beginning with cautious moves toward the Allied camp. Being the astute diplomat that he was, he started to woo the most powerful potential victor, the United States.

In making this new move, Pius XII was following the traditional grand strategy which the Church had used throughout her long history, namely, that of abandoning a losing ally to side with the winner. Thanks to his consummate diplomatic skill, timing and assistance from certain powerful personalities in the United States, he successfully laid the foundation for the Vatican's new alliance. As soon as the Vatican-Berlin axis began to crumble, the Vatican-Washington axis started to come into being.

But if a new alliance had been launched upon the ideological field, an alliance which affected most profoundly the domestic and foreign policies of America, another and more ominous one had also taken shape. That was the clandestine entete between a militant Communism and certain Catholic radicals active in the underground movements throughout most of Europe.

The pro-Communist elements had penetrated not only the rank and file of the lay Catholic cohorts; they had also infiltrated the very inner chambers of the Vatican itself. Disguised as diligent prelates or suave diplomats, they had also started to prepare for the day when, once Nazi Europe collapsed, a victorious Soviet Russia would emerge as a great military power, and Communism would take over a ruined Europe.

Their expectations proved partially incorrect. The Vatican, under the firm control of Pius XII and now an ally of the United States, pursued an anti-Communist crusade more fiercely than ever before.

Some of the dissidents in the Church, also still active in ecclesiastical obscurity, in due course became publicly known for their "un-enthusiasm" concerning the Vatican-Washington alliance. It was an alliance which, in their view, had promoted the Cold War against Communist Russia.

One of these dissenters was Monsignor Roncalli, an easygoing career diplomat, posted at various intervals to third-rate missions bordering Southern Europe and the Near East. His task was that of a minor functionary, charged with regional problems, and with issues of a purely ecclesiastical character.

At least, that was the official version.

In practice, however, once the war broke out, the character of his mission had changed. Turkey — before, during and even after World War II — was a well-known international listening post, a polite way of saying a centre of espionage. As such, it had become particularly important to certain anti-Communist nations, being as it was at the back door of Soviet Russia.

When Nazi Germany had finally collapsed and General De Gaulle had returned to liberated France, Pius XII's concern at the General's policies became acute.

De Gaulle, who from the day he returned until he resigned (1944-1969) managed to survive thirty-one assassination attempts, had declared in so many words that he intended to set up tribunals where members of France's Catholic hierarchy would be tried and condemned for collaboration with the Nazis.

The threat was a serious one and needed careful handling. It was even more serious in that behind it there was another, no less grievous, problem. This was the close association and cooperation of pro-Communist French Catholics, who were planning a joint political campaign for a take-over of post-war France.

The Communist threat

The problems were serious also for De Gaulle, since the French Communists had given notice that they intended to create large-scale trouble if their demands were not met, at least partially.

The French Communists were, of course, supported both politically and financially by Soviet Russia, then busy planning the territorial appropriation of Eastern Europe, with special regard to Poland, Hungary, Czechoslovakia and Eastern Germany.

At this juncture, Pius XII remembered the diplomat who had acted so sensibly and capably as a Vatican intelligence official in Turkey. His qualifications were impressive. He had had long training in the delicate art of conciliations, dealing with most desperate opponents. He had acted as Apostolic Delegate in Istanbul since 1934, as an administrator of the Latin Rite in Constantinople. There he had made friends with leading members of the Turkish government and with prelates of the Greek Orthodox Church. In Greece he had been spectacularly successful as a negotiator, when dealing with the Greeks during the German and Italian occupation.

In addition to his service record, he had another and no less interesting qualification: he was pro-Russian, pro-Orthodox Church, and for the people. He was popular with political leftists within and outside the Church. He was accepted by the Communists as one who understood them. In short, he was the ideal negotiator for dealing with the delicate situation which had developed in France.

An envoy from the Vatican, therefore, who although not a Communist, had expressed the opinion that the Russian Orthodox Church should consider a detente with the Soviets and also with Rome, was the man needed to solve the French Catholic-Communist tangle.

And so, one year before the end of the Second World War, Pius XII recalled Monsignor Roncalli, the radical diplomat in Turkey, and dispatched him to Paris to appease an embittered Catholic statesman, General De Gaulle.

At first, the leftist diplomat received a cool reception from De Gaulle. Then, De Gaulle's determination to punish the French hierarchy began to waver. Finally, his original plan to jail them or to have them dismissed, was dropped altogether. This, much to the relief of Pius XII and to the astonishment of many within and outside France.

What had occurred behind the scenes? The progressive Vatican envoy had demonstrated his skill to the full, a proficiency in the art of appeasing an opponent via the soft approach — that is, by the use of "political ecumenism." He had presented De Gaulle with a political bargain, namely that he, the Catholic diplomat, would deal with the French Communist guerillas. He would persuade them to forego their planned disruptive activities, provided De Gaulle would drop his plan to have the bishops and Cardinals of France tried in court for collaboration with the Nazis.

De Gaulle accepted. The charges against certain French bishops were dropped. How did Monsignor Roncalli, the radical diplomat, manage to persuade the Communists to soften their campaign of disruption in a recently liberated France?

He had convinced the Communists that the Church would soon re-orientate her policy towards Communism as a philosophy, as well as towards Soviet Russia as a former ideological opponent. To prove that he meant what he promised he blessed them and on one occasion in Paris even declared that he personnally was in sympathy with Marxism, since its tenets were in harmony with those of Christ.

His mission to France had been an outstanding success. Once back in Rome, however, the pink monsignor became quickly disappointed. Pius XII, instead of muting his opposition to Communism and to Russia, helped to launch the Cold War with his new ideological partner, the United States.

While not denying that the expansionist ambitions of Stalin in Europe and Asia were the main contributors to the growing military tension between East and West, Monsignor Roncalli remonstrated with the Pope for his "American anti-Communist bias."

When the Cold War became a hot war in Korea, the radical prelate objected to the support which the Vatican was giving, directly and indirectly, to the United States.

His objections to the domestic and European problems were no less frequent. He was very displeased, for example, when Pius XII suppressed the worker priests, and even more when he decreed excommunication for Catholics who dared to support a Communist candidate for political office.

One day, Pius XII finally sacked him. That is, he removed him from the policy-making centre of the Holy See to an ecclesiastical limbo.

To make the demotion less glaring, he was at the same time given a Cardinal's hat, but posted to the back-water Patriarchate of Venice. In other words, his promotion had been a veritable demotion — *"Promoveatur ut amoveatur"* as the ancient Romans used to say.

From the view of Pius XII, that should have been the end of an importunate radical, since the new Cardinal's only task would be, in the normal course of events, merely to prepare to die peacefully in Venice.

Fate had decreed otherwise. Not long afterward, the pro-Russian, pro-Orthodox, and pro-Communist diplomat succeeded Pius XII to the Chair of Peter.

CHAPTER 15

The Vatican-Washington Axis

If a Washington-Moscow entente had been the military axis upon which World War II had been made to revolve in a joint fight against Nazi Germany, the Washington-Vatican axis was the one upon which the Cold War was made to spin in a joint fight against world Communism.

Its two principal ideological opponents confronted each other across the globe, each determined to win the world's allegiance — the Pope in Rome and Stalin in Moscow.

Communist Russia, the main victor of World War II, now had at her command not only millions of armed men, but equally millions of Communists throughout liberated Europe. Amongst the latter were the pro-Communist, or even Communist, Catholics who emerged from the war more determined than ever to bring socialism into the reactionary corridors of the Vatican.

While these Catholics, including members of the clergy, became active in the ideological arenas, operating via socialist movements or through resurrected Catholic Parties now named Christian Democrats, the Vatican itself began a most formidable anti-Communist campaign, the like of which had never been seen before, nor has it been seen since.

The intensity of the crusade was fully justified by the world's political situation. The Bolshevist Dragon, which the Church had hoped to see destroyed or at least contained by World War II, now emerged stronger than ever. It threatened to engulf whole nations, militarily, ideologically, and territorially.

When the war had been going well for Hitler, the Vatican had tacitly and cautiously cooperated with him. When finally, the war had turned in favor of the Allies in 1933 and 1944, the Church had moved in their direction. France, England, and the other European countries did not matter much at the time, and were not courted as in the past. The chief object of the courtship was the country which had come out of the war as the second super-power — the United States.

As the war was drawing to its close, the U.S., no less than the Vatican, had become apprehensive about the spread of Communism in the countries being liberated by Allied arms. The cooperation between Washington and the Holy See, which had been tentatively initiated when Hitler's military machine began to go to pieces, turned swiftly into a veritable alliance. At first, the partnership was secretive and informal; but as the Russian menace became ever more evident, it became more open and direct.

The threatening postures of Stalin and the growing territorial appetite of the advancing Soviet armies, alarmed both the Vatican and Washington. While the Vatican became deeply concerned about the fate of millions of Catholics in Poland, Czechoslovakia, Austria, and Germany, the United States became no less concerned about the balance of power in the postwar world.

The ever-merging objectives of the Vatican and the policymakers in Washington gradually resulted in an integrated common cause — the containment of Russian geopolitics and Marxist imperialism.

Soviet Russia was not alone the sole threat. Communism itself became a formidable political force in the very midst of the victorious Western nations, in the form of national Communist parties which sprang from the ruins of war like dragon's teeth, ready to devour the victors.

Their ambitions knew no bounds. Belgium, France and Italy seemed to be turning red. Their leaders looked increasingly to Moscow for inspiration for setting up Sovietized governments.

It was in the interest of both the Vatican and Washington to see that these native Communist aspirations came to nothing. Since the ultimate goals of both centres of power were so similar, it was a simple matter to set into motion a common anti-Communist strategy directed at checking the spread of Marxism.

Pope Pius XII, now in full control of the Holy See, marshalled all the formidable forces at his disposal to consolidate the embryonic anti-Russian alliance. The diplomatic, religious, and emotional machineries of the Church were informed by the most animated anti-Communist attitudes. The Pope, a master tactician, saw to it that the cumulative result be felt throughout Europe and, above all, in the United States.

The Vatican-Washington partnership was widely accepted as being the Christian answer to the relentless advance of Godless Marxism. It came to be regarded as the chief means of rebuilding a democratic postwar society.

Thus it came about that within the shortest possible time, the Vatican and U.S. courtship turned into a concrete ideological wedding. The union was one of the most important political developments of the postwar period.

The traditional strategy of the Vatican — to discard a losing ally and to side with a victor — was once more adopted with predictable success.

The result of the strategy in the case of the U.S. — Vatican entente was to produce the Cold War. That war was not begun, as many came to believe, by a jingoistic Winston Churchill and other minor European statesmen. It was conceived in part within the walls of the Vatican, with the secret cooperation of certain religio-political and military activists in the United States.

The first indication of its birth emerged within the Church, not in the political, but in the religious field. This was embodied in the cult of Our Lady of Fatima one of whose objectives lent itself to a Cold War: Communist Russia would be defeated and then would be converted to Catholicism.

The Church is immensely skillful in such matters. Prior to launching any campaign, she takes preparatory steps, based upon strong religious emotion. We shall deal with this side presently.

Post-war hostilities

The Church did not originate the Cold War; but it was one of the first volunteers in the fight. The Western secular powers had already recognised the postwar threat of a victorious Russia, and were preparing to meet it even before the Vatican's move to join in the counter-thrust. Long before the defeat of Nazism, both Roosevelt and Churchill realised that Stalin had plans to annex half a dozen countries in Eastern Europe.

After the end of World War II, the two major victors — the United States and Russia — regarded each other with growing mutual suspicion. Instead of disarming, they both kept their military forces combat-ready.

Soviet Russia slowed down its demobilisation and kept a colossal army on a war footing. The United States, while debolising a large proportion of its wartime forces, nevertheless started preparing in other ways for a forthcoming confrontation with its recent ally. Only one year after Hitler's defeat, i.e., in 1945, the United States was already busy stockpiling essential raw materials, a 100-percent war measure. In July 1946, the 79th U.S. Congress gave official approval to the programme by passing Public Law 520 for that purpose. At that time the combined stockpile already stood at $4,546,000,000 worth of materiel. From 1946 to 1950, before the Korean War began, the U.S. stockpile almost doubled, standing at $8,300,000,000.

Soviet Russia's equivalent stockpiling of weapons and military goods was never disclosed, but one may reasonably assume that it was at least comparable to that of the U.S., if not more.

By 1947, throughout the world, there were 19 million men under arms. This less than two years after victory in Europe. From then onward, military expenditure rocketed to astronomical figures. By the time that Yugoslavia — who had begun to show her independence and to lean toward the West — the world had been split asunder.[1]

The American armament factories were made to hum, while the U.S. Air Force, Army and Navy were posted throughout the world in the principal strategic places. Colossal expenditures for maintaining this worldwide war readiness were voted by the U.S. Congress — e.g., $129,000,000,000 within less than two years (1950-1952). By 1953, in Europe alone, the United States had already built more than a hundred airfields, many of them specifically equipped for atomic operations, as defensive-offensive bases against Russia.[3]

In Communist Russia, preparations of the same magnitude were carried out, with an impetus to match that of the West. Within a few brief years, billions of rubles were appropriated for military purposes. As Russia became the Communist arsenal of the East, America became the anti-Communist arsenal of the West, and its most powerful political and military leader.

The other nations of the world, not yet recovered from the

Second World War massacre, now were obliged to make ready for the Third. Politicians, generals, heads of state, all spoke of atomic war. Armies re-assembled, ready to march.

Such a gigantic armament race undermined the economy of whole nations, thus rendering an eventual war between the two mighty Eastern and Western blocs not so much a probability as a certainty.

While these military preparations were under way, preliminary moves of a psychological, i.e., emotional, nature were also being carried out on the religious front by the Vatican.

This programme was formulated not only in the secret recesses of the Holy See, but also in those of Washington. It was then promoted on a global scale with the most consummate skill, typical of the genius of Pius XII.

Mounting emotional reaction to Communist religious suppression was engendered first by the trial of Archbishop Alojzije Stepinac of Yugoslavia, and then by that of anti-Communist Cardinal Mindszenty of Hungary.

The two trials, widely publicised, generated immense feeling of resentment against the Communists, in both the Catholic and the Protestant worlds. It provided Pius XII with two effectively spectacular bases from which to put political pressure upon the U.S. government, and to consolidate the Catholic-American alliance.

Archbishop Stepinac had helped in the setting up of a Catholic dictatorship in Croatia in 1940-1945, with the blessing of Adolf Hitler. Although he denied it vigorously, he was later charged with having collaborated with the leader of the Ustashis (a kind of Croatian Nazi party) led by Ante Pavelic. Croatia became a kind of Fascist state in which everybody had to belong to one political party and to one religion — Catholicism. There were forced conversions, sometimes of whole villages. Those who resisted were sent to concentration camps. Atrocities were committed, it was claimed, by the knowledge and connivance of the archbishop. By the time the pogrom ended, over 600,000 men, women and children had perished.[4]

Following World War II, Pavelic reportedly found asylum in the Vatican until he could flee to South America, the refuge of so many other Nazi criminals.

Archbishop on trial

The postwar Communist government of Yugoslavia arrested Archbishop Stepinac and put him on trial for his alleged cooperation with the bloody Ustashis. The Church declared that these were trumped-up charges, levelled against the prelate because of his unrelenting opposition to Communism. On October 11, 1946, he was sentenced to 16 years imprisonment, but Tito released him on house arrest in 1951. Pius XII named him a Cardinal the following year.

During 1948-1949, another ranking prelate of the Catholic Church was placed on trial by the Communists, this time in Hungary. He was Cardinal Mindszenty, who had staunchly supported the U.S.-Vatican campaign to overthrow the Communist regime in his country. Like Archbishop Stepinac, he became known to the West as an anti-Communist hero, and was given refuge in the American embassy in Budapest.

During this period, Pius XII was holding talks with prominent military leaders of the non-Communist world, particularly those from the United States. British and American generals came and went in endless procession to and from the Vatican.

To cite but one example: during a single day in June 1949, Pius received five U.S. generals in successive audiences. They were: Gen. Mark Clark, wartime commander of the U.S. Fifth Army in Italy and subsequently a field officer in the Korean conflict; Lt. Gen. J. Cannon, commanding general of the U.S. Air Force in Europe; Maj. Gen. Robert Douglas, Chief of Staff of the U.S. Armed Forces in Europe; Maj. Gen. Maxwell Taylor, Deputy Commander, European Command; and Lt. Gen. Geoffrey Keyes, Commanding General of the U.S. Forces in Austria.

All these top-ranking military figures went to confer with the Pope because they considered him, like themselves, the commander of forces involved in the Cold War.

With the Vatican now a busy centre of far-flung anti-Communist war strategy, it is not surprising that Catholic dignitaries in some countries would speak and act on the assumption that actual war was impending. The Vatican which, in an astonishingly brief period, had developed the most intimate relations with certain influential elements in America, was not merely indulging in wishful thinking. It was dealing with a concrete military reality of the time. This was demonstrated to a stunned world on August 27, 1950.

On that date, Mr. Francis Matthews, during a speech in Boston, called upon the United States to become "the first aggressor for peace." In other words, he was calling upon his government to launch a third world war.

Matthews was neither a crank nor an irresponsible citizen. He was, in fact, a key figure in the U.S. government – Secretary of the Navy. He was also a practicing Catholic, honoured many times for his services to the Church. More, he had been the head of the Knights of Columbus and a secret Papal Chamberlain to Pope Pius XII.

With such highly-placed Catholics in the American government, the Vatican could not help being informed of what was brewing in certain quarters, where the expression, "first aggressors for peace" was not merely a rhetorical device. The information passed along to bishops and Cardinals throughout the Western world helped them to shape the attitudes of people within their respective spheres of influence. The result was that while the vast ecclesiastical network of the Roman Catholic Church was setting in motion strong anti-Communist sentiments, the military, political and financial machinery of the United States was adding weight to a joint campaign that was soon to be identified by the media as the Cold War.

The Cold War — a child of Communist territorial and ideological aggression, plus the Catholic-American determination to resist it — was soon to break out into the "hot war" of Korea when, quoting U.S. Secretary of State John Foster Dulles, "the United States walked to the brink of war [atomic war, that is] three times.

The first time occured during the Korean truce negotiations in June 1953; and twice in 1954, when the U.S. warned the Chinese that if they intervened, atomic bombs would be dropped in Manchuria and Southern China.[5]

That threat was not a bluff. It was concrete and nuclear. Russian, European, Chinese, and World Communism took notice and slowed their pace.

Retarding the march of World Communism in this way represented a triumph for the Vatican's new Vatican-Washington alliance, the great political imponderable of post-World War II.

CHAPTER 16

Stalin's Plan For a Red Papacy

Even though World War III did not break out in 1952, as so many thought and some wished it would, the machinations which had been going on in Washington and at the Vatican were not lost upon Joseph Stalin.

He had set in motion some counter-moves of his own.

The general feeling of helplessness of those throughout the world who were caught between the two hostile powers, was experienced also by some within the Church itself. Indeed, this was the situation in the Vatican itself, which at this juncture had been turned into a centre for Pius XII's personal rule.

It was chiefly during this period that Pius had dispensed with the traditional diplomatic procedures and the customary exchanges of ecclesiastical and political representatives, the better to conduct a campaign which required more direct, resolute action.

The Kremlin had been no less active than Washington; yet, while concentrating upon U.S. affairs, it did not overlook the Vatican. Ex-seminarist Stalin's cynicism about the Pope during World War II, when he had inquired sarcastically how many battalions the Pope could put into the field, by now was a thing of the past.

Stalin had learned his lesson. In Eastern Europe, Catholics were giving him continuous trouble. In Western Europe, the newly-created Christian Democracy had set up major anti-Communist governments. Moreover, as far as the Cold War was concerned, Stalin knew that one of its chief promoters was none other than Pius XII himself.

It became obvious to the Kremlin strategists that the Vatican deserved not only careful attention, but unusual treatment as the diplomatic weapon of a religion with political muscle.

Men, whether they be Communist Commisars or Catholic Cardinals, cannot entirely discard their individual likes and dislikes, or minimise their weaknesses and preferences.

Stalin, who had dealt personally with thousands of people, whom he had elevated to great political heights or sent to be executed, was a master analyst of human behaviour. He applied the same rules vis-a-vis the situation at the Vatican that he had so successfully followed in dealing with secular political power centres.

Not those in which he had applied brute force, to be sure, but those where cunning had been most effective. What was required for combatting an amorphous, widespread menace such as the anti-Communism of the Vatican, was a similarly intangible weapon, one as invisible as a spider's web, and as deadly.

Accordingly, Stalin prepared for the actual demise of the Pope — nothing less, nothing more. Since the Catholic anti-Russian crusade emanated chiefly from the personal convictions of Pius XII, he reasoned, it should be possible to neutralise such anti-Communist virulence by the replacement of Pius XII with a pope whose personal beliefs were the opposite.

The success of such a policy, of course, depended upon the election of a new pontiff who would be ready and willing to dismantle the structure Pius had built over three decades, and to replace it with one of a political character more favourable to Communism. On the face of it, Stalin's objective was an impossible one. Only direct divine intervention could work such a miracle.

Former seminary student Stalin, however, although a professional atheist, was well versed in theological thinking. His dealings with the Orthodox Church had taught him that ecclesiastics, high or low, have their personal opinions about political problems. Through the skillful manipulation of its clerical roster, for example, the Orthodox Church — once the sworn enemy of Communism — had now become an ally.

The Orthodox hierarchy had faced the political reality, not only that Russian Communism was there to stay, but also that Christianity could be interpreted as being nearer to Communism than the traditional capitalist teaching of the Gospels had made it appear.

Stalin well knew that in the West there were pockets of Catholic clergy who were Communist sympathizers. Also, that large sections of Catholic workers and, indeed, of Catholic social movements, had their Marxist advocates.

These elements had always disapproved of Pius XII's anti-Communist activities, the more so since such policies dovetailed with those of the United States, whom they had been taught to regard as the fountain-head of imperialism. Inside the Vatican itself, there were some who had experienced the same war jitters as the average man in the various cities of Europe.

Spies inside the Vatican

In addition to such considerations, Stalin had processed certain information, not available even to traditional diplomacy. In other words, if the Pope had his agents in Washington, Stalin had his own informants inside the Vatican.

These were not the kind of agents so typical of the antediluvian Comintern and its related spy agencies. They were the very cream of the Kremlin's special elite.

Although a ruthless pragmatist, Stalin held un-Marxist beliefs concerning the irrationality of human behaviour. Also in the potency of deeply-held religious or ideological convictions.

These, if adroitly employed, could work miracles. Additional information about the opinions, personal habits, physical dispositions and monumental minutiae of certain individuals could do the rest.

Such information had been collected from all over the Catholic world. The world's number one Catholic, Pius XII, being the main target, yielded the most. His visions and mystical visitations were as familiar to Stalin as they were to the editor of the *Osservatore Romano,* or to the Cardinal confidantes who made them known to the world.

Back in 1948 and 1949, for instance, when Pius XII was fulminating against anyone who wished to vote for the Communists in the general elections of Italy and France, Stalin knew that the Pope was planning to proclaim a new dogma.

Piety and propaganda

But more significantly, he was aware that some Cardinals were firmly opposed to it, on religious as well as political grounds. As noted previously, the new dogma — the bodily assumption of the Virgin Mary — had been an act of piety on the part of Pius XII, but served at the same time as a focus of political propaganda, as was his subsequent experience of the Fatima phenomenon.

Stalin, the materialist, regarded these manifestations as indications of physical and psychological ailments, as clearly shown by the fact that following such visions the Pope became the prey of fits of depression. These, Stalin was told, were relieved by an ever-increasing dose of drugs, some of which were considered dangerous.

It was even rumoured (although the rumours were never confirmed) that certain doctors, in their eagerness to ameliorate his distress, had administered overdoses of tranquillizers. The files of the Kremlin, no less than those of the CIA, contain accurate details about these developments. They were of immense political significance because they directly influenced the Pope's decisions concerning diplomatic and political matters of grave importance.

Years later, it was reported that these periods of depression developed into veritable illness which, besides causing acute pain and recurrent discomfort, were thought to be the cause of mystical experiences of various kinds.

In 1955, for example, during one of his serious illnesses, Pius claimed to have been visited by Christ in person. "He saw the Lord close to him, silent in all his eloquent majesty." And later, according to the *Corriere della Sera,* Italy's largest newspaper, the Holy Father also heard "the true and distinct voice of Christ."

In Stalin's way of looking at things, such experiences indicated that the Pope's health was failing. In political terms, this meant that once Pius had passed from the scene, his anti-Communist crusade would come to a halt, or at least ameliorate.

The selection of a new pope would then assume a far-reaching significance, not only to the Church, but also to Washington and to Moscow.

The papal elections in 1939, on the eve of World War II, had not been forgotten, the missing papal testament even less. The Conclave of 1939 had, in a sense, been a farce, a triumph of "reactionary" forces of European and American right-wing elements. Middle-of-the-way Cardinals did not have a chance. The most *papabile* of them, for example, – Cardinal Dalla Costa, Archbishop of Florence – had been defeated almost at once, although many had expected him to be elected.

The coming papal election, Stalin reflected, had to be planned in a more satisfactory way. That meant long-range lobbying, both within and outside the Vatican. The most acceptable papal candidate had to have a well-defined personality; possess the right kind of ideological bias that would have the approval of the "progressive" forces inside the Church; and be potentially attractive to a vigourous group of activists within the Roman hierarchy itself.

Candidates, known and unknown, had been carefully monitored and nursed since the end of World War I. One or two of the more desirable had managed to infiltrate the Catholic Parties, but then had vanished without leaving a trace. During and after World War II, however, several individuals had seemed to make their mark, and were duly noticed. The three names which headed the list in Rome, Washington and – above all – in Moscow, were those of Msgr. Giovanni Battista Montini, the red pro-Secretary of State; Msgr. Gregory Agagianian, Patriarch of the Catholic Rite of the Armenian Church; and Msgr. Angelo Giuseppe Roncalli, diplomat and intelligence agent for many years in the Middle East.

Msgr. Agagianian had become noteworthy before World War II when Pope Pius XI, after his disillusionment with Hitler, had elevated him to the Patriarchate in 1937, a post which he held for 25 years thereafter.

In 1946, anti-Communist Pope Pius XII made him a Cardinal. This was at the start of the Cold War. At the time, the appointment raised many eyebrows in Washington and in Rome. The fact was that the move was a longrange one. Cardinal Agagianian was expected to play a major role during the developing Cold War and afterward, once Russia had been invaded or, at least, Eastern Europe had been liberated from Russian occupation.

The reason was that Agagianian was the top expert on the Soviet Union, Communism, and the Orthodox Church; a brilliant scholar and a devious diplomat. In addition to such qualifications, he had others no less interesting in the eyes of those who intended to use him for implementing their political plans.

He was of Armenian origin, but a Georgian by birth. He had known Communism at first hand, having lived three difficult years as a young priest in Tiflis, Georgia, whilest the Bolshevist Revolution was raging. He spoke fluent Russian, and was considered a very special Russian by the Russians themselves.

Agagianian was also considered very special by Stalin himself, the Cardinal having had the dubious distinction of attending the same Jesuit seminary in Georgia as Stalin had done. This was a small, but significant, fact, since Georgian Stalin had an extraordinary weakness for anyone born in Georgia.

Pius XII's successor, John XXIII, appointed Agagianian Prefect of the Congregation for the Evangelization of the People in 1960, intending to woo the Soviets through the Russian-born Cardinal.

Stalin's predilection for Agagianian proved to be the Cardinal's undoing, however, since several cardinals feared that Stalin's patronage might turn into a political liability.

Their apprehension proved to be well-founded even after Stalin's death. At the conclave of 1958, which elected the first pink pope, John XXIII, and even at the succeeding one which elected the first socialist pope, Paul VI, Agagianian's star suffered a sharp decline because of Stalin's past distant patronage.

That Agagianian had been a serious candidate for the papacy was due not so much to the fact that the progressive and pro-Russian elements within the Church took his candidature for granted, but that he was personally very popular with all the cardinals. This to such an extent that during the two conclaves of 1958 and 1963, he was frequently greatly embarrassed when people in Rome, upon meeting him, shouted: "Long live the

Pope!" as he passed.

The fact that he was Georgian-born, that he had attended the same seminary as Stalin, that he was known for his expertise in Russian and Communist problems, and that the Communists in Russia and Italy liked him, all were indicative that the general opinion was favourable for a radical reorientation of the Roman Catholic Church towards the left.

Although Agagianian had been a favorite ideological candidate of Stalin, nevertheless, the Russian dictator, prior to his death had reached the conclusion that Agagianian's election to the papacy might do more harm than good, since the break could have caused great alarm in the Catholic world, not to say in the United States. A softer approach was considered to be more diplomatic. This meant that, ironically, Agagianian was discarded for the very reasons which had made him such an ideal papal candidate. A Russian-born, Russian-speaking, Russian-educated pope would have created embarrassment for those who were seeking a smooth Vatican realignment.

A candidate with the traditional qualifications — European, Italian, and mildly progressive — had better chances to guide the Church towards a pro-Communist policy.

And so it was that Kremlin eyes turned towards two candidates who best qualified for a progressive new papacy, namely, the Monsignori Roncalli and Montini.

The Catholic comrade

Stalin's preference was for Roncalli, ever since his name was brought to his notice by the French Communists. Thorez, the French Communist leader, who had dealt personally with Roncalli when the latter had been sent to France to appease De Gaulle, gave a glowing report to the Kremlin about him. He was the ideal prelate, he reported. He understood Marxism like a Marxist; he had no hard feelings against anybody, and if Marxism had not been sponsoring militant atheism, he might have been the best Christian (*sic*) comrade in the Catholic Church!

Reports about the possible candidates and also about future possible cardinals, were sent regularly to Moscow. The files of many promising hierarchs after World War II were bulging with the most minute curricula vitae. The archives of the Kremlin have never been kept so up-to-date since that time. The smallest details concerning the top *papabili* − the stuff of which popes are made − were carefully filed and analysed in great detail.

Roncalli's assessment at the Kremlin was more favourable than that of Montini.

Roncalli had three qualifications that had endeared him to Moscow. He was a genuine socialist. He was easy with the left. He was of true peasant stock and "he sported peasant's hands," an observation which was later confirmed by none other than the daughter of the Soviet Premier, Nikita Kruschev, after her visit to the Vatican, where she met Msgr. Roncalli who, by that time, had become Pope John XXIII.

From a political point of view, Msgr. Roncalli's opposition to Pius XII's anti-Communist crusades had qualified him, more than anything else, to be their protege.

If this attitude had made Roncalli a favourite in Moscow, it had made him unpopular in Washington. There, Roncalli was regarded as a prelate of no great importance and no future − a mistake which the Vatican-Washington lobby repeated twice, having underestimated the strength of the anti-American, progressive elements in the Roman Catholic Church since the end of World War II.

Whether Msgr. Roncalli was aware of the attention he was receiving from the Communist command centre or not, has never been disclosed. That he was sufficiently perceptive about his personal popularity with the leftists of Italy is an undisputed fact. Italian socialists and communists were in frequent contacts with him, at different levels. Some of them had direct lines of communication with the Communist Party chiefs, and thus with

Moscow.

The leader of the Italian Communist Party, for example, Palmiro Togliatti, considered Roncalli the ideal man for reaching a workable compromise between the Church and Socialism, and so reported during his frequent visits to Moscow.

The campaign to make Roncalli *papabile* at this stage seemed somewhat devoid of any concrete success, particularly during the general elections of 1948 and 1949, when Togliatti had to counteract Pius XII's threats to any Catholic who dared to vote for the Communists.

In Washington, talk of progressive popes after Pius XII were dismissed and red-inspired moonshine. As for Msgr. Roncalli, the man who had disapproved of the Cult of Our Lady of Fatima, he was treated as a person with not a chance in hell of "denting in" the policies of the Vatican...or words to that effect.

Roncalli's views concerning the sundry Cold War problems, although put on record, were not (as they should have been) assessed in political terms, even by the policy-making people at the CIA subsection specialising in Vatican affairs.

Yet, most of them were pertinent and potentially important. Roncalli did not approve, for instance, of visions or so-called miracles. It is doubtful whether he personally believed in the validity of either. He prided himself on having, besides large hands, equally large feet, firmly planted on the ground. Visions, he said in private, were harmful to true religion. He disapproved of them specifically when they were used as a means of promoting political ends. Occasionally he had also made barbed remarks about Pius XII's apparitions, no less than about Cardinal Spellman — the "dollar boy scout," as he called him — not to mention certain other prominent Americans "eager to test their new atom bombs."

According to him, the Vatican-Washington alliance was leading to war. The Church had become more reactionary even than the United States, and was being transformed into the antechamber of American dollar imperialism (a familiar Communist epithet).

When Pius XII condemned and then disbanded the pro-Communist worker priests, Msgr. Roncalli first protested in private to the Pope, and then encouraged the worker priests to go ahead "but not too openly."

He was known for his eagerness to start a dialogue with the Russian Orthodox Church, as well as with the Russian Communists many of whom, he used to say, were more Christian in practice than certain Christians in the West. Atheism, according to him, was an intellectual fashion and was already on the way out. He had known Communists who were more believers than even he was.

A radical promise

Msgr. Roncalli, pretending not to notice the activities of the pro-Communist campaign in the Church, was always non-committal. Once he even said that if the Holy Ghost ever made the mistake of electing him to the Papacy, he would start a reformation the like of which the Church had not seen since the first one, a right-wing Cardinal who knew him well, told the present author.

Pius XII, although immersed in his grandiose schemes, kept a watchful eye on the few progressives in his immediate circle. Their private opinions reached him regularly through an internal intelligence service, adequate for the purpose. This consisted of Vatican gossip, Roman exaggeration, and genuine information. One of his principal informants was Count Della Torre, editor of the Vatican newspaper, the *Osservatore Romano.* Count Della Torre was honest, devout and loyal; and all kinds of information, much of it of a very private nature, reached him.

Pius's intimates were also fed with genuine and false reports by interested diplomats or agents. U.S. Intelligence had a very special channel — a hot line between the Pope's private study and its equivalent in the State Department in Washington.

John Foster Dulles, his brother Alan, and Archbishop Spellman saw to it that nothing should pass unnoticed in Rome. In a word, the intelligence exchange between the Vatican in Rome and the "Little Vatican" in New York was meticulous and accurate.

Roncalli's "lobby" was watched even more closely than the subtler subversive thinking of Msgr. Montini, the Church's other leading progressive. But if the dossiers of both were daily growing thicker in Washington, they were increasing even more in Moscow. The only difference was in the labels. CIA files (and those of cognate agencies) regarded them as "red," while those in Moscow called them "progressives."

The American and Russian intelligence systems, however, were no less keen of reciprocal reporting. At time, such information was released as "leaks." Some of them were genuine, some concocted. Many were meant to reach the ears of Pius XII, and more often than not, did so.

Finally, the two Dulles brothers, supported by Spellman, asked for Roncalli's removal from the Vatican. Plausible reasons were given: health, age, gentle subversion.

One day in 1953, Msgr. Roncalli was given a Cardinal's hat and then promptly transferred to the Patriarchate of Venice. So far as Pius XII, the Dulles brothers and Cardinal Spellman were concerned, that should have been the end of the pro-Russian prelate, now interred in a political backwater, where the best he could look forward to was an honourable death, unremembered and harmless.

The following year, Msgr. Roncalli's socialist fellow traveller was also transferred, he to the Archbishopric of Milan "to do pastoral work," something totally alien to the former pro-Secretary of State.

The two removals were made at the height of the Cold War, and therefore in political terms, were very significant. The

Stalin's favorite candidate for a leftist pope was his fellow Georgian, Cardinal Agagianian, Patriarch of the Armenian Church, here shown being greeted upon his arrival in London by black Cardinal Rugambwa, Archbishop of Tanzania.

transfers were duly noted in Moscow and also at the Russian Embassy in London, where the two men had come to be regarded as even more *papabile* than ever.

They were now mentioned as the potential means of breaking the Vatican's dependence upon the "war-mongering policies of the United States."

This information was imparted to the author by a person who was well informed about the Kremlin's thinking on the matter. He was first secretary of the Russian Embassy in London, who was in a very special position to know. He had been put into the diplomatic service by Stalin himself, a fellow Georgian. His observation proved to be very accurate, as we shall have occasion to prove presently.

Stalin's death ended his personal sponsorship of Roncalli as a papal candidate. Although the Russian dictator's protege, the First Secretary in London, also vanished following his patron's demise, (as did most of Stalin's Georgian compatriots) during the anti-Stalist purge, his successor — a Mr. Bruslow who was also a top KGB official — confirmed that the two progressive prelates were still regarded by the Kremlin as favourite *papabile.*

In 1958, Pope Pius XII's successor ascended the throne of St. Peter. To the surprise and dismay of many, he was the exiled and almost forgotten Cardinal Roncalli, Stalin's favourite old candidate.

The Conclave had been a laborious one; the fight for Roncalli's election was a heated one. It had taken no fewer than eleven ballots to reach a final choice. Washington's lobbying had been outwitted and had come into action when it was too late.

A number of Cardinals were alarmed. Several considered Roncalli's election a disaster. The pro-American element, in particular, predicted the opening of a gulf between the United States and the Vatican. The golden era of the Pius-Dulles-Spellman triumvirate had closed.

Some observers predicted that the new Pontiff would destroy the Church. And the first omen of his pontificate could not have been more indicative. He chose the name of a 15th century anti-pope, John XXIII. The assessment of the conservative element, as well as that of the Soviet embassy official in London, and others in Rome, was proved to be correct:

The Catholic Church would never be the same again.

CHAPTER 17

The Pontiff Who "Opened the Window"

In 1903, Msgr. Giuseppe Sarto, the good-hearted Patriarch of Venice, became Pope Pius X. He was the same Pius X, whose ghost in 1939 allegedly appeared to Cardinal Pacelli to predict the latter's elevation to the Papacy.

When that prophecy was fulfilled, Pope Pius XII, besides taking the same name in gratitude, canonised him. The Church had enrolled another saint — St. Pius X.

In 1958, another good-hearted Patriarch of Venice became a Supreme Pontiff of the Roman Catholic Church. He was John XXIII, formerly Patriarch Roncalli, the prelate that Pius XII had exiled a few years before as a punishment for daring to opposé his anti-Communist policies.

There was one important difference in the careers of the two Patriarchs of Venice, however. While Msgr. Sarto, back in 1903 had left Venice to attend the Conclave, with a return ticket, Cardinal Roncalli had not followed his example.

When someone, prior to his leaving for Rome, had jokingly reminded him of this, Patriarch Roncalli had smiled a knowing smile, as a reporter aptly remarked at the time, and made no comment.

Roncalli's smile on this occasion, far from having been ambiguous, had been a significant one. It was the smile of a *papabile* who had been aware of the subdued activities of a powerful lobby on his behalf.

His candidacy had been known to him as well as to others interested in the radical transformation of the Church, which they considered to be long overdue. They were not disappointed in their expectations, as they learned almost at once, even before they had left the Conclave which elected him.

The new Pope, in fact, ordered the immediate prolongation of the assembly by one day in order to hold a private Consistory before the Cardinals dispersed.

A small act, but indicative of the impatience the new Pontiff had to begin restructuring the whole Church, which he had determined to free from what he considered her petrifying religious and political dogmatism.

John treated his electors to an illuminating speech, in which he told them in so many words what he intended to do. Then he dismissed them, to start his radical reformation.

Pope John, "the good Pope," as he was called almost at once, or "John the anti-pope," as he was known in certain circles in Rome and in the U.S.A., has realised how bitterly his election had been contested, as evidenced by the eleven ballots necessary to achieve that end.

He turned his attention first to the ultra-conservative and pro-American cardinals, led by Spellman who had so relentlessly opposed his candidacy, an opposition which Pope John never forgot nor forgave.

He informed Spellman that from that time onward, he would not be welcome in Rome. The ban — for that is what in fact it was — had been the more telling because until then Spellman had visited the Pope with a frequency denied even the cardinals resident in Rome.

Spellman had had exceptional private access to Pius XII because he had been a personal friend and confidant of the Pontiff since the latter was a Papal Nuncio in Germany. His intimacy, however, had not been only of a personal nature. They had political significance as well. Through Spellman, Pius XII could deal almost directly with the Catholic lobby in Washington, with the Senate and the Pentagon, and other key figures in the U.S. government. Incidentally, it will be recalled that Spellman was also the Military Vicar of the American armed forces.

John's ban against Cardinal Spellman alarmed certain elements in the United States because the prelate, besides being a very privileged associate of Pius XII, had also served as the Pope's "grey eminence," acting as a spokesman for all the anti-Communist forces in America.

He was also the unofficial link between the Pope and John Foster Dulles, the U.S. Secretary of State and, therefore, the Secretary's brother Alan, head of the CIA.

Spellman's special relationship with the Vatican and with the U.S. State Department, made him a power in his own right at both ends of the axis. Thanks to such a status, he had become the channel through which certain U.S. government officials on a policy-making level (not excluding those of the Pentagon) could communicate with those in Italy and elsewhere.

John never forgave Spellman for the role he played in the Cold War, nor for propelling anti-Communist President Diem into a position of power in South Vietnam; nor indeed, for his steady propounding of an anti-Russian hard line.

The ban was even more significant in that it gave clear notice to Spellman and the forces he represented that the special relationship between Washington and the Vatican, which had flourished under Pius XII, was now permanently at an end.

The new pope was anxious for the American lobby at the Vatican to be completely neutralised. The more so, since the American group, aided and abetted by a substantial rightwing minority in the Curia, had almost won the day during the papal elections, in their passionate opposition to John.

The favourite non-candidate

At the 1963 Conclave, many of the progressives as well as some of the uncommitted Cardinals would have preferred Msgr. Montini to Roncalli as a candidate for the Papacy, because of Montini's long and distinguished diplomatic career.

But Montini could not be elected pope because he was outside the College of Cardinals from which the Supreme Pontiff must be chosen. The result was that Msgr. Montini, while being the preferred candidate by many, was in fact lobbying these same people on behalf of Roncalli. He had favoured Roncalli as the future pope from the beginning, successfully persuading certain noncommitted Cardinals to vote for him.

It was generally believed that it was Msgr. Montini's efforts which in the long run had tipped the scales in favour of Roncalli. This also was something which Pope John never forgot. His first act as Pope, in fact, was to make Msgr. Montini a Cardinal, thus ensuring that at the next Conclave, Montini would be eligible for election to the Papacy.

John's gesture was also meant to indicate that he considered Montini the man best suited to be his successor to the Chair of Peter, a leader who would be fully capable of continuing the radical reforms he planned to launch.

Montini's acceptance of a Cardinal's hat was proof that he supported John's proposed revolution in the Church with the same ardor with which he had opposed Pius XII's anti-Commu-

President Podgorny of Soviet Russia spends an hour in private audience with Pope Paul at the Vatican on 30th January 1967. The meeting set an historical precedent, being the first ever between a Pope and a Communist head of state. The encounter, brought about by the Soviet ambassador (centre) was the culmination of secret negotiations, carried on for years, since the son-in-law of Premier Nikita Kruschev paid the first visit of any top Soviet leader to the Vatican during the reign of Pope John XXIII.

Pope Paul VI extends cordial papal greeting to the Communist mayor of Rome, following the latter's election in December 1976. The Pontiff urged Romans to cooperate with the Communist administration.

nist campaign, refusing the Cardinal's hat when it was offered him by Pius.

It was the effective, clever lobbying of Msgr. Montini, therefore, plus the subtle Russian influence, which eventually made the large groups of uncommitted cardinals change their minds and gave Roncalli their votes, thus ensuring his election.

The lesson Pope John had learned about the influence of the "reactionaries" spurred him to reduce their power by enlarging the number of Cardinals in the Sacred College. To that effect, early in his pontificate, he created 23 new Cardinals. This brought the College's composition to 74 members, four more than the traditional number cherished by Pius XII.

By 1962, John had effectively neutralised "the ultras," as he called the supporters of Pius XII. He accomplished this by adding 12 Cardinals, all of whom were favourable to his political views and ecclesiastical aims.

Some of the new Cardinals were already well known for their liberal sentiments. Amongst these was Cardinal Godfrey, Archbishop of Westminster, with whom the present author had been in contact for years — ever since Msgr. Godfrey was Papal Legate in Great Britain.

The first external changes which John made after his ascension were those in the papal environment. He did this at once and with a rapidity that astounded everyone. Within forty-eight hours of his coronation, he set to flight the "pestilential rats" as he called them — that is, certain Jesuits, who had been prominent at the Vatican during Pius XII's 19-year reign.

He was ruthless with all those said to be the "intimates" of his predecessor. For example, he ordered the German nun who had looked after the person of Pius for more than thirty years, to quit the Vatican. At once.

He told the editor of the Vatican's official organ, the *Osservatore Romano,* — a man who had complied with all Pius's "idiosyncracies," such as publication of allegedly fake photographs — to be ready to resign. Count Della Torre, who had edited the paper for decades, duly got the sack. Later he was given a job as a librarian at the Vatican Library where he bemoaned his fate, "roaming aimlessly like a nostalic ghost" until his death in 1967, his nephew, Count Paolo Della Torres later told the author.

Pope John was even more severe with the surviving members of Pius XII's family. The late pope, in addition to his ruthlessness in political matters, had indulged in a personal weakness believed to be extinct − nepotism.

Nepotism, derived from the Latin word *nepos,* meaning nephew, formerly was used to describe the vainglorious selfishness of Medieval popes who granted indiscriminately titles of nobility and immense monetary privileges to their nephews.

Pius XII had revived this practice in the 20th century. He distributed privileges of all kinds to his nephews with an openhanded generosity that rivaled that of the pontiffs of the Middle Ages.

By contrast, Pope John's only official relationship with his family from the time he was elected until his death, consisted of two formal occasions: on the first, they came to Rome to witness his coronation; on the second, his funeral.

Radical changes in policy

John's pontificate became immediately identified with his personal outlook, both political and religious. This was felt almost at once, in Italy first, then abroad.

He gave a new editorial policy to the *Osservatore Romano.* He told the leaders of the Christian Democracy Party of Italy not to rely any longer on the Vatican for support, financially or politically. The days when the Christian Democrats had formed a political branch of the Vatican in the domestic affairs of Italy were over. The Party, accustomed to receiving financial aid, protection, and political directives from Pius XII, reacted with shock.

Many felt that the socialist attitudes of the new pope would mean the ascendancy of the Communists and of their political influence, fears which later proved to be well-founded.

The political structure of Italy began to shift almost at once. The Christian Democrats, who had taken almost for granted their divine right to rule, now felt politically naked. This was all the more true because the new pope, while abandoning them, went half way to meet the reds.

John opened a dialogue first with the Socialists, and then even with the Communists, making them understand that he would support many of their social reforms.

Following words with deeds, he lifted the ban which Pius had instituted against any kind of intercourse with the Communists, advising the latter to reach an understanding with Christian Democracy. At the same time, he asked them to relent in their fight against the Church, and to abate their anti-clericalism. He hinted that he would not condemn those Catholics who had supported them, not even those who came to the altar to receive Holy Communion, an act that until then had been considered an abomination.

His official acts proved that he was as good as his word. In May 1961, he published his first famous encyclical, *Mater et Magistra,* in which he reviewed the whole field of social doctrines, from the time of Pope Leo XIII, down to contemporary times.

With one stroke he placed the Roman Catholic Church on the side of the leftist reformers, insisting that the Church must be the cutting edge of social changes and urgent reforms, including aid to underdeveloped countries, Christian or not.

In April 1963, he wrote an even more celebrated document, *Pacem in Terris,* in which he openly advocated a compromise with Communism.

The tension between conservatives and the left wing in Europe, and with the Russian Communists relaxed as if by a miracle.

Relations between the Vatican and the Soviet Union also improved beyond recognition, thanks to the fact that Pope John initiated an entirely new approach to the Church.

Whereas Pius XII had envisaged a defeated and occupied Russia, John envisioned a Red Russia cooperating with the West, and the Orthodox Church eager to collaborate with Rome in the creation of a new Christian front.

This radical change of attitude towards the Soviet Union and the Orthodox Church meant an even more radical shifting of religious beliefs. This, indeed, was a most dangerous step, since once religious emotion is involved in political matters, the reaction of the two can provoke unpredictable and often disastrous results.

Pope John tackled the thorny issue with a bluntness which shocked many Catholics throughout the world. To be sure, the maneuver was not carried out directly. It was kept well in the background at first. But when his attitude towards the Fatima cult was fully realised, it was too late for the millions of devotees to do anything but accept the situation.

We have already seen how the anti-Communist crusade of Pius XII was conducted. Pius had planned a kind of holy war, whose culmination would have been a religio-ideological Armageddon.

This was supposed to have taken place when the third great prophecy of Fatima, which was to have been revealed to the world in 1960. By that year, according to the formidable anti-Russian trio — Pius XII, Cardinal Spellman, and U.S. Secretary of State Dulles — Russia should be defeated and occupied.

Pius, who always thought and planned in quasi-apocalyptic terms, had carefully planned his time of revealing the final secret of Fatima. One day he "confided" to a few intimates, who curiously enough seemed to have close connection with the Catholic and world press, how he had read the third prophecy. Upon reading it, Pius informed them, he had "trembled with fear and almost fainted with horror."

This episode was corroborated by two reliable Vatican sources, during conversations with the present author. It was also confirmed later by sundry Catholic publications prior to, and after Pius XII's death.

What the Pope would have revealed to the waiting millions of devotees of Our Lady of Fatima in 1960 is not known. What is certain is that Pius XII, being a very devout man — but at the same time an equally skillful manipulator of religious and political emotion — had prepared some spectacular event of his own, which might have had profound political repercussions.

Pope John XXIII, however, being the matter-of-fact man that he was, and fully realising the political implications of the Fatima revelations, ordered the Portuguese hierarchy to drop at once *"La pulcinellada",* a word which, in Venetian slang meant leg-pulling or burlesque.

Thus, the third secret was never disclosed. This notwithstanding the sporadic attempts made by members of the Fatima cult throughout the world. The lobbying was headed by various organisations and publications, as, for example, the Blue Army *Messengem de Fatima,* or "Action Fatima." In France, the French hierarchy, at the personal instigation of John, condemned the more extravagant followers of the cult. In Portugal, however, certain groups flatly refused to toe the line, notably the *Avoz* of Lisbon.

To Pope John, the Cult of Fatima, with all its various implications, was the tip of an iceberg of unhealthy attitudes towards certain contemporary social and political problems, attitudes stemming from the personality of the late Pius XII. Being a down-to-earth pragmatist, even in religious matters, John attempted to curb activities of the cult whenever he could.

To mention another example of the kind of mysticism which flourished during Pope Pius XII's pontificate, there was the cult of Padre Pio. The cult was built around the stigmata of an Italian priest, who made prophecies about the personal future of individuals and about the political future of nations. Thousands of followers flocked to his monastery from all over Italy and even from abroad. Advance booking had to be arranged months before a visit. Large sums of money were involved and religious and financial scandals became regular features.

The Second Vatican Council

Pope John's most important act by far, during his pontificate (it was heralded as "the religious event of the century") was his summoning of the Second Vatican Council. It was first announced by him in January 1959, opened in October 1962, and concluded in December 1965 under his successor, Pope Paul VI.

The story has been told of how, during an interview, he opened the window of his study, explaining that the reason he had decided to call the Second Vatican Council was to permit a new and refreshing wind to blow through the stuffy edifice of the Church.

The chief purpose of the Council, he said, was to bring Roman Catholicism into tune with the times; indeed, to make it jump ahead of them.

Such a call sounded sweet to the ears of many and commanded heavy coverage in the media. It became as irresistible as the siren's song to the sailors of old. And like them, with the exception of a few, having ignored the hidden dangers, they were eventually to founder upon the submerged rocks of ecclesiastical and radical ideological innovations. There they would be devoured by a devastating spirit of revolution, which was to transform the very foundations of the Roman Catholic Church.

CHAPTER 18

Red Flag Over the Vatican

The passing of Pius XII and the election of John XXIII end-ed, and at the same time initiated two different eras, totally op-posed in religion, in diplomacy, and in politics.

The centuries-old tradition of dogma, of inflexibility, and of absolutism terminated with the burial of the dead pontiff. That of appeasement and tolerance of systems which until then had been fundamentally inimical to the Church, became the key-note of the new pontificate.

At seventy-seven, Pope John was called, almost at once, the "care-taker" pontiff. Such a hasty assessment, no matter how plausible in human terms, proved to be wide of the mark in-deed. For that matter, recent ecclesiastical history could have that Pope Leo XIII (1878-1903), who wrote his famous ency-clical, *Rerum Novarum,* at age eighty-one, had continued in office until he was ninety-three.

In the case of Pope John, such a judgment proved wrong, not so much because it ignored the hidden forces which propelled him to the papacy, or because it minimised the eagerness of the progressives within the Church — who had made him their can-didate — but because it overlooked the impassioned radicalism of the man.

Although John's affability and straight-forward manner of speaking reflected his true personality, behind this *persona,* nevertheless, was a dedicated revolutionary. Deep within him there was a radicalism that was profoundly integrated with his very nature. Personal background and empirical, socialist-orientated convictions did the rest.

His physical coarseness, even if attenuated by his ecclesiastic-al training, and by his papal status, was as self-evident as was his warm-heartedness. His strong peasant features helped millions of ordinary Catholics and non-Catholics alike to identify with him. A pope made in their own image. Hence his widespread popularity.

John's immediate abatement of the Church's elaborate cere-monies, his eagerness for informalities, his homeliness, his acceptance of familiarities by the faithful and his mode of ad-dressing them, did the rest.

The contrast with the ascetic, aristocratic and authoritarian figure of Pius XII could not have been more striking.

Those who had promoted his candidacy, with the specific objective of forcing the Church into a fundamentally different and new outlook, could truly congratulate themselves on the rightness of their choice.

The more so since they had, knowingly or not, made the same evaluation as that of Russian Intelligence. The latter's special section, dedicated to the problems of the relationship between the state-controlled Orthodox, and the Catholic,

Churches, the name of Roncalli figures prominently as a man who held no animosity towards Christian Orthodoxy, nor the Russian people, nor the Revolution.

This Russian profile of the new Pope, filed years before he was elected, is a revealing document. It is a fascinating dissection, not only of Roncalli himself, but even more, of the Russian mentality and their mode of assessing individuals for political and ideological potentialities.

"Roncalli," stated the *curriculum vitae,* written in 1938, "...likes frugal meals, has frugal habits, is naturally informal. He indulges in soft drinks and likes Lebanese tobacco, but not to excess. The offer of good cigarettes makes him very jovial. He is inclined to an earthly sense of humor and can be a practical joker in his immediate circle. Once, having put the clerical headress of an Orthodox priest upon his head, he spotted a flea, which Roncalli collected with great care. Thereupon, having put the flea inside an envelope, he told the Orthodox priest that he was going to send the Orthodox flea to His Holiness in Rome. According to Roncalli, fleas — whether Christian Orthodox, or Roman Catholic — being reasonable creatures, had no religious prejudices. This was proved by the fact that the flea had felt at home on the head of a Roman Catholic prelate like himself.

"The Orthodox priest did not take the joke as it was intended, and Roncalli, to appease him, cooked his favourite porridge — polenta. They drank three bottles of Greek wine, and ate a large basket of Armenian figs."

A more accurate, down-to-earth description of the future pope could not have been written. Soviet intelligence agents, however, had anything but a sense of humour. They were in dead earnest when they thus recorded the personal background of individuals, as indicators of their present and future ideological and political potentialities.

Roncalli, they noted, was the eldest son of a peasant (small holder) who had to keep twelve children. He (Roncalli) had descended from a stock of small farmers, who had worked their small plot more than six centuries. He had remained a proletarian, with a proletarian radicalism and zeal for reform, "notwithstanding a traditionally reactionary religious training."

During World War I, they observed, Sergeant Roncalli had "consistently favoured the comradeship of his fellow working-class soldiers, to that of higher station. And even after he left the army and had become a prelate of promise, he preferred to eat polenta, the maize porridge typical of the peasant of North Italy.

The importance the Russians gave to the fact that the future pope liked maize porridge is telling. Although it may appear strange to Western eyes that an inference could be drawn from Roncalli's eating polenta, such a conclusion was perfectly plausible to the Russian Communist way of thinking.

For it was assumed that Roncalli's preference for porridge went with his personality, since it indicated his basic outlook, whose primitiveness was bound to foster socialist thinking.

The forerunner of Communism

The fact is that the Russian assessment of such trivialities proved prophetic. It aided them in their choice of candidate to support in a future papal election, an election in which their influence, even by remote control, helped to bring socialism into the Church, socialism being the forerunner of Communism.

Once socialism had achieved an important place in the Church, they reasoned, the door would be half-opened to the acceptance of certain basic left-wing tenets which appeared to be in harmony with the Gospels.

Christianity had much in common with Communism. Had not Jesus himself declared that he had come to "preach good news to the poor...to proclaim release to the captives...to set at liberty those who are oppressed?" (Gospel of St. Luke, 4th chapter).

And how many passages of the same Gospels did not coincide with those of Marx and Lenin, concerning the poor and the oppressed — that is, concerning the millions of workers throughout the world?

This was the rationale that in Catholic Latin America had already become known as "the liberation theology," the acceptable mixture of Jesus and Marx, which was eventually to spread throughout that continent, producing Marxist Catholic priests and Marxist guerilla Jesuits, as we shall see in a forthcoming chapter.

Whereas the process of Marxist-Catholic integration in the religious field would have taken time, in the political area certain objectives could be more quickly achieved. For example, a tacit entente between the Roman Catholic Church and Soviet Russia.

In diplomatic and political parlance, this meant the birth of a Vatican-Moscow alliance.

Such a partnership had been envisaged by many progressives in the Church long before Roncalli's election, during the many years they had languished under Pius XII's anti-Communist crusade.

Upon Roncalli's becoming pope, they surged to the fore with renewed vigour, determined to do away with the past. They wanted to re-shape the present and, above all, the future according to their neo-Christian Communist conceptions.

They realised at once, however, that in temporal terms, the time at their disposal to accomplish their aims, was short. At 77, Pope John could not last long. Their concern proved to be well-founded, since the new pontiff did, in fact, die at age 81.

And yet they did not foresee that radical reforms would have to be half-hearted and minimal because of the shortness of time. That was not John's way; but even the most go-ahead amongst them had not expected the radicalism of John to be so radical. In fact, far from merely making the long-overdue reforms that had been discussed, John launched a veritable revolution.

A revolution meant sweeping away many of the cherished values of yesterday and bridging the gap which until now had separated the Church from a Communist-orientated society.

In the field of world politics, this had to mean a radical re-alignment. The Church from now on, instead of relying upon the United States as her major partner, would have to ally herself with her former opponent, namely, Communist Russia.

Pope John met the demands of the radical progressives much sooner than they had hoped for or expected.

He issued the two famous encyclicals, which have already been mentioned as the foundation stones of his revolution: *Mater et Magistra* in 1961; and *Pacem in Terris* in 1963.

In the first, he extended the social principles of the socialist pope, Leo XIII of the previous century, enlarging upon the duty owed by society and especially by the privileged classes to the "underprivileged and to the exploited," telling the wealthier nations of the world that it was also their duty to share their wealth with the poorer countries of the Third World.

In his second encyclical, *Pacem in Terris* (Peace on Earth), he declared that it is "vitally important that the wealthier states... should provide assistance to the poorer."

The passage, however, which alarmed most traditionalists, was that concerned with error. Error, said John, should not be confused with the "erring person," since false philosophies regarding man and the universe are not identical with their associated historical movements, in which there might be patches of good (read the Bolshevik Revolution of 1917).

Then he concludes by saying that a drawing together or a meeting for the attainment of some practical end, which was formerly deemed inopportune (a clear reference to Communism) might be considered opportune and useful "now or in the future."

His startling references to socialism and even to Communism were not the expression of rhetorical banalities. They indicated the direction in which the Church was now moving. John had been formulating re-orientation with the Russians privately during long months. He had secretly conducted negotiations with the Kremlin through the mediation of none other than the leader of the Italian Communist Party; and a progressive cardinal who was aided by a specialist in religious affairs from the KGB, then resident in Rome.

Rumors that something was going on were current in certain Roman circles at the time. These rumours were denied again and again by the Vatican. Then, one day it was announced that Pope John had been awarded the Balzan Peace Prize. A significant feature of the price was that the Balzan Foundation, whose international committee included amongst other left-wingers, no fewer than four Russian Communists, all of whom voted for the Pope.

Another interesting event followed. Pope John addressed a group of selected journalists which included Alexei Adzhubei, the son-in-law of the Soviet Premier, and who was editor of *Izvestia,* the official organ of the Soviet Communist Party.

The secret audience

Notwithstanding the Vatican's repeated denials that Adzhubei had been among the journalists to whom he had granted an audience, the fact is that the Pope invited him and his wife to the papal study for a private audience afterward.

The Vatican continued to deny that the meeting had ever taken place. As the *London Times* put it, in their issue of March 3, 1963, "even now, the Vatican is refusing to confirm officially that the two men met in private."

That the editor of *Izvestia* had indeed met with the pope, was later confirmed by none other than the daughter of the Soviet Premier, who was present at the meeting.

"Pope John," she stated, "has large, good hands...like those of a peasant..." (echoes of the Soviet secret police report back in the 50s). "The Pope's hand," she continued, "reminds me of my father's hands." Mrs. Adzhubei then admitted also that she was tempted to tell this to the Pope, but she did not have the courage to say so. Pope John gave her and her husband gifts, one of which, the pontiff said, was "for your father" (i.e., Soviet Premier, Nikita Kruschev).

So much for the private meeting that never took place. When, finally, the Vatican confirmed the encounter, the *Osservatore Romano* recorded simply that a number of journalists were present for the ceremony, amongst them Mr. Adzhubei, who had expressed a desire to meet His Holiness.

At their private meeting, Pope John and the Russian editor confirmed what the Vatican and the Kremlin had been discussing for months, namely, the mutual acceptance of a general guideline for the newly-born Vatican-Moscow alliance.

The necessity of a personal meeting was due not so much to a formal agreement on the entente's abstract principles, but to the practical confirmation of a concrete, working agreement between the Vatican and the Kremlin in the ideological and diplomatic fields.

The presence at the Vatican of the Russian Premier's son-in-law, therefore, far from being a mere coincidence, in reality was the climax of a secret rapproachment between Russia's rulers and the Pope who, as the *London Times* expressed it, "is ready to carry out an uninhibited approach...towards the Soviet Union."

It is significant that prior to the original audience, Pope John had defined the new position of the Church as "one of perfect supra-national neutrality," which he then hastened to explain, "should not be understood in a purely passive sense."

The full significance of this declaration can be grasped by recalling the fact that until then the Vatican had been vigourously anti-Communist and had been fighting Russian expansionism with the utmost energy

Pope John's attitude and words at this stage, therefore, were the clearest proof that now the Church had reached a practical, albeit secret, accord with the Soviet Union.

The accord was verified by Moscow itself in the constant communication which Adzhubei carried on with his father-in-law, Kruschev, via the coded hot line between the Soviet embassy in Rome and the Kremlin.

Premier Kruschev told his son-in-law to ask the Pope for a "positive" siding of the Vatican with Russia in Europe, including the Iron Curtain countries. Also about the possibility of an official visit by the Soviet Premier to the Vatican. In short, Kruschev wanted a personal confirmation of the birth of the new Vatican-Moscow alliance.

Five days later, Adzhubei was back at the Vatican. To look at the Sistine Chapel, he explained. The Italian socialist leader, Pietro Nenni, welcomed the pope's attitude to the Soviets as important. Conservative Catholics regarded John's open courting of the Russians as adopting left-wing neutralism at best.

The papal flirtation with Communism had its immediate effects in Italy. At socialist, and even at Communist, rallies it was enough to mention Pope John's name to spark off a storm of applause. This, it should be noted, from traditional anti-clerical audiences to whom, until recently, the papacy had meant anti-Communism.

Conservative and Catholic opinion were alarmed. Even moderates made barbed comments. "Communists and socialists, including the Russians, are becoming more papist than the Pope," declared a leading Rome daily, *Il Messagero* – a comment which Christian Democrats repeated all over Italy.

Shortly afterwards, in May 1963, at a public ceremony again connected with the Balzan Prize, another high-ranking Soviet official, president of the State Committee for Foreign Relations of the Soviet Council of Ministers, was present. It was the first time since the October Revolution of 1917, that a senior representative of the Soviet Union had been officially in St. Peter's Basilica, where the ceremony took place.

The comings and goings of such high-level Russian personages, although significant for the world at large, represented the mere tip of the Catholic-Communist iceberg. The fact that both the Vatican and the Kremlin now felt sufficiently confident not to hide any longer the Vatican-Moscow rapproachment, indicated how far they had gone in consolidating their newly formed alliance.

The externalisation of the Vatican-Moscow partnership created tremors in Washington and open discontent in Rome. Pius XII's old guards were shocked. Millions of socialist- and Communist-orientated voters, however, were overjoyed.

These included the maintenance workers at St. Peter's. One day, several of them, having accosted the Pope while he was talking a stroll in the Vatican gardens, sounded him out about raising their wages. After which, finding him in an affable mood, they asked that they might be permitted to hoist a Red Flag from one of the windows of the Vatican.

Pope John appeared to take the request with his notoriously pragmatic sense of humour. He asked how large the red flag was. He was told it was about three metres long and two wide. How much did it cost? The workers mentioned a sum. Too expensive, commented the Pope; we can't afford such a price for one single visit, can we? Let's wait for more of our Russian comrades to visit us.

The political result of a visit to the Vatican by the editor of the Russian Communist Party's official organ was not so much that she should be welcomed by one symbolic red flag, but that he boosted the fortunes of the Communists in Italy.

The millions of Catholics who, although secretly supporting the reds, until then had never dared vote for them for fear of being excommunicated, as Pius XII had warned, now openly voted Communist.

The result was seen during the general election which followed, when the Communist Party became overnight a major political force.

The progressives of the Church were elated no less than the Communists or the Sanpetrini, who celebrated the Communist victory, foreseeing a steady stream of Russian visitors, headed by the Soviet Premier himself, if not by the whole Russian Politbureau.

The red procession

It was an expectation that was eventually fulfilled by the increasing number of top-ranking Russians who went up and down the Vatican stairs in the years which followed.

Viewed in this light, Pope John could no longer be considered a "caretaker pope;" but the deliberate propounder of a revolution, and a double-headed one at that.

The ideological and religious ecumenism was the ecclesiastical counterpart of his political somersault.

Ecumenism, by trespassing into the inter-denominational field, could help the Vatican reach long-range ideological goals, which were integrated with its political revolution. For ecumenism as a policy of *detente* with other Christian bodies, could help to undermine the Vatican's main rivals, the Orthodox and the Protestant churches.

This was proved by the fact that even prior to launching the programme, Pope John had taken the first steps by sending his secret envoys to the various capitals of Orthodoxy — the Patriarchates of Athens, Istanbul, and even Moscow.

Such moves would have been impossible unless an ideological *detente* had been agreed upon with the Soviet Union, and vice-versa. Witness the sundry visits made by Msgr. Willebrands to the Russian capital as the personal envoy of Pope John. Later, the same prelate visited Moscow to have special talks with the leaders of the Soviet Union.

These exchanges could not be dissociated from political issues, both being but the two facets of the same Vatican-Moscow rapprochement. Such a *detente* could be summarised as: a) the launching of ecumenism; and b) concrete reconciliation with the Russian Orthodox Church.

Both objectives were for the purpose of dismantling the elaborate apparatus which Pius XII had so laboriously erected against the state-controlled Orthodox Church, and the Soviet Union.

Judged from this coign of vantage, therefore, ecumenism was a blinker imposed upon the religious communities to distract them from the political reality – that is, from the sudden volteface of the Vatican towards the Church's mortal enemy of yesterday.

It made possible the acceptance of, not only theological, but also of ideological tolerance. In other words, it was a *detente* not only in religion, as advertised, but equally in ideologies, beginning with Communism.

Pope John was essentially a practical man, and as such he set out to implement his revolutionary policies as quickly as possible. These were encompassed into a grand strategy, the development of which was subdivided into three concurrently running phases: 1) abandonment of the Church's close ties with the United States as a principal political partner; 2) entente, cooperation, and tacit alliance with Soviet Russia; and 3) *detente* with the entire Communist world.

The grand strategy itself was promoted simultaneously on two fronts – the religious and the ideological. The religious movement became identified with ecumenism; the ideological with Communism. While ecumenism opened the doors to an entente cordiale with the Orthodox Church and with Protestantism generally; the ideological revision of Church policy opened the way for a prudent but bold rapproachment with Russia and world Communism.

In practical political terms, this meant first, the immediate normalisation of relations between Moscow and the Vatican; second, the harmonising of ideological strategies between Communism and Catholicism; third, *de facto* recognition of the Communist regimes in Eastern Europe; fourth, cessation of Catholic hostility against national communist movements in Italy and France; and last, but not least, an official and radical change of attitude on the part of the Catholic Church towards Communism in general and Russian Communism in particular.

The practical external manifestations of all this was that very soon an incredulous world and an astounded America witnessed the (until recently) inconceivable spectacle of a stream of Communist leaders into and out of the Vatican as though they had suddenly been converted to Catholicism, although, as some cynics were quick to observe, just the reverse was true. It was Catholicism which had suddenly been converted to Communism.

Behind these diplomatic formalities there was to be found evidence of a solid practical strategy aimed at bringing the two erstwhile enemies into close co-operation. The strategy at this period could be summarised thus:

The very active opposition of the Church against Communism ceased in the political, religious and diplomatic fields. A novel approach to the Orthodox Church was initiated. Dialogue with the Communist parties of Europe began in earnest. The Catholic parties — that is, the Christian Democratic Party in Italy, in France, and even in Germany were told not to expect any more direct support from the Vatican. They were also advised not to campaign against Communism, as they had done under Pius XII. The very active hostility of the Catholic Church behind the Iron Curtain was stopped; the Vatican gave *de facto* recognition to the Russian integration of Eastern Europe into the Soviet Empire; and finally, the Vatican began a policy of active cooperation with Russia in the diplomatic and ideological fields.

It was a grand strategy of the first magnitude.

Pope John XXIII, "the good pope of the people," could truly say that by opening the window of the Vatican to let in the fresh air of ecumenical reforms, he had also opened the same window to let in the whirlwind of socialism and, indeed, of Russian and world Communism.

At his death, the Sanpetrini, instead of putting out a white and yellow papal flag from the Vatican balcony, should have hung the red flag, with the sickle and the cross well displayed on it — the true symbol of the revolution which John XXIII had started within and outside the Roman Catholic Church.

CHAPTER 19

Election of a Pink Pope

The revolution which had been launched by "the radical shepherd," John XXIII, was continued and expanded by his successor, Pope Paul VI.

From the moment of Paul's ascension, the forces set in motion by his predecessor, gained momentum. He lost no time in setting precedents — as a person, as Supreme Pontiff, and as a politician.

For instance, he was the first pope since Peter (although, strictly speaking, Peter was never a pope) to set foot in the Holy Land; the first in history to visit Australia and India; the first to go to North and South America; and to visit the heart of Africa. He was the first to address the United Nations in New York.

All this was a far cry from the life style of the preceeding popes who, only two generations before, had incarcerated themselves in the Vatican in protest against the seizure of Rome by Italy in 1870.

Pope Paul VI brought innovations, suppressed ancient traditions, and Protestanised the beautiful Catholic liturgy. He also abolished the ancient language of the Church to such an extent that it became an ecclesiastical crime to say or to hear the Mass in Latin.

His innovations disconcerted the faithful, bewildered untold millions and cast doubt in the hearts of many who, until then, had taken their Church to be immutable — a fixed point by which to steer their spiritual course.

The desertion from historical Catholicism had never been carried out on such a large scale since the days of the Reformation.

"Four hundred years of history have been changed in four years," as a saddened American Catholic put it. An understatement.

Yet Paul VI himself appeared to be anything but a revolutionary. He was mild mannered, considerate, gentle, and exceptionally diligent in the performance of his papal duties. The mere fact that there were periods when he had to deliver eight speeches a day, and to see more than one million visitors in a year, testified to that.

When he became Pope in 1963, he found the Second Vatican Council in his hands, and even more, a full-scale revolution within the Church itself. If there was ever an individual fully prepared to deal with both, however, it was he. He possessed two outstanding qualifications to act as Pope John's successor: he had breathed diplomacy all his adult life, and he was also a radical, politically more to the left than even Pope John.

He had had first-hand experience with the intricacies of the Vatican's multifarious activities, mostly in the authoritative confines of the Vatican's Secretariat of State — the equivalent, in diplomatic terms, of the U.S. State Department, the Pentagon, and the CIA combined. Twenty-nine out of his 32 years of service in the Church had been spent working in the Vatican. That was in itself a unique record.

With the exception of Pope Pius XII, he had the widest knowledge of the most sensitive and far-flung operations of any other top-ranking diplomat in the whole of the Roman Curia.

From 1945 to 1955 — that is, from the end of World War II until the height of the Cold War — his pro-socialist leanings had come openly into view, notwithstanding Pius XII's anti-Communist policies. He had sided, even if somewhat equivocally, with liberal Catholics on almost all social and political issues. In other words, he favoured the pro-Communist members of the Church.

Despite his ecclesiastical rectitude, his radical views, even then, had become so well known that he was widely labelled the "Red Pro-Secretary of State."

Pius XII tolerated him and accepted his services because of his diplomatic skill and also because of his scrupulous obedience in carrying out orders, even when they were contrary to his personal convictions.

At the same time, Pius had counter-balanced Montini's progressive ideas with those of another, no less skillful, diplomat. He was Cardinal Domenico Tardini, a dour conservative, as anti-Communist as Pius himself, and as determined as he to work the downfall of Soviet Russia and of world Communism.

Tardini and Montini worked for years in tandem as Pro-Secretaries of State, busy in the promotion of diplomatic objectives, but privately favourable to their respective beliefs.

Thus, whereas Montini was constantly suggesting reforms and changes, Tardini was advocating the reverse, convinced that his colleague was a cryptosocialist, if not worse.

Thanks to his traditional conservatism, Tardini had been considered by many as the logical successor to anti-Communist Pope Pius XII. A succession, by the way, which had been taken almost for granted at the U.S. State Department. Washington's conclusion was based not so much on an estimation of Cardinal Tardini's personal capabilities, as on their cool assessment of what they considered a political reality. That was an uninterrupted continuation of the Vatican-American anti-Communist campaign. The expectations of both Washington and Pius XII, however, were cut short when Cardinal Tardini died. The field had been left wide open to socialist Montini.

But if there was consternation at the CIA and in Rome, when Montini was elevated to the papacy, there was tacit jubilation amidst the silent radicals on either side of the Atlantic, not to mention Moscow.

It must be remembered that the Cold War was then in full swing and was reaching dangerous proportions. Also, because of the apprehension it had given to Stalin and to others, the Russian Communist lobby had already embarked upon a campaign for the election of a suitable progressive papal candidate to succeed Pope Pius XII.

The leading favourite at this stage was, as we have already seen, Stalin's former schoolmate, Cardinal Agagianian. Cardinal Roncalli, although in the running, was still considered a third alternative, both at Rome and in Moscow.

Roncalli's name jumped ahead when it was realised, at Pius XII's death, that Msgr. Montini could not be elected pope, owing to a technicality. Montini had, in fact, excluded himself from the Sacred College, from which a pope must be selected, by refusing a cardinal's hat when Pius had demoted him to the see of Milan, North Italy.

Had it not been for that obstacle, it was almost a certainty that he would have been elected pope in 1958, rather than Cardinal Roncalli.

Yet, had Msgr. Montini been technically eligible to the vacant papacy, it is doubtful whether the election would have been that easy. Not because he did not possess the right qualifications, in the eyes of the progressives and the pro-Russian cardinals, but on the contrary, because he was endowed with too many of them. His election would have made his extreme ideas so obvious that he might have scared too many and too soon. In other words, a radical pope like him would have been premature at the time.

Hence, the selection of Roncalli as the obvious best choice.

The velvet steam-roller

After John's death, however — that is, at the Conclave of 1963 — Montini, now a Cardinal, was recognised at once as John's heir apparent, the man best qualified to carry on John's revolution. Moreover, he could do the job without too sudden a breach and by means of the velvety softness of super-diploma-cy, behind which was the irresistibility of a steam-roller.

Cardinal Agagianian, although still *papabile* in the view of many, now would have been too much of a liability, had he been elected instead of Montini.

The progressive assessment had been a practical and sensible one, since it reasoned that the election of a Russian, pro-Communist pope following the death of a revolutionary like John, would have constituted too blatant a break with the traditional acceptance of a traditional pope, no matter how progressive.

Most of the Catholic millions, still confused by the upheaval in their Church, might not have reconciled themselves so easily to a Russian-born pope, a former protege of Stalin. Such a pontiff, while might have rallied around him the great number of left-wing Catholics in Europe and those in the uncommitted nations, would nevertheless have alienated hundreds of millions in Western Europe and the United States.

A gentler policy with a gentler pope, therefore, seemed the most judicious course. And what better choice than Montini, the former Pro-Secretary of State?

Had not Montini opposed the anti-Communist policies of

Pius XII? Had he not been always a convinced leftist? Had he not been consistently anti-American? Last, but not least, would not his election ensure the continuation of the pro-Russian, pro-Communist, and anti-American programmes of the late Pope John?

The days of the American hegemony at the Vatican under Pius XII had not been forgotten. Cardinal Spellman, one of the voting cardinals, in the eyes of his colleagues, was still the representative, not only of New York, but also of the Dulles brothers, the U.S. Secretary of Navy Matthews, and of all the hard-line anti-Communist officials in Washington.

This working machinery of the Vatican-Washington partnership had been conceived by an American Jesuit, promoted by an American Catholic politician, and strongly supported — notwithstanding official disclaimers — by the Catholic hierarchy and their friends.

It was a fact, well known by the whole Conclave, that Montini had been consistently opposed to all this. Also, that during the potentially most dangerous moments of the Cold War, certain ultra-secretive diplomatic activities had gone inexplicably wrong, e.g., frequent misunderstandings with the United States, or unexpected leaks that more often than not compromised the ideological operations of the Vatican-Washington axis.

Montini's sacking from the Vatican in 1954, following that of Roncalli the previous year, had indicated very clearly the reasons Pius XII had in mind when he "promoted" him to pastoral work in Milan.

His transfer from the Vatican had been the equivalent, in military terms, of a general who had been directing the grand strategy of an army, being promoted to supervise the kitchen batteries of a regiment.

Montini had responded to the Pope's snub by refusing to accept a cardinal's hat, a refusal which probably cost him election to the papacy in 1958, as we have already noted.

His protest — the most daring he had ever made against Pius

XII — had been greatly appreciated by the growing number of anti-American elements within and outside the Vatican. It had given the greatest satisfaction, however, to Montini himself, who had known all along what had caused his being sent into exile.

His demotion had, in fact, originally been conceived in Washington, where Montini had always been adjudged a real danger to the Vatican-American partnership. It had first been suggested by Cardinal Spellman, acting as the mouthpiece of Alan Dulles, head of the CIA, although the last word had been left to his brother, John Foster Dulles, then U.S. Secretary of State. Secretary Dulles was anxious about having fool-proof security concerning Vatican-American relations.

The frequent attempts to remove Montini from the Vatican were known in Moscow, something which the present author also knew at the time, thanks to hints given him by one of the top Soviet intelligence officials at the Russian Embassy in London.

In Washington, Alan Dulles had built up an enormous dossier on Montini, beginning with his family background. Montini's father, while a member of the Italian Parliament as a deputy of the Catholic Party of Italy, seemed to have influenced his son towards the left, ever since Montini's student days. The author was informed about this, not by Russian Intelligence, but by a prominent Catholic — none other than the founder and leader of the Catholic Party of Italy, Msgr. Dom Sturzo, while Montini was still a minor prelate at the Vatican.

Alan Dulles, who worked very closely with his brother John, had compiled a tale-telling file about the red Pro-Secretary of State. Cardinal Spellman, the closest personal friend to Pope Pius XII, had the opportunity to scrutinise it whenever certain delicate operations of the anti-Communist strategy were to be promoted, or when fresh information about Montini's activities were added to the CIA files.

Some of Montini's political doings which had been unknown

even to Pius XII, at one point were disclosed to the Pope by Cardinal Spellman, who had been briefed by Alan Dulles.

The accusations were mostly based upon suspicions. It was not so much that Montini had been guilty of any crime or really dangerous disclosures. His honesty was never questioned. What was questioned were his political leanings to the left.

These were considered a serious liability. It will be recalled that his dismissal from his Vatican post took place at the time the CIA-Vatican intelligence apparati were busy with the Catholic and anti-Communist forces inside Hungary, where they were seeking to foment an anti-Communist uprising.

The intended coup was aimed at restoring Hungary to the comity of Western Europe as an important facet of the Cold War, and the subsequent liberation of Eastern Europe from Russian domination.

In the case of Hungary, one of the objectives was the installation of an anti-Russian and pro-American administration, headed by Cardinal Mindszenty. The attempt failed, owing chiefly to the refusal of the United States to become openly involved after Russia crushed the rebellion by sending her tanks rolling into Budapest in 1956.

The preparatory moves in the Hungarian build-up, initiated about 1952-1954, required the strictest measures of security; hence Montini's removal.

It was said afterwards that the "promotion" of Montini to the See of Milan had been prompted by Pius XII as a step for Montini to succeed him. The reverse had been the case. And the simple fact that Montini dared to defy the pope by refusing a cardinal's hat, was the most convincing answer Msgr. Montini himself could give to such speculations.

When Pope John died, therefore, the anti-American and pro-Communist clique at the College of Cardinals decided to act as swiftly as they could, before the popular enthusiasm for the "wind of change" subsided. Lobbying, which had been going on since John's elevation, was intensified. The pro-red cardinals presented diplomatic packages, according to which a continuation of the policy of rapproachment with Communism would yield immense benefits to the Church, not only inside Russian-dominated Eastern Europe, but even more outside of it.

Soviet Russia, so they argued, would ease its iron grip on the Church in the Communist countries. Moreover, she would direct the various Communist parties of Europe to slow down their attack on European democracy. At the same time the real, or imagined perils of the Vatican-Washington partnership were magnified, as were the "miraculous advantages" to be reaped from the embryonic Vatican-Moscow alliance.

A logical succession

Further to that, it was recalled that Montini had been a favourite of Pope John XXIII. Also, that the two had shared the same ideological outlook regarding a progressive re-orientation of the Church in accordance with the revolutionary programme initiated by John.

The practical results had been that as soon as John had opened the window to the wind of change, he dispatched Cardinal Montini on a worldwide tour. His task was to report especially on the conditions of two of the poorest areas of the globe — black Africa and Latin America.

The mission had been significant and well-planned. For it was precisely in black Africa and Latin America that was to be found the greatest reservoir of revolutionary forces could be promoted by the new Vatican.

During the Conclave, therefore, when the cardinals were faced with choosing Pope John's successor, the result had been predictable.

In 1963, Cardinal Montini — the first cardinal whom John had nominated, became Pope Paul VI. True to the spirit of John, he set himself the serious task of carrying on his predecessor's transformation of the Church.

The direction his new pontificate was taking was indicated in his first encyclical — *Ecclesiam Suam* — issued in August 1964, fourteen months after his coronation. In it, Paul denounced atheism, but at the same time he also encouraged keeping the line open to Communism. "The Church," he said, "should enter into a dialogue with the world…" since "we do not despair that ideologies [communism] might one day be able to enter into a more positive dialogue with the Church."

Thereupon he began, in an unprecedented and unbecoming manner, a global tour, setting foot in sundry areas of the world, beginning with Jerusalem and ending up in the Yankee Stadium in New York.

The wayfaring new pope was seen by millions: seated in open helicopters, or boarding jet planes in tourist fashion, or sitting casually in superficial conversation with politicians (e.g., chatting with President Johnson on a setee of a commercial hotel).

These were spectacles which, notwithstanding Paul's well-meant intentions, mortified millions of believers, accustomed to thinking of the Roman Pontiff as the Vicar of Christ on earth, with the aura of a distant Vatican, de-materialised by mysticism, by history, and by religion.

Pope Paul VI, however, true to his own convictions, had given them but a preliminary glimpse of the behaviour to be expected of tomorrow's progressive papacy.

CHAPTER 20

The Countermine That Failed

Before embarking upon a panoramic scrutiny of Pope Paul VI's activities, it might be instructive to glance at an episode which, perhaps more than anything else, can indicate Paul's attitude towards partnerships.

The first of these was that of the Vatican-Washington entente; and the second, the Vatican-Moscow alliance. Once seen in their historical perspective, it is easy to realise how radically Vatican policies were made to change from the anti-Communist crusade by an anti-Communist Roman Catholic Church, to the pro-Communist activities promoted from the moment the first generation of progressive popes took over.

We shall begin by reviewing most of the facts which we have

already examined in relation to the general background of the Cold War.

What had distinguished the actions of the Vatican-Washington axis during the long pontificate of Pius XII, was not only its virulent opposition to Communism and to Soviet Russia, but that the crusade had been fathered by the joint Catholic-American hostility to both.

To contain, check and possibly destroy Communism, various campaigns were promoted in different countries of the world, chiefly in Europe and in Asia.

In Asia, the larger burden fell upon the United States, who conducted military operations there, with doubtful results. The most bitterly remembered was the war in Korea in the 50s, and the protracted war in Vietnam, from about 1960 to 1975.

In Europe, the anti-Communist operations, while no more resolute, achieved spectacular results. The Communist bid for power through the democratic machinery was nipped in the bud, thanks largely to the well-coordinated Vatican-Washington combined operations. While the Vatican used religious pressure e.g., the pope's threat against Catholics who voted for Communist candidates — the United States intervened with the timely use of the CIA and allied intelligence agencies, supported by wealthy individuals, and the still-undisclosed large sum of U.S. dollars supplied from the federal treasury.

It was otherwise in Eastern Europe, already occupied by Soviet Russia as a result of the Second World War. There, former non-Communist countries such as Poland, Czechoslovakia, Rumania, Bulgaria, Hungary and others, had been forced to accept Communist regimes.

One of the main objectives of the Vatican-American partnership at this time was, besides halting Russian territorial and ideological expansion, to deprive her of her colonies. In short, it was to liberate all those countries upon which Communism had been imposed by native and Russian commisars.

The spearhead of the Vatican-American operations was the

overthrow of certain Eastern European Communist regimes, to be followed by governments friendly to the United States and to the Vatican.

One of the first terrains was Hungary, designated to become the initial stepping-stone for the first overthrow of Soviet Communism in Europe.

While the United States infiltrated Hungary with her agents, the Vatican set in motion its religious and diplomatic machinery.

The joint Vatican-U.S. operations revolved around a high prelate of the Hungarian church, a protege of Pius XII. He was Cardinal Josef Mindszenty. Certain U.S. officials, operating inside Hungary under diplomatic immunity, co-operated with him.

The strategy was simplicity itself: a) the overthrow of the Communist Hungarian government; b) its replacement with a new anti-Communist regime, friendly to the United States and the West; and c) restoration of the monarchy.

Mindszenty's role in the whole operation was a paramount one. After the overthrow of Hungary's Communist rulers, the Cardinal was to issue a document by virtue of which he, Mindszenty, would be legally entitled to assume power as Prince Primate of Hungary.

There were historical precedents according to which the Prince Primate had done so before. To that end, Mindszenty charged Professor Miklos Gruber with the task of making an historical survey and producing the legal justification for Mindszenty's taking power, once the Communist regime had been abolished.

Mindszenty considered the event so close at hand that he even ordered the necessary stock of newsprint to be ready in the new government's own printing office.

After having dealt with sundry operations at home, Mindszenty became active abroad. He contacted the Hungarian king in exile, Otto of Habsburg, first through the Marquis Palavicini, then via a Belgian cardinal, Van Roey; and finally with the co-operation of a former member of the British Parliament.

In June 1947, under the pretext of visiting the Congress of the Virgin Mary at Ottawa, he travelled first to Canada and then to the United States, where the confessor of the Habsburgs arranged meetings with the widow of Charles Habsburg, and with Otto Habsburg. Those present at these meetings agreed upon a plan to overthrow the Hungarian regime. They also agreed that for the attainment of this political objective, Josef Mindszenty should contact Selden Chapin, the U.S. Minister to Hungary. After Cardinal Mindszenty had done so, he saw Cardinal Spellman, with whom he discussed the whole operation, in the presence of Dr. Andras Zakar, the archi-episcopal secretary.

Liaison with the U.S.

Once back in Budapest, the plotters created the Legitimist organization whose task was to legalise the government which was to be set up.

One of the principal objectives of this Legitimist body was to establish regular liaison with the U.S. Minister in Budapest. The purpose was to enlist the aid of America, from which they sought the necessary supply of money, as well as the exercise of diplomatic pressure. Even U.S. military intervention was envisaged should worse come to worst.

Intervention in the circumstances, of course, would have meant the risk of war. It should be borne in mind that at this period, there was talk that war between the United States and Soviet Russia was not impossible.

Mindszenty became increasingly active at home and abroad. The Catholic lobby in the United States was approached with utmost confidence. Spellman was at the centre of the affair, the Mindszenty operation being considered part and parcel of the anti-Russian grand strategy elaborated by Pope Pius XII.

The encouragement received in Washington, especially from certain agencies of the U.S. intelligence service, was so sanguine that Mindszenty and friends went further and compiled a full list of cabinet members they planned to nominate as soon as they formed a new government.

It was the first concrete triumph of the newly-born Vatican-Washington anti-Russian axis.

A touch of old-fashioned romanticism came to the fore when the plotters asked the United States to put the royal crown of Hungary in their hands. Possession of the crown was considered necessary to ensure the legalisation of the whole operation, since it had to be used for the coronation of the king, following the planned overthrow of the Communist Hungarian government.

The difficulty, however, was that the crown was under custodial care in the United States.

The correspondence which took place between Mindszenty and U.S. officials, and various cardinals — for example, Archbishop Faulhaber of Munich, Archbishop Innitzer of Vienna, and even Msgr. Montini at the Vatican — provides a fascinating study of the religious, diplomatic, and ideological climate of the period. Letters were sent to Pius XII himself, who, of course, was kept minutely informed of the progress of "Operation Hungary."

Some of the strategists, however, started to worry, since promotion of the scheme, which at first had been confined to Hungary itself, now had begun to tresspass into the international area. The involvement of the U.S. in the internal affairs of a country like Hungary, which was under the direct protection of Soviet Russia, entailed risks which had to be considered with the greatest attention by the American State Department.

The ecclesiastical, diplomatic, and intelligence nets had become so widespread that the pressure to involve the United States in the Hungarian venture was assuming dangerous proportions. The more so since several well-known cardinals had been drawn into it; to mention only one, Cardinal Innitzer.

The number of U.S. agents operating within and outside Hungary, at the Vatican, and elsewhere, and their close involvements with ecclesiastics and Hungarian Nationalists, was turning the whole venture into a traditional operetta.

The whole affair was even more tragic because the Russians were watching with the silent attentiveness of a cat, ready to pounce upon a mouse.

Mindszenty's activities went on multiplying, and his efforts to have the U.S. help him increased. He contacted, again and again, the U.S. diplomatic representative in Budapest, asking for help.

On the 6th of December 1946, for instance, to quote but one of such requests, he wrote directly to Arthur Schoenfield, the U.S. Minister to Hungary, informing him that American support was urgently needed. Intervention by the United States was now extremely important, he wrote. Ten days later, on December 16, 1946, Mindszenty wrote another urgent message:

"I ask for the help of America," he told the U.S. diplomat. "A solution is possible with outside help. I can indicate the ways and means by which this can be done."

Mr. Schoenfield, who had at first sympathised with Mindszenty, finally found the Archbishop's requests excessive, if not imprudent. He refused to comment.

Mindszenty then, after consultation with the Vatican — a conference, incidentally, in which Msgr. Montini was passively involved — went over the head of the American diplomat in Hungary and, on June 12, 1947, appealed directly to President Truman.

Cardinal Spellman meanwhile had set to work at the U.S. State Department with the definite objective of having the uncooperative Mr. Schoenfield recalled from Hungary. Spellman asked for a truly cooperative man and one was duly appointed — Seldon Chapin.

From that time onwards, things started to move in the right

direction. The Vatican, Hungarian and Catholic lobby in Washington was fully mobilised. Money arrived, legally and illegally. Certain currency channels and couriers were used. Mindszenty himself was personally involved. The intrigues, letters, and diplomatic exchanges multiplied. Copies of letters were sent to various ecclesiastical and political terminals. Pope Pius XII, although remaining in the background, was discreetly promoting the Hungarian venture since it was an essential operation to be fitted into the larger background of his and America's anti-Communist campaign in Eastern Europe.

The go-between Cardinal

Msgr. Montini, then one of Pope Pius XII's loyal lieutenants, was acting with even more discretion, as a subservient but nevertheless very efficient go-between of Mindszenty, the Pope, Spellman, and others, as the verbatim report of the trial which took place later so clearly proved.

It has been said with justification that Paul VI's silent hostility to the United States, apart from its purely ideological nature (he was always a man of the left), might have been initiated by the intrigues which he had willy-nilly to spin between the Vatican and the U.S. at this period.

The fact that Cardinal Spellman had such a disproportionate influence at the Roman Curia and in Washington, did nothing to endear him to Msgr. Montini, then or ever afterwards.

At one stage, Spellman went directly to the very centre of U.S. military power and appealed directly to Kenneth C. Royall, Secretary of War. The latter promised to act, although with discretionary ifs and buts.

Major and minor issues — all connected with Hungary — came to the fore and were the subjects of various exchanges of letters between the Secretary, Cardinal Spellman, Msgr. Montini at the Vatican, and Mindszenty in Budapest.

One of these dealt with the Hungarian crown. Missives of Cardinal Innitzer were sent by Msgr. Montini to Cardinal Mindszenty on September 19, 1947 assuring him that action would be taken for the purpose of assuring him that the Royal Crown would not be left in Europe, but transported overseas, possibly to the United States.

Mindszenty was anxious that the crown not be stolen by the Russians, since by gaining its possession they would have prevented him from becoming legally the Prince Primate — that is, the Prime Minister of the new, anti-Communist Hungary. Its safety was necessary, wrote Mindszenty in a letter to Seldon Chapin, U.S. envoy to Hungary, so that it would not meet "a tragic fate."

Mr. Chapin, the cooperative American diplomat, in a letter dated December 9, 1947, promised Mindszenty that he would support his request.

Following various colourful exertions by the promoters of the Vatican-Washington axis, not to mention those operating inside Hungary itself, the scheme collapsed.

Cardinal Mindszenty was arrested, tried and, in 1949, sentenced to life imprisonment.

He was universally hailed as a hero of freedom and a crusader against the Godless tyranny of Communism Overnight, he became a point of focus in the spirited Vatican-Washington alliance.

Seen from the Church's point of view, Cardinal Mindszenty had symbolised the sacrificial lamb at the altar of the anti-Bolshevik crusade — a religious symbol of the Church's efforts to contain the spread of Bolshevist atheism which, the prophecy of Fatima had warned, would spread throughout the world, "provoking wars and persecutions against the Church."

In the eyes of Pius XII and of those of his co-ordinators, as indeed in the rest of the world, the assessment was correct.

In the eyes of those who opposed the anti-Communist crusade, however, the assessment was incorrect, unjust, and dangerous. Many within the Church itself had disapproved of the whole Mindszenty affair. Their condemnation had been silent, sullen and resentful. Certain progressives and Church dignitaries had, in fact, gone further than mere hidden disapproval. They had taken steps aimed at neutralising, if not actually over-turning the joint Vatican-Washington Hungarian venture.

There had been rumours, never confirmed, that certain vital leaks had reached the Communists from within the Vatican itself, as a high Soviet official told the present author two years after Cardinal Mindszenty's trial.

It also appeared that certain agents of U.S. intelligence, then involved in the Hungarian operations, had been more than lax when dealing with the activities of Catholic personalities while these were in the United States. According to the same source, Russian intelligence had known for years what was going on in Budapest, and about what they regarded as the absurd plot to restore the Catholic Austrian-Hungarian monarchy.

Whatever the truth, the fact remained that the elaborate Mindszenty scheme collapsed like a pack of cards. All those intimately involved in the plot reacted with traumatic shock to Mindszenty's arrest and subsequent trial. The effects reverberated throughout Europe and the Americas.

After the initial stunned disappointment, however, the Vatican and the United States resumed their activities, but with greater precautions. The hotting up of the Cold War required it. The whole picture assumed a more ominous aspect, since the potential risks involved had escalated and could draw the two super-powers nearer to war.

From that time onwards, diligence and promotional intelligence became the keynote for ensuring the venture.

The whole operation burst into the open a few years later, with the Hungarian uprising of 1956. It was a landmark in the annals of the joint Vatican-Washington anti-Communist strategy, shortly to close with the death of Pope Pius XII only two years afterwards.

CHAPTER 21

Red Hat vs. Red Tiara

If the exertions of the anti-Communist campaign carried out in Eastern Europe by the Vatican-Washington entente, came to nothing, at least their propounder in Washington, Rome and Budapest learned a very important lesson.

In the second engagement of the conflict, intelligence activities were translated into quasi-commando tactics with a ruthlessness which this time allowed no room for any political dilettante, no matter how distinguished.

The general political climate of Europe at the time was of considerable help in the execution of the new campaign. The momentum of the Cold War, although slowing down on the military front, was still sufficiently hot, ideologically, to permit the continuation of the fight against the expansionist policies of Soviet Russia.

The Soviet aggression, even if magnified, was real and pressing. After the fiasco of the Hungarian "Holy Crown" revolution, Russia had tightened the screws upon Eastern Europe as a whole, and upon Hungary in particular.

The Communist regimes of Poland, Czechoslovakia, Rumania, and other countries became ever more conformist. In the rest of the continent, the various national Communist parties were becoming more belligerent. In Asia, the French defeat in Indo-China was laying the foundation for the Communist take-over of Southeast Asia. The spectre of the war in Vietnam was already raising its head. Within a few years, in fact, the United States was sending arms to the French, while grooming the future Catholic dictator of South Vietnam, President Diem, for his office. The Cold War, half a decade after the ill-fated Mindszenty plot, had turned emotionally dangerous with the Fatima crusade.

Behind the Iron Curtain, the muted rumblings of revolts in the making were being heard with increasing frequency, accompanied by the sacking and arrests of Communist dissidents who resented Russia's iron hand.

But while most of these were locally fomented, others were inspired, when not actually promoted, by outside forces.

The explosion which occurred in Hungary in 1956 was a case in point. That the 1956 Hungarian revolution was a spontaneous reaction of the Hungarians against Russian hegemony, is an historical fact. But that such reaction had been promoted by Catholic and American agents is also an important reality.

This time, however, unlike 1947, the whole operation had been meticulously planned, in both the religious and the political areas. Its prime movers were Pius XII and the CIA.

The latter, as organiser of the semi-military aspects of the operation, had depended to a degree amounting to indiscretion upon the active participation of the Catholic Church.

The CIA had come to depend heavily upon the intelligence network of the Vatican, more even than in the past, because of its ramifications. By operating under the mantle of religion the Church agency could be far more effective than a lay intelligence service, no matter how experienced or well financed.

The spontaneous revolt, which had originally been planned for 1954, however, had to be postponed. The fear of repeating the 1947-8 fiasco was very much present in the deliberations of the planners. The health of the Pope had also to be considered when, during the following year — 1955 — Pius XII had serious bouts of nervous exhaustion, owing chiefly to the anxiety which his crusade had been causing him, coupled with the religious emotionalism engendered by the Lady of Fatima's messianic campaign.

The Pope's most serious illness occurred during the autumn of 1955, the time which had been set for the Hungarian revolution to happen. The plan misfired once more, also because of certain internal preparations having gone wrong. The result was that the insurrection had to be postponed a third time — to 1956. It was said afterwards that the Pope's nervous ailment was due also to the uncertainty about the outcome of the Hungarian venture.

Cardinal Mindszenty, of course, figured prominently in all of this because, although relegated to a kind of loose supervisory confinement by the Communist authorities, he was approachable through secret lines of communication, which had been maintained with him from outside.

Mindszenty had been designated to play the major role in the whole affair, not as an activist during its preparation, he being a prisoner, but as a participant once the insurrection had burst into the open. That is, he had accepted once more the role of Premier-designate of a liberated Hungary.

Whether spontaneous popular forces had joined the domestic and external promoters of the revolt of their own volition, it is for history to judge. The probability is that they did. What is indisputable, however, is that Pius XII, prior to and during the Hungarian tragedy, had a leading hand in the whole affair, although CIA agents were the most immediate sponsors of the internal conspiratorial uprising.

Leading figures of the previous plot, like Pretender Otto Habsburg and other prominent Catholics, were kept in the background. The Catholic groups which had muddled things so badly the first time, were left out, while new ones were organised on professional lines by the CIA and its allies, both inside and outside Hungary. The spontaneous insurrection this time could not be permitted to fail. The genuine discontent of large sections of the Hungarian people was tapped and directed towards making the second attempt a success.

The Hungarian Communist government, taken by surprise, was duly overthrown. And Cardinal Mindszenty, who had been whilling away his time in a monastery, became once more the focus of the revolution.

When, in October 1956, the insurrectionists took over the Hungarian capital, their first and most significant move was to liberate Mindszenty.

"The Prince Primate Cardinal Mindszenty returned to Budapest today for the first time since 1948," declared a communique. "The Cardinal, who was freed last night from the monastery in which he was confined...drove into the Capital escorted by three Hungarian tanks...

"Thousands of the faithful crowded around his house when the news spread that he was back, and knelt in the dust as the Cardinal gave them his blessing."

Within twenty-four hours of the Cardinal's triumphal return, speculations were flying to the effect that Mindszenty might head a new Hungarian government as the only public figure to command wide support.

A liberation symbol

That in the minds of millions, Mindszenty by now had become a liberation symbol, there was no doubt. That he was the most plausible figure to command the support of the masses was equally an undisputed political reality.

That he had been chosen to be both, from behind the scenes by the insurrectionist forces, beginning with the CIA and by the Vatican, was equally an undisputed political fact.

This was all the more so, since Mindszenty figured prominently not only in the internal affairs of Hungary, but also in those of a vaster, anti-Communist network, namely, the Vatican-Washington campaign against Soviet Russia.

Hungary, being the first stepping-stone to the concrete unfoldment of the wider area of attack, the victory there was considered a triumph of the first importance. With Mindszenty as legal head of an anti-Russian Hungary, the first success would have opened the way to the second — further spontaneous revolts in the neighboring Communist countries such as Poland, for example. The result of the second phase would have been the third and final — the invasion and occupation of Soviet Russia, as envisaged by certain groups within the Catholic Church and in the United States, as we have already seen.

With the initial success of the Hungarian revolution, all the many individuals and organisations charged with the future occupation and conversion of Russia were alerted.

Religious fervour was mobilised. Special novenas, prayers and vigils were organised in the churches and convents of many countries, and even in Hungary itself. Our Lady of Fatima was invoked. Her prophecy at long last was about to be fulfilled.

Even before the Hungarian uprising, Pius XII, driven by his own religious and ideological fervour, had already issued statements which shocked some people and newspapers, such as the *London Times,* which we have already quoted, proposing "what almost amounts to a crusade of Christendom."

After the original exhileration following the successful Hungarian coup, fear gripped Europe. Would Soviet Russia intervene? If she did, would the United States oppose that action?

Days of anxiety followed. Then Russia, in defiance of the rest of Europe and of the United States, dispatched columns of Russian tanks into Budapest, and the Hungarian revolt was crushed with the utmost, bloody ruthlessness.

For awhile there loomed the prospect of a U.S.-Soviet armed confrontation — in a word, of the outbreak of World War III.

Despite the fact that certain political and military elements in the United States advocated intervention, however, President Eisenhower overruled these and the extremist coterie of the CIA. The latter's task, once it was realised that their offensive strategy had met with defeat, was confined to organising the evacuation of plane-loads of Catholic refugees, many of whom had worked for the agency, and most of whom were sent to the United States.

How close to war the world had come at this juncture, eventually was disclosed by one who was in a position to know — namely, John Foster Dulles, the U.S. Secretary of State.

Dulles's paramount obsession was Communism, the common denominator which made him the staunchest associate of Pius XII, as we have already noted. The association was the more critical because Alan Dulles, the Secretary's brother, was head of the CIA and could mobilise the vast intelligence resources of that agency in cooperation with the Vatican-Washington diplomatic campaigns.

The two brothers at one time worked so closely together that President Eisenhower on more than one occasion had his official policies nullified by CIA activities. The most spectacular example was the collapse of the American-Russian summit meeting of 1960, when the CIA sent a spy plane over Russia so as to prevent the American President and the Russian Premier from reaching an agreement that would terminate the Cold War. The proposed meeting, thanks to the incident created by the CIA plane, was cancelled. It was one of CIA's greatest triumphs.

John Foster Dulles (whose son, incidentally, became a Jesuit) and Alan Dulles, in total accord with Vatican intelligence, conducted their own foreign policy based on threats of "massive retaliation," that is, of atomic warfare.

After the Russian army had brutally suppressed the Hungarian revolt, Cardinal Mindszenty took refuge in the American Legation in Budapest.

Although U.S. regulations specifically forbade giving asylum to political , the CIA, prompted by the Vatican, succeeded in having this proscription waved aside. Secure in his American retreat, Mindszenty waited for another favourable opportunity. The opportunity never came. Less than two years later – in 1958 – his protector, Pius XII, was dead. The two red Popes who succeeded him made the Hungarian cardinal's position hopeless. Pope John began discreet negotiations for his release. The Communists agreed.

Cardinal Mindszenty was told that he was free to leave the Legation. He would be given safe conduct to either Rome or to the United States. He replied that he wished to remain near his people, even if separated from them by the walls of the American Legation. This he wished to do as a protest against Communism, which he still considered anti-religious, anti-Christian in particular, and altogether evil.

Pope John persevered, however, and dispatched various individuals whom he charged with persuading the Budapest "prisoner" to leave as a free man. All without success.

After John's death, efforts to have him set free were restarted all over again by Pope Paul VI, with the same result. Mindszenty's stubborness on the Communist issue was beginning to be an ideological anachronism to the increasingly Communist-oriented Vatican. Lay and ecclesiastical persuaders travelled back and forth between Rome and Budapest, a telling reminder that Paul VI was becoming more anxious even than the Communists themselves to get rid of anti-Communist Cardinal Mindszenty.

Finally, in October 1967, Paul VI sent none other than Cardinal Koenig of Vienna, who flew directly from Rome after a private audience with the Pope, and into Budapest, as he had done so many times before, with specific instructions from Paul to have Mindszenty "forced" free.

The issue had become the more pressing because the United States had by this time restored diplomatic relations with Communist Hungary. The American ambassador was given instructions to persuade Mindszenty to leave the building. The U.S. needed the Cardinal's two-room suite.

After receiving the eviction notice from his erstwhile protector and ally, Cardinal Mindszenty was threatened with excommunication by the Vatican, plus hints from the Communists that unless he left the country, he might be re-arrested and charged with the original crime of insurrection, which imported life imprisonment.

A shameful betrayal

Everybody seemed to have ganged up against Mindszenty — yesterday's hero — because he continued to remain loyal to those very principles for which he had risked so much. His enemies, the Communists; his friends, the Americans; and even his Church, were now accusing him of plotting against their interests.

True, some people at the CIA were bitter at the treatment which the United States had given the Cardinal, no less than at the efforts of Paul VI, "the Marxist," as they labelled him, for his relentless efforts to efface the very memory of their hero.

The truth of the matter, however, was that Mindszenty had been bypassed by events. The shifting of ideologies and of political influence had transformed the diplomatic horizon, where he no longer figured as a significant or valid symbol. For, since both Pope John and the U.S. had initiated a kind of anemic detente with Russia, the Vatican had proceeded much farther than detente. It had concluded a veritable realignment with

Moscow and now was engaged in a grand strategy of reorientation of the whole Church.

The time for the apotheosis of anti-Communist heroes had been long passed, at least in the eyes of the new Catholic Church.

The element of personal tragedy was the more poignant because many years before, Paul VI — when still Msgr. Montini — had acted as a link between Pius XII and the United States (and therefore with the CIA) in propelling Mindszenty into his ill-fated anti-Communist struggle.

Msgr. Montini, the red Pro-Secretary of State, now as Pope Paul VI, had not only reversed the former Vatican anti-Communist strategy; he had seen to it that the last champion of the defunct Vatican-Washington axis, namely Cardinal Mindszenty, was reduced to a mere half-forgotten footnote of history.

Notwithstanding the mounting pressure from the Communists, from the United States, and from Rome, Cardinal Mindszenty never accepted the red revolution of the two progressive popes. A symbol, and perhaps a warning to the Church, which, in order to further her dominion in a "progressive" world, had compromised so blatantly with a mortal enemy — an enemy which, according to Mindszenty, and even more to Pope Pius XII, would never change; indeed, would ultimately attempt to destroy her.

At long last, the U.S. officials at the embassy in Budapest told Mindszenty to go. The command of the Pope did the rest. The Communists, as anxious as they to get rid of him, said thanks to both, and forced the issue.

Cardinal Mindszenty arrived in Rome in September 1971. At the Vatican Pope Paul received him with genuine personal warmth. There is no doubt that Paul, a very sensitive and humane person, shared the freed Cardinal's anxieties and individual sufferings.

This he demonstrated in a spontaneous gesture, which proved it to be so. After embracing Mindszenty, Paul took his personal gold ring from his finger and gave it to the newly arrived cardinal in a moment of generous acknowledgement of the latter's personal worth.

Yet it was equally clear that, after expressing these personal feelings as man to man, prelate to prelate, the ideological gap which divided the two men, had become unbridgeable.

Mindszenty had entered the Vatican, no longer as a martyr, but as an awkward reminder of an anti-Communist past, which now for the New Vatican was already long dead and buried.

After visits to sundry members of the Roman Curia, who, he thought, might support him, Cardinal Mindszenty yielded to the painful efforts of the New Vatican and left Rome, a sad, rejected and broken man.

Pope Paul had ideologically avenged himself against all the dangerous policies and promoters of his predecessor by rejecting the surviving symbol of Pius XII's pro-American, anti-Russian past — Cardinal Josef Mindszenty.

Mindszenty flew away, never to see Rome again.

He died in exile, alone and forgotten, holding a picture of Pius XII, his Pope, in his hands.

CHAPTER 22

Soviet Spies and Vatican "Observers"

Nations fight not only with armies but also with the intricate mechanisms of intelligence, popularly known as spying. The mightier the nations, the mightier their intelligence systems. The more autocratic their governments, the more ruthless their covert activities. Communist Russia under Stalin had the most formidable espionage system in the world; the Roman Catholic Church, the most experienced. When the two met, therefore, there was bound to be a clandestine battle of heroic proportions.

Each system, staffed by masters of their respective crafts, has to exert itself to the best of its ability to outwit the rival. For, upon the success or failure of a given mission might depend the outcome of policies affecting not only current issues, but also the promotion of each side's grand strategies. Because of this, it became imperative for both Rome and Moscow that the intentions and plans of the opponent be known as accurately as possible, the better to assess the next move and thus to be in a position to formulate meant to counteract them.

Such an objective implied the penetration of each other's intelligence apparatus. The two systems were unique, sharing in equal measure as they did, the same rigidity and flexibility — two factors which permitted them to inter-penetrate each other with a subtlety denied to other espionage systems that were lacking in the messianis motivation of Catholicism and Communism.

The singular nature of each was that each represented something peculiar to itself: an autocracy sponsoring a world ideology in the case of Soviet Russia; and a theocracy radiating a global religion in the case of the Vatican.

Each was a monolith; rigid, immovable, and unbreakable, the enforcers of conformity, of collective acceptance of ideological or religious formulae, outside which there was no salvation.

Both theocracy and autocracy have always excommunicated those who dared to dissent. It is their nature to do so; hence the authoritarianism and the theocracy of the present are but slightly modified replicas of those of the past.

Stalin had dissident Trotsky expelled from Soviet Russia because Trotsky, even though he was one of the saints of the Bolshevik Revolution, had failed to conform and thus became an outcast from a rigidly organised Communist Party. Political deviationism is the secular equivalent of religious heresy.

Not only was Trotsky expelled from the Party, he was even eliminated physically, when Stalin ordered his assassination in 1940.

The murder of Trotsky provoked accusation and counter-accusation as to its real inspirer, for almost two generations. Although the most plausible author of the crime would obviously

In their secret files, the Soviet Secret Police recorded the minutest details of the life and habits of Pope John XXIII (here shown with his favorite brand of Turkish cigarette). Even before World War II, they noted that he had three important features as a possible future pope: 1) he was a genuine "progressive"; 2) he was of "true peasant stock"; and 3) he had "peasant's hands." They also gave importance to the fact that his favorite dish was "maize porridge, even when stale."

be Stalin, proof of his culpability was not brought to the fore until forty years later, when those individuals who had carried out the homicide came into public view.

The assassin, one Ramon Mercader, was exalted as a Communist hero by Soviet Russia. During an official ceremony attended by the top Communist leaders, held in Moscow in February 1977, he was officially declared a Hero of the Soviet Union and awarded the Gold Star, an equivalent to the Victoria Cross in England.

Pius XII dealt in a similar manner with Catholic dissidents. He had them ecclesiastically executed; e.g., the Catholics who dared to vote for the Communists in 1948 and 1949 elections; or Cardinal Suhard of Paris, the inspirer of the worker priests; or scientist-philosopher Theilhard de Chardin because of his revolutionary theories.

Theocracy and autocracy, being twin brothers, both use ruthless suppression when dealing with their opponents, or when it comes to operating their espionage systems, whose tentacles embrace the world.

Catholic and Communist intelligence networks have another feature in common. Unlike other intelligence systems, they offer their operatives rewards which are transcendental and beyond the reach of any other spying system based upon weak patriotism or financial guerdon.

It is not our intention here to deal with the nature of their activities, but only to relate, however briefly, typical instances in which their tentacles reached the present author in matters connected with both Moscow and the Vatican. Some were due to mere accidental contacts with persons closely connected with historical contemporary events, others with the operations of agents active in both intelligence apparatuses. Hence their significance to the present work.

Italian priest and Russian prince

The first of such key personages was the founder and leader of the Catholic Party of Italy, Dom L. Sturzo, whom we have already discussed in these pages.

Dom Sturzo at one time became the most serious obstacle to Mussolini's Fascist dictatorship. After founding the Catholic Party of Italy with the personal help of Pius XI, he later had to liquidate it on the Pope's order to let Fascism strike roots. As a result, he took refuge in London, where the present author met him some years before World War II. The man was reserved, devout, and loyal. He had every reason for bitterness. Yet he never once condemned the Supreme Pontiff. When finally Pius XI changed his mind about Fascism, contacts of a very delicate nature were resumed with the Vatican.

The OVRA or Fascist secret police, nevertheless kept a careful watch on Dom Sturzo, whom they considered potentially dangerous. Their interest increased about 1938, during and after the Munich crisis.

The outbreak of World War II made inevitable the machinations of political refugees in France and England. This writer had seen some of them while a student in Paris. There, he encountered various groups, all intent on plotting against either the Fascists or Nazis, or alternatively, against the Communists.

While most of their cabals were confined to verbal rodomontades, or others involved actions which had tragic results.

Of the latter, the case of the two anti-Fascist brothers Rosselini is an example. The brothers, being members of an active anti-Fascist group of which Socialist leader Pietro Nenni was a member, were kidnapped by the OVRA and murdered under the nose of the French police.

It was in this periods — 1933-34 — that the author became involved indirectly with the case of the murder of the King of Yugoslavia. The assassination was carried out by the Ustashies, an extreme Catholic nationalist group, whose objective was the independence of Catholic Croatia, then an integral part of Yugoslavia.

During the official visit to France of the King of Yugoslavia, while that monarch was riding in the company of the French Foreign Minister Bartou, two Ustashies jumped on the carriage and murdered both.

One of the assassins, prior to killing the king, had stolen the passport of a friend of this writer, with the result that both he and his friend were suspected of complicity by the French police who arrested, but later released them.

Afterwards, the Ustashies remained active under Communist Tito, spreading throughout the world — Europe, Australia, the United States — where they carried out dangerous missions, e.g., the assassination of one of Tito's ambassadors in Sweden in 1974.

In the case of Dom Sturzo, the OVRA was soon joined by a more subtle intelligence agency, that of the Vatican. The latter, although posing no physical threat, nevertheless was very effective in using ecclesiastic pressures.

During the winter of 1938-39, the Communists also suddenly became interested in the Italian priest, who was at the time quietly writing his books in a slummy section of Notting Hill Gate, in genteel poverty. He was a protege of Scotland Yard's special branch. Their interest in him was triggered by the Nazis. The Nazi intelligence network had been very busy in the purely domestic affairs of Britain. Their fields of operation were the British upper and middle classes. The latter was identified with the movement of Sir Oswald Mosley and his undisciplined battalion of black-shirted followers, the terror of the native Communists and Jews in East and North London.

Many sections of Britain's so-called high society were flagrantly pro-Nazi in public and even more so in private. This author knew several of them. Amongst the most notorious was Unity Mitford, the siter-in-law of Sir Oswald: a talented and beautiful girl and a fanatical admirer of Hitler. At the time, she was reputed to be Hitler's friend and a rival of Eva Braun herself.

When World War II broke out, Unity Mitford was shot. It was reported that she tried to commit suicide because of her disappointment about Germany and England going to war instead of fighting together against Communist Russia.

The probability was that either the Gestapo, which had suspected Miss Mitford of being a British agent; or even the British intelligence itself, might have had a hand in the whole affair.

It became somewhat disconcerting, therefore, when Dom Sturzo, whom the Nazis until then had totally ignored as a political nonentity, discovered that he had become the centre of their attention.

Their sudden interest was the more significant because it coincided with reactivation of certain unofficial Vatican contacts.

Hints of renewed political activities in Italy, coupled with those of ecclesiastical advancement, appeared unjustified under the circumstances. Dom Sturzo's main activities at this period were centered upon a book he was then writing, entitled *State and Church*.

The operational intelligence network had been alerted by specific motivation, that Dom Sturzo had been in contact for some time with Pope Pius XI.

The contact, which had been vaguely casual for some years, had become more discretionally frequent in 1938-39; that is, as soon as the Pope had hinted to several of his most intimate friends that he was planning to write his famous political testament, which we have discussed elsewhere.

This interest indicated the following: a) that the Nazi and Communist espionage systems had the Vatican under strict observation; b) that they must have had a special channel inside the Holy See, which reached the Pontiff himself, possibly a man in the Papal entourage; and c) that Dom Sturzo, because he had been made to partake of the Pope's intention, might have been in danger from one or the other, or both.

Yet Dom Sturzo never said anything to anybody. Certainly

not to the present author, who came face to face with the Russian presence by mere accident.

This appeared in the person of a Russian Orthodox priest, a "convert" to the Roman Catholic faith.

One day the convert priest addressed this writer in Russian, having wrongly assumed that he was of Russian origin. The mistake derived from the fact that Dom Sturzo had told him how the author had an original portrait of Leo Tolstoi, which had been drawn from life at Tolstoi's farm by one of the author's close friends — Prince Paul Troubetskoy.

The two names had immediately evoked from the "converted" priest impassioned rhetoric and revolutionary zeal.

Referring to Prince Paul's father, he enthused: "A great martyr of the Revolution!"

He then related a story for Dom Sturzo's edification. The elder Troubetskoy, he said, had been the Czar's great chamberlain, powerful at court, and immensely rich. Yet he had plotted the assassination of the Czar, "to free the Russian people." Unfortunately, the plot had failed. That failure, he added, "postponed the Revolution until 1917." It had been the will of Divine Providence to see that Lenin should finish the task, so nobly undertaken by Prince Troubetskoy in the 80s.

Significantly, the priest seemed to have an extraordinary knowledge of Prince Paul: of his past history, his work as a sculptor, his political beliefs.

He recounted, for instance, how the Bolsheviks, after having pulled down all the monuments erected to the Russian Czars throughout Russia, had spared only one — that fashioned by the hand of Prince Paul Troubetskoy.

This was true. The monument done by Prince Paul of Czar Alexander the Third, which the Czar's son had commissioned before World War I, had been spared. The Bolsheviks had contented themselves with changing its inscription, to read as follows:

"*Scarecrow*. My son and my father were executed, and I reap the harvest of immortal shame. I am standing here as a cast-iron scarecrow for the country which has forever thrown off the yoke of despotism."

Subsequently, Dom Sturzo admitted to the author that the Russian convert was, in fact, a Communist agent.

Hammer-and-sickle priests

In retrospect, the admission was an interesting one, since almost forty years later — in 1977 — West German intelligence revealed that the Soviet spy agency had flooded Europe with Orthodox priests, trained in both Europe and the U.S. by the Russian secret police in illegal activities.

Before and even during World War II, this use of priests by Russia was opposed by both Protestants and Catholics on the ground that religion, which was persecuted in Communist Russia, would never provide priests worthy of their calling to work as spies.

It might not be amiss to mention the fact that the CIA — the U.S. counterpart of Soviet intelligence — also employed clergymen as spies, e.g., in the French Riviera, where this author was badgered by one of them with subtle indirectness at Cannes in 1952, and again in 1954.

Prior to the revelation by West German intelligence sources, the CIA declared — in October 1976 — that it had stopped recruiting clergy.

Dom Sturzo admitted that he also had been approached by the Communists, long before he had created the Catholic Party of Italy. He had been contacted by none other than Chicerin, Lenin's personal confidant and the first Soviet Foreign Minister, via an Italian Communist leader. It had been Chicerin's approach which had spurred Pope Pius XI to give immediate support to the Catholic Party.

The Russian convert-priest continued his activities in London, even after the outbreak of World War II. This author encountered him a second time when he turned up unexpectedly at an important public affair in 1941.

One evening in November of that year, a banquet was held in the Dorchester Hotel in London, at which a top British journalist named Cummings from the *News Chronicle* was the featured speaker. He had just returned from Moscow, where he had had several meetings with Stalin, who charged him with delivering a very important message to Russia's Western allies.

The leaders of all allied governments-in-exile, then in London, together with their generals and diplomats, plus several ministers of the British government, were present.

Stalin's message was: his personal assurance that he had no intention whatsoever of trying to establish Communism outside Soviet Russia."

The importance of such an assurance must be measured against the political background of the period. Less than two years before, Stalin and Hitler had created the Berlin-Moscow Axis. That spelt a mighty combination of Communist-Nazi power and the general fear of an impending Nazi-Communist take-over of Europe. Soon afterwards, in 1940, Hitler invaded France, Holland and Belgium; routed the British, and had Europe at his mercy.

Then, in June, Hitler attacked Soviet Russia. Russia asked the West for help. Britain and the United States began to pour out weapons of all kinds. Many objected; the Stalin-Hitler treaty was still fresh in their minds, and the fear of Communism was real everywhere.

Stalin's assurance, therefore, had great impact, especially upon the Poles who, in 1939 had had their country invaded, occupied and partitioned into two halves by Hitler and Stalin.

By November 1941, Soviet Russia was in desperate need of war material; hence the launching of a psychological campaign to have the West accept Bolshevik Russia as their new fighting companion. Mr. Cummings was listened to with the rapt attention given an ancient oracle. His words — or, rather, Stalin's "message" — was drowned in ten-minute long applause.

Everybody appeared to be enraptured at Stalin's assurance, even though it was not given via diplomatic channels, but in the mouth of a journalist. When the audience quietened, the present writer indicated that he would like further clarification of the message. Was Stalin's assurance valid only for the duration of the war, or also for the post-war period?

Mr. Cummings replied: "Questions not permitted."

A heavily be-medalled individual shouted that Mr. Cummings should give an answer to the question.

Following a general uproar, Mr. Cummings finally nodded assent. Thereupon, this author asked the journalist whether he considered Mr. Stalin an honest and trustworthy man. The reply being in the affirmative, the author then made this comment:

"If that is the case, then Mr. Stalin's most sacred duty as a genuine Communist is to assure that Communism be established all across the rest of Europe, and up to Portugal, there to stop only because of the Atlantic Ocean."

Pandemonium followed. Krishna Menon, an Indian Communist and rabid Stalinist, who was present, was so incensed that he left the table.

Then, unexpectedly, the Russian converted priest first met at Dom Sturzo's, appeared from nowhere. He knew Menon well, even though the latter was a professed atheist and enemy of all religions. The priest, after expressing his disapproval of questioning Stalin's assurance, gave an ambiguous warning: "The arcana of the great religions," he said, "should be imparted only to the initiated. So, why not keep them to ourselves?"

The "ourselves" included, of course, not only the author, but also Krishna Menon. Menon, at that time, was a lonely Indian nationalist operating in London with little money or support, and even less a prospect for a political future. Yet Soviet intelligence had kept a watchful eye on him. Having sensed his political potentialities, they nursed him as they had done Dom

Sturzo.

The results were interesting. While, in the case of Dom Sturzo their efforts came almost to nothing, with Menon their perseverance paid off.

When India became independent in 1947, Jawaharlal Nehru, Indian premier and personal friend of Menon, made him Minister of Defense. Menon, a pacifist, armed India to the hilt, and then attacked the tiny and defenseless Portuguese colony of Goa, which was invaded and occupied. Further to this, he was responsible for steering India towards Soviet Russia, a foreign policy that that country has pursued to this day.

The Soviet's ideological pampering of Menon produced rich dividends indeed. The strength of Soviet intelligence, like that of the Vatican, resides in the fact that besides being animated by abstract objectives, they set in motion long-range policies which, oblivious of the time factor, work tirelessly to reach their targets.

As for Dom Sturzo, his political fortunes never rose again. It was not so much that the Russians had miscalculated his potentialities in the political area as that perhaps they had minimised the personality of Pope Pius XII. Hence the failure of Stalin's efforts to effect the election of a progressive pope after Pope Pius XI's death.

The novel political climate following World War II had made it utterly unfavourable for Dom Sturzo's resurgence. For, while the Vatican under anti-Communist Pius XII spurned him, the Communists, confident of their newly-found power, chose not to compromise themselves with a political Catholicism which had belonged to a Fascist past. Christian Democracy, which Dom Sturzo helped to create, nevertheless ruled Italy without interruption during thirty-three years, until 1977, when finally it capitulated, if not in name at least in fact, to Communist power, by accepting the "historic compromise" with the Italian Communist Party.

Dom Sturzo died a disappointed man, in a world which no

longer had any use for his brand of Catholicism, which both his Church and the Communists considered had outlived its original objective.

A Soviet eye at London's keyhole

The most striking example of the Kremlin's watch on key figures in Britain, as far as the present author is concerned, occurred during the fifties, during the cold war. It came straight from the top, and it penetrated via the cultural field.

That operation is worth recounting, no matter how much it is, of necessity, summarised.

One day in the early 1950s, this writer called at the Soviet Embassy in London, expecting to have the door slammed in his face, as had happened at least half a dozen times since 1948. He wished to ask why the Soviets had published a Russian translation of one of his books, *The Vatican In World Politics,* without any permission, notification, or remuneration.

As the door was ajar, the author entered the Embassy. There he came face to face with a gentleman in striped trousers, black jacket, and a stiff white collar. He was courtesy personified. He explained that he had just arrived from Moscow, had not yet entered his office, and was not familiar with diplomatic protocol. He asked the nature of the writer's enquiry.

Once in his office, where he listened patiently to the author's account concerning the recurrent rebuffs by Soviet officials, he gave his personal assurance that he would help to the best of his ability, although Russia was under no obligation to pay royalties, having never signed the Berne Convention.

He well understood the problem. He had been a writer himself. Following this initial rather stiff formal meeting, the Russian, whom we shall call Mr. Vladimir K and the author became friends. What provided the basis of their friendship was literature and religion.

Vladimir was the first secretary of the Soviet Embassy in London, second in authority only to the ambassador himself. He was a Georgian by birth, and had been a professor at Moscow University. His ambition had always been to write, but he had been forced into diplomacy by the direct order of Stalin, a fellow Georgian, as Vladimir pointed out with his enigmatic Mona Lisa smile.

The encounter took place at the time when the Cold War was at its most dangerous point, and the hot war in Korea at its hottest. The anti-Communist Hungarian coup in 1948 was still resented, and the embers of a counter-revolution were still aglow in Poland and Czechoslovakia. Andrei Gromyko, then Soviet ambassador to Great Britain and later Secretary of Foreign Affairs for the Soviet Union for many years afterward, was playing a major role in the delicate diplomatic chess game between East and West.

It became evident from the very beginning that Vladimir was more than a mere diplomat or even than the second most important official at the Embassy. His ideological sophistication, hidden beneath the stupid procedures of a crude diplomacy, was too striking to go unnoticed. His exceptional cultural background — he was at home with the most obscure and subtle ecclesiastical or theological themes of Christianity, whether Orthodox or Catholic — was an intellectual smoke screen behind which was something far more subtle, as the author was about to discover, namely, the elite of the Soviet intelligence service.

Vladimir always bade his time, never got cross, and maintained the same ambiguous smile regardless of what was said. Simultaneously, he explored with the utmost thoroughness, disguised as casual interest, the backgrounds and personalities with whom the writer was or had been familiar.

For instance, while dining at some expensive restaurant in Soho, he mentioned as off-handedly as possible the founder of the Catholic Party of Italy, Dom Sturzo. Vladimir knew, of course, that he was an Italian Senator, but what was the Pope going to do with him? What was the author's opinion about the role which Dom Sturzo might play with Christian Democracy? He was interested in hearing a personal assessment of Sturzo's political potentiality, since the author had known him intimately since before World War II.

Such a casual mention of the past and of current affairs became ever more noteworthy as time went by. And more curious. For instance, Vladimir once hinted that he would like to visit an English fair, encamped on Wimbledon Common, just outside London.

Having arrived there, he and the writer mounted the brightly-painted wooden horses of the merry-go-round, seemingly for a lark. As the carousel revolved, however, Vladimir pointed to some grey, Edwardian buildings in the distance and asked very casually, if the author's friend who lived there, was faring well.

It so happened that the grey buildings he indicated comprised the Vatican's legation in Great Britain. The papal legate, the unofficial ambassador of the Pope, obviously lived there. But it happened also that the author had known him well for years. He was Msgr. Godfrey, later archbishop of Liverpool and finally Cardinal and Primate of Great Britain. He was an unassuming, cultured, and highly diplomatic individual with whom the author had discussed the Church's role in world affairs, while researching material for his book, *The Vatican in World Politics.* Very few persons had known of these conversations with the prelate.

On another occasion, Vladimir mentioned the name of Sir Bruce Lockhart. His curiosity concerning Lockhart seemed a pointless one at the time. Viewed in retrospect, however, it made sense, as it was clearly a long-range intelligence pointer, full of hidden, explosive charges.

Lockhart was no obscure personality. During World War II he had become deputy Undersecretary of State at the British Foreign Office, and finally director general of the Political Warfare Executive, from 1941 to 1945. The author had met him socially during and after the war, once in the office of Mr. Eduard Benes, the Czech Prime Minister in London; and several times with St. John Philby, famous Arabist and father of the no-less celebrated Kim Philby, spy of the century, as he later turned out to be.

Sir Bruce Lockhart had been a well-known British intelligence agent before and after the Bolshevik Revolution. In 1918, he had been sent to Russia by Lloyd George, then British Prime Minister, to establish contact with Lenin and Trotsky — not to bring about their downfall, but, on the contrary, as he himself wrote, "because he was in favour of intervention by the Allies (then at war with Germany) on the side of the Bolsheviks."

The Allies, at this period of the 1914-1918 war, consisted of Britain, France, the United States, Russia, and others.

Allied policy did not support Sir Bruce's desire to aid the Bolsheviks, and, under orders, he sent a British force of about one thousand men to Archangel to help the counter-revolutionary movements, which were trying to keep Russia in the war.

The result of such contradictory activities was that he came under suspicion from all sides, and became entangled in accusations and counter-accusations, of plots and counterplots, which he could never openly explain. The last straw was his implication in an attempted assassination of Lenin himself. The charge this time was too much, even for the Bolsheviks. He was arrested and shut in the Kremlin.

It so happened that one of Lenin's comrades, Maxim Litvinov, at this time was "diplomatic agent" for the Bolsheviks in London. The British promptly arrested him as a hostage and told Lenin that Litvinoff would be released on one condition: instant freedom for Sir Bruce. The two men were set at liberty one month later.

At the outbreak of World War II in 1939, he rejoined Britain's Political Intelligence department. It was there that the author originally met him, introduced by one of Churchill's war ministers, Hugh Dalton, then responsible for broadcasts to guerillas in Nazi-occupied Europe.

Vladimir's mention at this juncture of Sir Bruce, a spent intelligence force, although seemingly innocuous, had a hidden significance, since it was at this very period that the author had also met Kim Philby, the son of St. John Philby, then engaged in triple intelligence activity in a network which spanned Washington and Moscow. A few years afterwards, the whole affair exploded into one of the major intelligence scandals of the mid-twentieth century.

Vladimir's conversations made it clear to the author that he knew all about St. John Philby's activities in the Middle East; the influence which he had exercised in the formulation of Britain's policies during and after World War I; and his disputes with his opponent, the legendary Lawrence of Arabia, whom he once had succeeded in the British Mandate of Palestine as High Commissioner.

He knew also something which St. John Philby had told the author in strictest confidence: how Lawrence of Arabia, while posing as the Arab's champion, had gone to London in secret, at least on two occasions, "to confer with Churchill and the Zionists," who were then planning the future state of Israel, even before the end of World War I. In addition, Vladimir referred to other episodes which Philby had never put into writing, then or afterwards.

Vladimir suspected that the elder Philby was still a great influence at the Foreign Office and in Mecca, Arabia, a sort of grey eminence of Middle East politics.

The son was introduced to the author by the elder Philby at the Atheneum Club in London. Kim Philby was a quiet-spoken, typical public school boy, possibly a former boat-racing defender of the Oxford and Cambridge Boat Race, or an excellent amateur cricket player. Politics was never mentioned. It seemed hardly worthy of discussion.

Vladimir's reaction to this writer's reaction to Kim Philby

was typically a sophisticated one. Seen in retrospect, it was also one charged with a very far-reaching intelligence objective.

He asked, as casually as ever, whether Lockhart's triple role — i.e., at first, helping the Bolsheviks, then aiding their enemies, and then being implicated in an assassination attempt against Lenin — could be repeated.

The author's reply brought a mysterious smile to Vladimir's face:

"Yes, provided there is the right man."

Such a reply to such an apparently hypothetical question, representing to the author a mere abstraction, was at that particular moment, linked by Vladimir with a very concrete, far-reaching operation.

It was at this period that Kim Philby, having climbed the career ladder to the top of British and American intelligence, was spinning his most subtle web between London, Washington, and Moscow, acting as one of Soviet Intelligence's chief double or treble agents.

A few years later, he was almost caught. The KGB prevented his arrest by helping him to escape to Moscow, where he has lived ever since.

Vladimir, as a ranking Soviet official, had not asked a silly question nor hypothesised a situation. He was dealing, however obliquely, with a real situation.

The vanishing spy

Following the death of Joseph Stalin in 1953, most of the Georgians with whom the Russian dictator had surrounded himself, including Beria, chief of the Soviet secret police, were liquidated.

Six months later, when this author called at the London Russian Embassy to make enquiries about Vladimir, he was informed by a Mr. Brushlow, the new First Secretary, that there had never been such a person.

When the writer printed Vladimir's full name on paper, to prevent a misunderstanding, his successor repeated once again that he had never heard such a name.

Vladimir had vanished as mysteriously as he had appeared, at the very embassy where his successor insisted that he had never existed.

CHAPTER 23

The Vatican's Watch on Israel

The Russian KGB is a global octopus. Intangible and yet concrete, it is seemingly unconcerned with abstract problems. Yet, it sets in motion long-range operations, inspired by objectives undetected even by those under its scrutiny.

Some of its tentacles are so shadowy and gossamer as to appear non-existent or non-operational; or even useless. Yet, each is operating to reach a definite target, no matter how elusive or remote.

Super-star Vladimir, whom we have discussed in the preceeding pages, was a master at the ancillary promotion of what appeared to be unrelated activities, whose imprecision at times verged on the immaterial.

The operational skill required of him was exceptionally mystifying, since its formulation employed what, for lack of a better description, we shall term a "Catherine's wheel" intelligence technique.

This technique was basically a simple one: a) concentration upon individuals or issues apparently unrelated to the current objective; and b) the creation of invisible intelligence foci from which to transmit "background-to-be-stored" information.

Unless handled with subtle coordination, such peripheral operations would have little usefulness, as for instance in the case of Dom Sturzo, or Sir Bruce Lockhart and the two Philbys — father and son.

A few typical instances of phase *b* will illustrate the *modus operandi* employed in the technique.

Before meeting Vladimir, this writer published a book about the Ustashies, the same Catholic extremists who had assassinated the King of Yugoslavia in 1934, and Marshal Tito's ambassador to Sweden in 1974. The Yugoslav Embassy in London had purchased 2,000 copies of the work, which they distributed free to members of the British government.

One day, after asking about the effect the book might have on the members of the British Parliament, Vladimir casually, and seemingly as an after-thought, enquired concerning the culinary skill of a Yugoslav friend of the author's, who used to prepare Serbian meals in the kitchen of the writer's London residence.

There was no apparent motivation for Vladimir's interest in the subject, since the man in question — Gen. Bora Mirkovich — was no longer active in either military or political affairs. He had retired from both, but remained stubbornly anti-communist.

It soon became evident, however, that the point of interest of Soviet intelligence was anything but regional cuisine. They were busy storing ancillary information about individuals whose future use was "potentially feasible" and "strategically desir-

The author chats with Yugoslav ambassador to Great Britain and his wife, at embassy reception. Yugoslavia's entry into the Vatican-Moscow alliance marked a sudden cooling of the formerly cordial relationship.

Yugoslav Gen. Bora Mirkovich (right), a vigorous opponent of both Nazism and Communism, who played a paramount role in the fight against Hitler. At one point there were plans to flatten the Vatican and St. Peter's with squadrons of bombers, but these were foiled only 24 hours before the attack was due to take place. Shown with Gen. Mirkovich is the author.

able," in some political abstraction as in the case of Krishna Menon.

Theoretically, their sagacity was laudable. For General Mirkovich, although retired from active political life, still retained exceptional credentials. These gave him credibility in the event of some ideological emergency.

During World War II, when Hitler destroyed France's Maginot Line and, having routed the French and British forces, invaded French territory, the Yugoslav government — faced with a victorious Nazi Germany on her borders — decided to prevent a Nazi invasion by signing a non-aggression treaty with the Germans.

Although the situation seemed, and was, a desperate one, Mirkovich overthrew the Regent Prince Paul, seized the administration, and tore Hitler's treaty to shreds.

Hitler, who had already mobilised Germany for an attack on Russia, and who had signed the Yugoslav treaty to protect his southern flank during the Russian campaign, was taken by surprise. His dilemma was dramatic. He could not spare any of the divisions already assigned to the Eastern front, yet he could not risk Merkovich's anti-Nazi stance to imperil Germany on the South.

On the 6th of April 1941 — only five weeks before Germany's attack on Russia — he finally invaded Yugoslavia, with the exception of one province, that of anti-Orthodox, anti-Communist, and pro-Nazi Catholic Croatia.

In 1945, when Nazi Germany collapsed and Yugoslavia became a Communist dictatorship under Marshal Tito, General Mirkovich sought refuge in England, where he lived in obscurity un-thanked by Allies and friends alike.

But while Western democracies have always spurned men of integrity and ideals, the Communists have seldom disregarded them. Communist Tito, although aware of the General's unbending anti-Communism, wanted him back. He offered him a national hero's welcome in Belgrade, the reinstatement of his status in the army, and finally, even the ambassadorship to England. All in vain.

Soviet Russia, while harboring no such illusions, also kept a watchful eye on him and, after assessing him as "potentially useful" in the diplomatic war of attrition which had developed between Soviet Russia and Tito's dissident Yugoslavia, put him in cold storage, in keeping with their Catherine's wheel technique.

Russia did this for three reasons: a) because of a sense of gratitude to a man who, by diverting precious German divisions from the Russian front, had in all probability saved Moscow from being occupied by the Germans (a fact which was subsequently acknowledged by Churchill); b) because Mirkovich could be used as a nationalistic tool by Tito, had Russia invaded Yugoslavia; and c) because of Mirkovich's still formidable capacity for plotting, had he once again become active in the political or military fields.

His reputation for skill in such matters was high, not only in Belgrade but also in Moscow. It was justified. For Mirkovich had been one of the few individuals who, even if indirectly, had precipitated the outbreak of World War I. He had been a youthful member of the *Black Hand,* a powerful secret society dedicated to the liberation of Serbia. During Serbia's occupation by the Catholic Austria-Hungarian Empire, forces of the latter government has tried to destroy the Serbian character of the province by, among other things, attempting to convert the Orthodox Serbs to Roman Catholicism.

The role of religion

Mirkovich greatly resented this kind of religious coercion, hence his joining *The Black Hand.* Following various attempts at persuading Austria-Hungary to desist, the Black Hand society finally decided upon the assassination of the heir to the Austrian throne. When Crown Prince Franz Ferdinand, therefore, went on an official visit to Sarajevo on June 28, 1914, one Gravillo Princip murdered him. This act gave Austria-Hungary the pretext to declare war on Serbia. The conflict developed into World War I.

In Mirkovich's view, the occupation of Serbia had been possible because of intrigues involving the Vatican. This was, indeed, a factual assessment of the situation at that period. What he resented even more, however, had been the attempts of the Roman Catholic Church to destroy the Serbian Orthodox Church.

The effort had been revived during World War II by a leading Croatian Catholic named Ante Pavelich who, with the help of Archbishop Stepinac, tried to wipe out the Orthodox population of Croatia by liquidating more than half a million Orthodox people.

The religious motivation underlying the activities of General Mirkovich were duly noted by Russian Intelligence which, although acting as the instrument of an atheistic regime, never minimised the importance of religion as a prime factor in prompting Mirkovich to act as he did.

This early recognition of the important role played by religious issues in political matters was confirmed some years later, not in connection with General Mirkovich, but with that of Tito's government in the formulation of its foreign policy.

After publication of the present author's book about Yugoslavia, he became a regular guest at the Yugoslav Embassy in London, as did many other writers, diplomats, and politicians, with the exception of the Russians.

In November 1970, at an embassy function, this writer greeted the Yugoslav ambassador as he was accustomed to do; but, unlike past instances, the ambassador — a personal friend of Tito — was now anything but cordial. After making certain pointed comments, he mentioned this writer's Yugoslav books. They were creating trouble. When asked to be more specific, the ambassador explained that Yugoslavia no longer cared about works which were critical of the Vatican's diplomatic activities.

When it was pointed out that certain past events, e.g., large-scale massacres — whether committed by the Nazis, the Russians, the Allies, or anybody else — should not and could not be forgotten, lest they be repeated in the future, the ambassador's reply was a curt one:

"In our case, they had better be forgotten, since they are endangering our relationship with the Vatican."

Just at that moment, a smiling, suave individual joined the conversation. He was wearing a black suit and clerical collar, silver crucifix and violet rabbi.

The ambassador made a formal introduction. The man was Archbishop A. Cardinale, the papal legate (that is, the Pope's ambassador) to Great Britain. It was a sight never encountered before at the Communist Yugoslav embassy.

His presence there heralded what had been in the wind since the formulation of the Vatican-Moscow alliance, namely, a latter-day Vatican-Yugoslav rapproachment. The Catholic Croats, who were still fighting for their independence from Yugoslavia as a political entity, and against Tito as a Communist dictator, obviously had been sacrificed by the new Vatican on the altar of its policy of detente.

The Croats' bitterness came to the fore not long afterwards when they began systematically to assassinate Tito's "Communist-Catholic creatures," as they called them. One day in 1974, as already mentioned in a foregoing chapter, they killed Tito's ambassador to Sweden. He was the first on their list. Their plan to kill another three was foiled by Scotland Yard, which passed on information, via Interpol, alerting the authorities concerned.

The significant feature of this and of similar killings, was that they were conducted by the Ustashies, or rather by the Croatian Nationalists who, although devout Catholics, nevertheless had rejected the Vatican's Marxist reorientation.

A few months after the Yugoslav ambassador's rebuke in the

presence of the Pope's ambassador, Communist Yugoslavia fell into line with the grand strategy of the Vatican-Moscow alliance. In April 1971, Dictator Tito paid an official visit to Pope Paul at the Vatican. There, after having had "a very private audience," the two men declared, in so many words, that a new era had dawned for yet another Marxist country in its relations with the Catholic Church.

But by then General Mirkovich was dead. Had he been still alive, it is possible that he might have joined the Croats in their fight against a Marxist Yugoslavia, which had aligned herself with a Marxist Catholicism.

The question of Israel

The KGB, or rather the Cominform, while concerned with Europe, never missed an opportunity to compile data, no matter how unrelated to current problems, as long as these helped to analyse and anticipate potentially dangerous realities of tomorrow, or even of day after tomorrow.

The problems of Israel provide a case in point.

Sometime in 1951-52, the author dined with a New Yorker named Rodman, who was visiting London on behalf of the Zionist Federation of America. He had one definite mission: to purchase agricultural tractors for Israel.

The British factories could not or would not commit themselves to any firm delivery date. Mr. Rodman was despondent, not only because he was about to return to the United States empty-handed, but also because he had been told that in a country behind the Iron Curtain, namely, Czechoslovakia, tractors were being produced in great numbers.

This writer volunteered to help solve the dilemma. He asked Vladimir whether Russia could not do something about it.

Vladimir turned suavely patriotic. Russia could not help anybody. Her agriculture had been devastated; she was short of farm implements herself; there was a scarcity not only of tractors, but also of labor; 22 millions had perished during World War II. And so on.

After prolonged reflection, however, he responded to the request by asking a disconcerting question:

Would the Vatican approve or disapprove of such a Russian gesture of goodwill towards Israel?

At first, the question seemed wholly out of place. Indeed, it seemed absurd. It must be pointed out that the conversation took place when the Cold War was at its most critical stage. Upon closer scrutiny, however, the query made sense.

During several days, the whole affair was kept in a kind of limbo. Rodman made ready to leave for New York. The night before his departure, however, Vladimir announced that he had "a very special permit" for him to visit Czechoslovakia.

Mr. Rodman did indeed go to Czechoslovakia, where he purchased a number of tractors for shipment to Israel, and returned happily to America.

Vladimir then explained. Soviet Russia, he said, had never been and could never be anti-semitic. First of all, more than five million of her citizens were Jews. They were good comrades. Besides, Jews had contributed more perhaps than any other minority to the Bolshevik Revolution. Marx, Trotsky, Chicherin, Litvinov and many others had been the founders and pillars of Communism.

Secondly, Marxist tenets forbade religious and racial bias, and protected minorities. Zionism, however, was not a religion, but an imperialism. Had not this writer's friend, S. J. Philby, thought the same? What about Philby's rival, Lawrence of Arabia? Had not Lawrence, while posing as the Arabs' champion, worked for the Zionist cause from behind the scenes?

The reference was to something which the elder Philby had related many times to this author during World War II. Lawrence of Arabia, at the height of his triumph, had, according to Philby, been contacted by London's Zionists. They wanted his

his help and counsel in formulating a policy in connection with remapping the Near East.

Lawrence had gone twice in secret to London to confer with the top Zionist leaders, Foreign Office experts, and Winston Churchill concerning the future implantation of Israel in Palestine.

S. J. Philby, as one of the most experienced authorities on Middle East affairs, has opposed Lawrence's policy, which in effect was that inspired by the British Zionists. The policy advocated the creation of a Middle East composed of numerous small Arab states whose economic and military weakness would have permitted the birth of a Jewish nation.

Philby, on the other hand, wanted a limited group of strong Arab states to give the Middle East stability.

Zionism, according to Vladimir, was a branch of American Imperialism. As such, it had to be opposed. It was a rival of Soviet Russia and of World Communism. Israel, being Zionism's territorial offspring, therefore, should not have been helped.

The present author, prior to the purchase of the tractors, had put forward the view that a strong Israel was in the interest of Soviet Russia.

How so, Vladimir asked.

Because a powerful Israel, the author argued, as a visible expression of Zionism in territorial, political, and military matters, in the long run was bound to antagonise the Vatican. The interests of each would clash, religiously and politically. The result of a forthcoming hostility between the Vatican and Israel would mean that the Vatican would be compelled to diminish its opposition to Soviet Russia. Indeed, the Church would seek a form of cooperation with her, the better to contain Israel's ambitions.

Not Israel's ambition in geographical, economic, or even political areas, to be sure; but her ambitions in the theological field. It was these latter aims which the Vatican feared more than it feared Communism itself. That is why it was bound to oppose

Zionism.

The Vatican did not view Zionism as a branch of American imperialism, as did the Communists — at least in public — but as a dynamic promulgator of Israel's eschatological mission.

Briefly, in Vatican thinking, the stronger Israel became, the stronger would be the ambitions of world Zionism. And vice-versa. Apart from the geographical presence of a Jewish state in the Middle East, the most controversial characteristic of an Israeli establishment, with Jerusalem as a territorial and mystical omphalos, was its messianic nature, the central focus of the Hebrew teleological dream.

Because of this, the Vatican could not and would not tolerate the establishment of an Israel which claimed messianic privileges, or rather, messianic uniqueness and which, therefore, would compete with the Roman Catholic Church as the centre of a future spiritual kingdom.

It was sound strategy, therefore, for Soviet Russia to strengthen Zionism with the precise objective of accelerating the inevitable Catholic-Zionist antagonism. So argued the present writer. Had Russia pursued such a policy, the resulting political situation would have compelled the Vatican to seek an ally in Soviet Russia.

It is important — although it may be difficult for some — to recognise the religious nature of the Communist-Zionist-Catholic political configuration. Although deliberately muted in public pronouncements, behind the Zionist banner there was to be found the ancient messianic hope for the coming of a global theocracy, as predicted by all the seers and prophets of Zion. It was to be a theocracy in which Jehovah, not Christ, would be king.

The spectre of the creation of such a theocracy has haunted the inner chambres of the Catholic Church from her earliest inception, and is still a dominant fear. Hence her equivocal role in world affairs surrounding the birth and existence of the State of Israel. Such a State was defined as a territorial entity erected upon racial and religious tenets, whose ultimate objective is the teleological triumph of the Jews whose Messiah will not be the Founder of Christianity, but of a future "unique presence" whose coming will nullify the messianic claim of Christ.

In Vatican eyes, therefore, the millenarian yearning for a global Hebrew theocracy represents a deadly threat to the eschatological teachings of the Catholic Church. When translated into concrete political terms, such a view spells not only rivalry, but implacable enmity.

It could not be otherwise, because both Zionism, as the herald of the ancient ancestral fulfillment of the Jewish mystic dreams, and the Catholic Church as the singular embodiment of the final uniqueness of Christ, owe their respective allegiances to a Messiah.

The Vatican's allegiance is to a Messiah who has already come and who will reappear in spiritual triumph at the end of time. Israel's allegiance is to a future Messiah, who is about to come. These two are mutually exclusive, since the first denies the claims of the second; and the second is the automatic denier of the claims of the first.

Such mutual nullification, when transposed from the mystical to the religious and political areas, can only become the source of mutual antagonism in the ethical, social, and political fields. In short, it will inevitably produce hostility between the established representatives of the two inimical Messiahs.

A Vatican fundamentally opposed by a powerful Jewish theocracy, therefore, would become not only hostile to Zionism and consequently to Israel; it would seek powerful allies to neutralise both. In political parlance, it would seek as an ally another imperial power — the Russian or the Communist, or both, to checkmate the imperialist dream of Zionism.

This is so because an imperialism like that of Soviet Russia, even if atheistic in ideology, in the Vatican's view is far less menacing than the mystical imperialism of the Zionists determined to prepare the Kingdom of the coming Hebrew Messiah.

It would therefore be good strategy for Russia to help Zionism expand, in order to accelerate the creation of a political climate conducive to the eventual confrontation of both with the Vatican.

The dawning of such a day would herald the coming together of Russia and the Vatican. The two, although remaining basically hostile, nevertheless would cooperate in their joint opposition to the other two imperialisms — namely, that of Zionism as opposed to the Vatican, and that of capitalist America, as opposed to Communist Russia.

The Vatican-Moscow partnership would have respective targets: 1) Zionism in the religious field on the part of the Vatican, because Zionism is the promoter of the messianic role of Israel and therefore the spiritual foe of the Catholic Church's messianic imperialism; 2) The United States on the part of Soviet Russia, not so much because the U.S. is an ally of Zionism or of Israel, but because the Kremlin hierarchy believe that the U.S. represents an imperialism which is antagonistic to Soviet Russia on ideological and military principles.

In other words, whereas Zionism wanted eventually to dominate the world as a theocracy, the United States wanted to dominate it by means of dollar imperialism. The materialistic interpretation of human events, even the rejection of spiritual life implicit in militant atheism, were far less dangerous to the Catholic Church than the claims of a Second Messiah. While the economic and military might of the United States were less threatening to Soviet Russia than support of messianic Zionism, with its dreams of a global Hebrew Empire.

After discussions that lasted for weeks, Vladimir finally asked if the author would provide him a formulation of the basic conflicting messianic interpretations between the Vatican, Zionism, and the United States.

This was done. It appeared under the title of *Catholicism, Americanism, Zionism and Communism (Four Imperialisms in Search of a World)*.

Vladimir dispatched it to Moscow without comment. There "a fellow Georgian" found the elaboration "potentially plausible" and, given time, even "feasible."

In the end, Vladimir was happy about the whole affair. He even admitted being happy about having helped Israel with the purchase of the tractors in Czechoslovakia.

CHAPTER 24

Russian Dossier on Three Popes

Messianic imperialism, whether Catholic or Zionist, is basically hostile to Communist expansionism. A combination of the two could have formed, quoting Vladimir's own words, "a monstruous cartel of organised mass superstition." Such a combination would have become a real peril to the security of Soviet Russia.

It was in the interest of Russia and of Communism, therefore, that such a partnership should never occur. While waiting for the expected conflict between Zionism and the Catholic Church to reach a realistic stage of concrete hostility, it was essential that the Vatican be reformed from within and possibly from the top.

Pope Pius XII was certainly a tool of American capitalism in the Russian view, because capitalism supported religion. But assuming that Communism no longer identified itself with capitalistic religion, and accepted the social tenets of Christianity, what then? The Church would stop her opposition to Communist doctrine (except for atheism) and, consequently, would stop her opposition to Soviet Russia.

This could happen via a revolution below and one from the top in in the Roman Catholic Church.

On one occasion, the present author asked Vladimir whether he had ever envisaged a Russian pope?

Yes, he had — but in the distant future. And even then, a pope as head of all branches of organised Christian "superstition." In such a day, however, any pope would be capable of giving the right social interpretation of the tenets of Christianity, which by that time would have been purged by the realistic principles of Marxism and Leninism.

The purified Christianity would make possible the fulfillment of a famous prophecy concerning Moscow, namely, that it would become "the Third Rome." Not a Third Rome as prophesided by Christianity, to be sure, but a Third Rome as the Rome of Christian Communism.

Before that, however, the Vatican and the Catholic Church had to be "marxistised."

His startling reply was significant because Vladimir had not expressed a personal opinion, but rather the "official line" of the Kremlin:

As Rome had been the capital of Christianity, and Constantinople had been the capital of Greek Christian Orthodoxy, so — in the future — Moscow would become the Third Rome, first as the capital of the Russian Church, and then as the capital of Christian Communism.

Such an opinion, expressed at the height of the Cold War when the Vatican was the focus of the most anti-Communist crusade in the Western world, a campaign energised by religious zeal, was, to say the least, surprising. It was also important; for it proved, if nothing else, that Moscow had already begun to think of some kind of rapprochement with the Vatican in the early 50s.

The contemplated accomodation was obviously not of a diplomatic or even of an ideological kind, per se. It envisioned nothing more, nothing less than the interpenetration of Marxism with Christianity, and hence the creation of the forthcoming Christian-Marxist hybrid of today.

Its implementation, however, required the accelerated promotion of a new climate in the Vatican, where a new type of Curia, or better still, of Pontiff, could give such a revolutionary entity the stability it needed.

That such a possibility had already been contemplated at the Kremlin, no matter how embryonically, was proved also by the fact that Stalin, as already mentioned, had somewhat naievely set in motion his lobbying for a Russian Pope.

The chances of electing a Russian Pontiff in the foreseeable future, as Vladimir had to admit, were about the same as, in his own words, "the Italians ever admitting that the Holy Shroud of Turin was a counterfeit copy of one we have in Georgia."

Stalin's papal candidate, as we have already seen, had been Cardinal Agagianian who, for Stalin, was *papabile* because he was Georgian, like the Soviet dictator himself.

But while Vladimir discounted the early election of a Russian Pope, he certainly at the same time feared the election of an American one.

The Vatican ruled by an American pope would have meant war, he used to say. It was one of the few occasions when his perennial Mona Lisa smile would vanish from his face. An American on the Throne of Peter would be a disaster for everybody, starting with the Catholic Church herself.

Americans knew nothing about theology, he said; and even less about Communism. They were naive, political adolescents. Any charlatan could lead them to right-wing extremism by appealing to their emotions.

If Spellman and some of his reactionary American prelates had succeeded Pius XII, there would have been real war. Pius XII himself had already made Spellman *papabile* with the probation of the U.S. State Department.

Asked by this writer to elucidate his assertions, Vladimir said the Soviet Intelligence had been informed about it all "by the Holy Ghost, acting as that agency's homing pigeon." Furthermore, they had kept abundant files about all the progressives in the Vatican, as well as those in Europe and in the United States.

He mentioned the names of bishops and Cardinals, names which afterward vanished into obscurity.

After Spellman, at the top of Vladimir's *bete noir* list, came Msgr. Tardini, the Pro-Secretary of State to Pope Pius XII, whom he called "the chief reactionary at the Vatican."

Other reactionaries and progressives were mentioned with startling familiarity. Amongst the "good men" were the Monsignori Roncalli and Montini, two progressives who have become part of contemporary history since then because of their having become respectively Pope John XXIII and Pope Paul VI.

A Communist at heart

According to Vladimir, Msgr. Montini had two Achilles's heels, one political and the other personal. As for the political, he was considered to be at heart a true Communist, but a Communist wrapped up in bourgeois formalities and curial caution, which meant "curial paralysis."

Personally, he was incapable of taking definite and prompt decisions. Although he was prone to favour Communism, he lacked the moral courage to do so in the open. On the other hand, this handicap was neutralised by his anti-Americanism, inspite of his bourgeois background.

Certain petty, unsubstantiated allusions to personal idiosyncrasies are not worth recalling. Soviet agents, however, true to their reputation, put them on record, believing that the utmost trivialities were of interest as long as these might reveal personal weaknesses of character, or indicate psychological trends.

Cigarettes and "red polenta"

As far as Msgr. Roncalli was concerned, he was too fond of Armenian tobacco; he favoured certain brands of cigarettes; and was fond of "red polenta," that is, he had Communist proclivities. (This last observation was made also by a U.S. intelligence report). Also, he liked to be whipped by "grey nuns" after he had a good portion of both.

At that time, the author could not fathom what the "grey nuns" were supposed to represent. Several years later, however, a friend who had long family connections with the Vatican, related some typically Roman gossip. According to these aspersions, Pope John used to be whipped with sticks by nuns who were brought to Rome especially for that purpose.

It was a despicable gutter report which, nevertheless, had circulated in Rome for many years without any substantial evidence to support it. The author's guess is that Pope John took sauna baths to reduce his corpulence. The customary beating with twigs or small branches following such a bath could have led to the stories launched by over-heated Roman imaginations.

Vladimir was optimistic about Msgr. Montini's playing an important role after the demise of Pope Pius XII. Curiously enough, however, he never considered Montini *papabile.* This on the ground that a man who, after many years of serving Pius XII, stubbornly insisted on standing when in the Pope's presence, as Montini did, even after he had been asked to sit, could *not* lead anything or anybody. This was a glaring demonstration that Soviet intelligence could also miscalculate.

Such "creatures" as Vladimir used to call them, were more useful than if they were popes. This was an indirect reference to the mystery of who had actually warned Stalin about Hitler's impending attack on Russia.

General Mirkovich had had no doubts that Stalin had been warned by "some prominent radical prelate working behind Pius XII's desk," and did not believe the official version released afterwards. He justified his scepticism on the ground that he had suffered a similar experience, which had cost him the loss of almost the whole of the Yugoslav Air Force.

Hitler had destroyed practically the entire Yugoslav Air Force prior to its taking off to carry out "a very special mass bombardment against a very special city." He gave credit for the leak to Catholic intelligence.

Hitler's intervention on this occasion may have saved one of the most important as well as the most celebrated centres of culture in the world, since an important part of that same air force had been assigned to the actual flattening of Vatican City and St. Peter's. The loss of artistic, literary, and historical treasures would have been irreplaceable.

The General never confided to anybody except a fellow Serb and the present author, who it was that had planned the actual bombardment of Vatican City. Vladimir, however, knew, and gave hints that the Russians had in fact been warned of the forthcoming destruction of the Vatican. His version differed with that of General Mirkovich only about who told Hitler to destroy the Yugoslav Air Force while it was on the ground, prior to its "very special" mission.

That there had been some contradiction in certain intelligence matters concerning the Vatican there was no doubt. It is possible that counter-intelligence working within counter-intelligence, closely connected within religious institutions of differing ideological sympathies, could have been responsible for the confusion. Vladimir used to refer to the Vatican's cipher book, as we have mentioned elsewhere, as a trivial example of "how things could help and not help," as he put it.

He was proud that the cipher book had played havoc with the American-Vatican plan "to invade Russia, Hitler style, but without Nazi efficiency," and "make us all Catholic Americans, baptised by Niagras of Coca-Cola and Neopolitan [sic] priests."

During World War II, the British had discovered the means of intercepting and decoding the most secret directives of the German High Command to its field commanders. The device was called *Enigma.*

Soviet intelligence and its subsidiary branches were just as efficient, if not more so, since "they could tell, for instance, how many times the Pope changed his socks."

More and more prelates were wearing red shirts under their black cassocks, figuratively speaking, Vladimir used to boast. They were waiting for the day when Christianity would divorce itself from capitalism "and side with the workers."

That divorce was inevitable, he added, since Marxist tenets were in harmony with those of the Gospels. In economic matters, atheism meant nothing. The Catholic proletariat were beginning to realise this, as were the lower clergy. The latter, once in higher echelons, would turn the Church into a "progressive institution." This would mean a progressive Vatican. And a progressive Vatican would spell the reduction of hostility in the world.

Most of the bishops behind the Iron Curtain — or in the Eastern democracies, as he put it — had already accepted this. They had come to terms with Communism, having discovered that Communism could co-exist with religion. This reality was demonstrated by the "co-operation" of the Soviet government with the Orthodox Church.

The coming of a progressive pope was an historical inevitability. Soviet Russia wanted such a Pope. It was also an historical necessity. It could and should have been accelerated before the Pius-Spellman-Dulles trio had launched a war against the Soviet Union.

Vladimir felt personally optimistic about the coming of a leftist pope, because in his own words, "we are moving in the proper direction under the very nose of Pius and his henchman, Spellman."

The U.S. had already begun a promotional campaign for the election of another reactionary prelate — Msgr. Tardini. Several Americans had put money into the hands of certain bourgeois Cardinals, to that end. The U.S. lobby was in full swing now. (In 1952).

When this writer expressed doubts about the validity of Vladimir's assertions, he would repeat the familiar refrain: "We know what's going on in the Vatican of Rome [sic] better than they know at the Little Vatican of New York. Our 'Vatican' in Moscow keeps hidden eyes on both."

To prove his point, there were occasions when Vladimir related certain gossip which was difficult to assess, contradict, prove, or even less, to check. One of his reports was to the effect that the Pope once had tried to marry Hitler to a Catholic woman reactionary of Spain.

"That's why your English friend, Unity Mitford attempted to kill herself," he used to tease the author — a reference to the mysterious circumstances surrounding the death by gunshot of Miss Mitford at the beginning of the war, when the Gestapo and the British intelligence service were both suspected of having had a hand in the affair. The more so, since one of Miss Mitford's sisters in the meantime had become a card-carrying member of the Communist Party in the United States.

The aim of the proposed Hitler-Spanish woman's marriage was to bring into being the brain-child of Pius XII, namely the resurrection of the Catholic Austrian-Hungarian Empire (destroyed during World War I) to act as a Catholic bastion against the expansionistic ambition of the Russian Orthodox Church, once Soviet Russia had been defeated.

General Mirkovich confirmed the truth of the story, which he had heard as early as 1942-43, and which had worried him no end, concerned as he was about the future prospects of the Serbian Orthodox Church. According to him, General Franco had agreed to appease Hitler in order to soften the Spanish dictator's continual refusal to enter the war on Hitler's side.

Vladimir's greatest fear, in the event of Pius XII's sudden demise — "because we know he suffers recurrent hallucinations" — was that the Americans might strike a successful deal with the Roman Curia and "buy" (his words) the next pope.

Another pro-American pope, according to him, would prove a disaster; the more so since the world was bound to become socialist — another inevitability.

One day he flew unexpectedly to Moscow. On his return, he offered the author a bottle of vodka he had carried away from a private party at the Kremlin. Then he came out with an astounding proposition:

In Russia there existed a Marx-Lenin Institute. Its course lasted four years. Only individuals with special gifts were enrolled there. Vladimir had himself spoken with the highest authority. If the present writer would accept the offer to attend that very special college, the course could be reduced to a mere nine months.

Simultaneously, he proposed that the author contribute a fortnightly article to the Soviet newspaper, *Pravda.*

A source of political power

Vladimir had become obsessed with the necessity for the election of a progressive pope. It had become ever more clear that the Kremlin's direct experience with the tremendous influence the Vatican could exercise within the Eastern European countries now under Russian control, had taught the Soviet authorities a hard lesson. Even more, they had come to realise that the Vatican, far from being a mere religious focus, was a mighty source of political power, the use or misuse of which could alter the balance of Europe, and in fact of the entire Western World.

This, it must be remembered, was a time when the Cold War was at its height, McCarthyism was rampant in the United States, and mysterious whispers about the impending invasion of Soviet Russia were being heard in some world capitals. This writer was even shown badges by more than one Catholic refugee who had volunteered to free the persecuted Christians from the oppression of atheistic Communism. Vladimir himself once had three such badges which he showed the author.

Perhaps his anxiety, and that of the policy-making forces he represented, was a reflection of the inner uneasiness of the Kremlin itself. Or — and this is even more plausible — there was a genuinely-felt desire on the part of Russia for a change in Rome.

Such a desire, of course, had nothing to do with theological considerations, or even with the planned resuscitation of the Russian Orthodox Church vis-a-vis a forthcoming confrontation with the Catholic Church, as an instrument of georeligious, ideological imperialism.

It was seen and was justified on concrete political grounds. The mounting unrest behind the Iron Curtain, led by the Catholic hierarchy, and thus by the Vatican, was menacing the stability of the Communist regimes. The Hungarian plot of 1947 had not been forgotten. The one which was about to burst out in 1956 was being watched by Soviet intelligence with deadly fascination. All this, with the accelerated tempo of the Catholic-American crusade being mounted by the West, had obviously created serious apprehension in a mellowing and ailing Stalin.

Vladimir's almost obsessive thinking about the coming of a "progressive" pope, therefore, might truly have been a reflection of such anxieties pervading the Kremlin at this particular juncture.

Nevertheless, Vladimir would sometimes become inexplicably optimistic. "Certain of your Cardinal friends," he used to say, "are already wearing red socks. Tomorrow one of them will become a pope. And then what?"

It was impossible to know, whenever he said this, whether he was jesting or whether he was alluding, no matter how circumspectly, to certain promotional intelligence activities perhaps already at work somewhere in the higher echelons of the Roman Catholic Church.

The answer came five years later. In 1958 there was elected a "progressive" pope. Soon afterwards, John XXIII — to the astonishment of the entire world — opened the windows of the Vatican to the air of socialism; indeed, to the whirlwind of the most radical revolution ever experienced by the Catholic Church since the Reformation.

Could Vladimir's other predictions: the identification of Russian intelligence with a Communist pope, also turn out not to have been in jest?

Only the Conclaves of the future will tell.

CHAPTER 25

The First Historical Compromise

In the same way that, after World War I, Italy created a novel political formula which was identified with Fascism, so, during the seventies, that same country set the pattern of another novel formula identifiable as Catholic Marxism.

The appearance of such an ideological hybrid will have incalculable implications for the future, since it could speel the ultimate transformation of Europe into a Communist-orientated continent.

Should that happen, the transition of a democratic West into a monolithic, Catholic-dominated red bloc, will imperil not only the national liberties of the European countries, but, equally, those of the United States. For, the sullen hostility of a sulking

Europe ultimately would be transformed into an anti-American alliance; indeed, a belligerency.

The ideological honeymoon between Catholicism and Communism in Italy, therefore, should not be dismissed as a local marriage of convenience, but on the contrary, an early indication of the shape of things to come for the entire West.

Italy has always been an extremely sensitive country as far as new ideological currents are concerned — a kind of political barometer, indicating with uncanny accuracy the nature and direction of political weather to be expected.

The Catholic-Communist partnership must, consequently, be studied with the utmost attention lest its real significance be minimised to the detriment first of Europe and then of the entire Western world.

It was to be expected that Italy, as the territorial centre of Catholicism, should be affected by the basic ideological transformation wrought by Popes John and Paul.

The physical proximity of the Vatican itself, the Italian-orientated machinery of the Curia, and the peculiar inter-penetration of the Church and State on all social and political levels of the country made it almost inevitable that the first "pilot experiment" of a Catholic-Communist partnership be conducted on the Italian peninsula.

All the elements for a Vatican-Kremlin entente had existed, even if in embryo, for decades preceding the Vatican revolution.

When the indigenous Marxist Catholics, who since Vatican II had drawn their inspiration from the Vatican, united with the Marxists who drew their inspiration from the Kremlin, they found a common ground of interest without any serious difficulty.

The theo-ideological bridge was crossed with incredible ease. The Catholic radical did not see any conflict between a Communism which preached economic and social justice and a Catholic Church, which advocated the same. While looking to Russian Communists for guidance in ideological and political matters, they considered Russian Communism to be a national phenomenon, which concerned only the Soviet Union. If Russian Communism was atheist, that was a purely internal Russian problem.

The Italian Communists, on the other hand, while anti-clerical on historical grounds, regarded separation of purely personal religion from ideological requirements of their party as a matter of individual conscience. According to them, therefore, religion and Communism could co-exist on these terms. Indeed, they could co-operate and work together for the establishment of a society in which Catholics could practice their religion without interference from the party.

The result was that in a very short time the few individuals who had once defied the fulminations which Pius XII had made against them for supporting the Communists, now emerged as leaders and promoters of a movement which multiplied a thousandfold.

Churches were packed with Catholics who were also Communists, or Communists who were also Catholics: going to confession, to mass, to communion, carrying in their pockets membership cards of the Communist Party of Italy.

It was a spectacle to sadden the Old Guard, which had denounced Paul VI's *Progressio Populorum* as the most radical encyclical ever written. In their opinion, the document had motivated millions of otherwise neutral Catholics to vote for the Communists.

It had done more: it had helped to weaken Christian democracy and thus to neutralise the movement which had defended the Catholic Church since the end of World War II. Yet, to Paul VI as to Pope John, Christian Democracy had already fulfilled its original role. Since the Vatican revolution, it had become almost obsolete. Indeed, it would be only a question of time before it would dissappear altogether as a political force.

The parallel of the situation of the Catholic Party following World War I and that of Christian Democracy after World War

II, is a striking one. In each case, once the party's role had been carried out, it was ruthlessly discarded without a backward glance.

When the Vatican sided with Fascism, having assessed Fascism as the dominant ideology of the time, it abandoned the Catholic Party and, in fact, disbanded it, to make way for an oncoming Fascist society.

Now, after thirty years of Christian Democracy, the Vatican — having assessed Communism as the ideology of a Communist-orientated society — has abandoned Christian Democracy to its fate. To be sure, it could not in the present instance, order the party to commit hara-kiri as it did the Catholic Party of Italy in 1927, or the Catholic Party of Germany in 1933. Its current tactic has been more in harmony with the new political climate, being that of gradual abandonment. The culmination of such a policy has been the final demise of Christian Democracy vis the gradual injection of Communist power into its political and hierarchical structures.

The two "red popes," after all had sympathised with the left, whether Catholic or Communist, practically since World War II, as had many other prelates throughout the world. Many Communist rank-and-file, including Communist leaders at local and national levels, had for years discreetly planned future understanding and even cooperation between the Communists and the Church.

The preliminary groundwork had been laid, therefore, for the new breed of Catholic-Communist creature who could identify himself as a practicing devotee of both Leninism and Catholicism, without any qualm of conscience or of religion.

A political volte-face

How could it have been otherwise, since Pope John, for instance, had asked top Communist leaders to visit the Vatican and had written documents praising socialism and saying that other religions and political parties, beginning with the left-wing ones, were no longer condemned, as Pius XII used to tell them?

The practical result of such a radical change was seen after Pope John had issued his encyclicals. At the general elections, which took place soon afterwards, the Communists polled their largest number of votes to date.

It is not an exaggeration to say, therefore, that it was Pope John who put the Communist Party of Italy on the political map at one stroke, making it the major ideological influence, second only to Christian Democracy.

Yet that was only the visible beginning of the decline of the former party of the Church, and of the rise of the Communists. Since 1963, many waters have already passed under the ideological bridges of Rome. The red waters became a flood under Pope Paul VI. And that flood, since his coronation, has menaced — indeed, inundated — not only the Vatican, but the whole of Italy itself. The highest level reached by the tide occurred in 1976, and again in 1977, the two most historical dates as far as Christian Democratic and Communist integration is concerned.

At the general election of 1976, the Communist Party in fact emerged as a party of growing dominance, having become the second largest in the country. Of the total votes cast, they polled 34%, as against only 38% for Christian Democracy.

It was truly a date to remember, since to Christian Democracy — which had ruled unopposed during the previous 33 years — that is, from the end of World War II, and had formed no fewer than 39 administrations during that time, the results of the elections represented a serious defeat.

The defeat had been rendered even more humiliating because they were unable to form a government unless they had the support of another party in some kind of coalition, or behind the scenes, when it came to voting in the new parliament.

And which other party could do that, except the country's

now second largest, namely, the Communist Party?

Many Catholics were reluctant to pay such a price. Finally, after a series of bitter dissentions, the Vatican ordered the Christian Democrats to cooperate.

It was in this way that the incredible happened. The Catholics — that is, the Christian Democrats — and the Communists reached a working agreement and assumed "co-responsibility," a face-saving formula which did not fool anybody. It was a device meant to reassure the anti-Communist forces of Italy, the Catholics who were still anti-red; and above all, to deceive the international conservative elements, beginning with the United States.

The Communists, after consultation with Moscow and deft private discussion with Pope Paul VI, volunteered to maintain a low profile, which in fact they did while waiting for further developments at home and abroad.

Yet, if the low profile worked for the masses, for those who had accurately interpreted the omens, facts were staring them in the face. A Communist speaker had been elected in the Italian Parliament for the first time in history. A Communist president of the Senate was presiding over that important chamber, again for the first time in the history of Italy. Most of the key positions in government, although ostensibly in the hands of the Christian Democrats, were in reality dominated by the Communists.

Communists were to be found everywhere along the echelons of a nominally Christian Democratic government, which not only tolerated Marxist officials, but was effectively supported by them.

That such is not an exaggerated estimate of the situation was proved by the fact that no fewer than seven Parliamentary committees whose task was to draft governmental legislation supposedly formulated by Christian Democrats, were in reality chaired by members of the official Communist Party.

It was a political phenomenon whose exceptionality was

noticed with utmost satisfaction at the Kremlin and at the Vatican, but with hidden dismay in Washington.

The pro-Communist grand strategy of the Vatican had started to produce the first concrete political results. The historical compromise reached between the Catholic Party and Christian Democracy would have been impossible had the Vatican pursued a policy of hostility to the Communists and to Soviet Russia as it had done in the past.

While rejoicing at their joint triumph, however, the Vatican and Moscow agreed not to press their political luck too far too soon. It was recognised by both that a Communist government in Italy, with or without the cooperation of the Catholic party, would have damaged the political image of both the Catholics and the Communists. The take-over by the Communists, or rather, by the Catholic-Communist alliance, had to be accomplished by a policy of gradualness on both sides.

Accordingly, the Communist Party in 1976 decided to support the Catholic government by abstention, that is, by not opposing it. It was the first compromise by the Catholics for the *sharing of power* with the Communists, in the history of Europe. It represented the most startling success of the Vatican-Moscow alliance in the field of European politics.

Such cautious strategy pursued by the Vatican-Moscow partners proved effective almost immediately in the international sphere as well as in the domestic one. The anti-Communist powers — America, Britain, France, and West Germany — fearing a full-scale Communist take-over, reached a secret four-power agreement in Puerto Rico during a meeting held in July 1976, directed at denying Italy financial assistance had the Catholics openly shared the government with the Communists. This was a threat which was never carried out, thanks to the historical compromise reached between the two.

Soviet leader Brezhnev declared that the four nations wanted "to take Italy by the throat" to keep the Communists out of the Italian administration. He never mentioned the Vatican.

This was due to the fact that he and the pope had already agreed on a policy of caution, that is, of waiting for the Catholic and Communist climate to mature, the better to permit a joint Catholic-Communist assumption of power without "undue political and social disturbances."

At the time that this secret cooperation between the Vatican and the Kremlin was agreed upon, the Church had to use discretion so as not to come out too brazenly on the side of the Communists, lest she be accused by millions of anti-Communist Catholics of having sold out to Russia.

Political imposture

Anti-Communist governments also had to be considered, and diplomatic balance maintained, at least in the eyes of the world. Pope Paul therefore had to make the customary gesture of anti-Communism now and then, mostly on religious grounds. He even went so far as to threaten ex-communication. In 1976, for instance, he issued some mild warnings as gestures meant to appease millions of Catholics who had become alarmed at his pro-Communist policies.

To demonstrate his good will to them, especially to the American hierarchy, he even sacked some prelates who had become too much of a political embarrassment to the Vatican's more subtle policy of gradualism in rapprochement with the Communists. Witness the case of the Rev. G. Franzoni, the Abbot of St. Paul's Outside the Walls, one of Rome's major basilicas, who during the general elections had repeatedly declared that he was giving his vote to the Communists, and advised other Catholics to do the same. He was unfrocked on the recommendation of Cardinal Poletti, the Vicar of Rome.

The tide, however, could not be stopped. And this to such an extent that priests, bishops, and even Cardinals, not to mention Catholic laymen, continued to flock to the Communist banner at an ever accelerated pace.

The following year, 1977, Paul became alarmed at the pheno-menon, and warned Catholics against moving from one political party to another in search of the one that would offer the most advantages.

Paul's words were aimed especially at groups with openly pro-Marxist objectives, like the "Christians for Socialism," and against Catholic politicians, and priests who had joined, and were still joining Marxist parties, in increasing numbers. The ranks of the Communist Party were swelling not only with priests, but also with members of the religious orders. Promi-nent cardinals were openly towing the Communist line; for example, Cardinal Koenig of Vienna who, when speaking at the Vienna Institute for Business Research in 1977, attacked busi-ness and the big industries. Again, during the celebration of the 70th birthday of Cardinal Hoeffner of Cologne, he stated that "the fight between good and evil is not one between East and West, and even less between Christians and Marxists, a declara-tion which was duly noticed in the Communist countries of Eastern Europe, no less than in Rome itself.

Meanwhile, the Pope began to lay the foundations for an even closer collaboration with the Communists nearest the Vati-can, namely, with those of Rome.

The Eternal City by now had become a Communist strong-hold, with the capture of the Rome administration by the Com-munist Party. Pope Paul VI launched the year 1977 by formally receiving the Marxist-led Rome Council in special audience at the Vatican. Addressing Marxist Mayor Giulio Argan, and eighteen of his aldermen, known as the Red Junta, Paul stressed the singular nature of Rome and City Hall's duty to maintain "freedom of conscience."

In return, the red Mayor of Rome spoke of the city's "sacrali-ty," and hinted at cooperation between the Vatican and the Marxist Council. Indeed, he went so far as to exonerate the Holy See from implication in the recent "Vatican's Land Speculations."

It was the first time in history that the Rome Council had been headed by a Communist. After the official reception, the Pope and the Marxist Mayor retired to the Pope's study, where they discussed their future cooperation in private, after which they joined the other Marxist councilmen for the official speeches in the Throne Room.

That was not all. Mayor Argan, with other members of Rome's Communist-controlled city council had already met with Pope Paul *three times* in the previous month, a record unbeaten even by his non-Communist predecessor.

The telling result of the official and, above all, very private meetings between Paul and sundry left-wing cardinals with the Marxists of Rome's civil administration, were to be seen a few days later.

Speaking to the Roman people, Pope Paul told them that it was their duty to cooperate with the Communists:

"The special position of the Church in Rome imposes the duty of exemplary comportment of Christian life, to the benefit of all the Church, since, he added, "the faithful are called on to coordinate the initiatives of diocesan promotions with those of the municipality, with Christian principles, and with those invested with authority, as a contribution to the common good.

"This requires on the part of Christians presence and participation, with an acute sense of responsibility."

Prior to that address, the Communist mayor of Rome had assured Pope Paul that "the sacred idea of Rome is the exact opposite of all that is the exclusive search for profit," that is, capitalism, and the epitome of capitalism, the United States of America.

The Roman mayor was familiar with Paul's encyclical, *Progressio Popularum;* he knew it by heart. And he had started to propagate its Marxist principles from the very centre of the Roman Catholic Church.

The reality of the alliance between the Vatican and the Communists could not have been a more striking one.

It had been a truly "unprecedented and historical occasion," as Pope Paul himself said afterwards.

It was, as someone remarked, of the shape of things to come: for Italy, for Europe, and thus ultimately for the entire Western world.

CHAPTER 26

Cardinals and Commissars

Cardinals are the princes of a theocracy, namely that of the Roman Catholic Church. Commissars are the pillars of an autocracy, that is, of a Communist dictatorship. Both are foundation stones — the first, of an ecclesiastical administration, the second of an ideologically inflexible bureaucracy.

When an absolute theocracy and a Communist dictatorship formulate policies, the promotion of which requires coordination, it it essential that the executors of such policies — the cardinals and the commissars — act in harmony, with a view to their successful implementation.

The Vatican and the Kremlin, the foci of Catholicism and Communism respectively, being aware of this, set out to interate the activities of both, from the very beginning of their secret entente. This they did via the careful selection of hierarchies acceptable to both sides. They pursued a course of careful selectivity and gradualness, the combination of which helped to create a balance of ecclesiastic and ideological exchanges designed for the promotion of a common objective; in short, the creation of hierarchs simultaneously acceptable to both the Vatican and the Kremlin. The word hierarch, in the present context, means not only cardinals and commissars as such, but also top-level leaders active within the administration of both the Church and the various Communist bureaucracies.

The basic criteria of the agreement are concretely indicative: the advancement by the Vatican of prelates acceptable to Moscow; and the advancement of commissars acceptable to the Vatican on the part of the Kremlin.

The apparent feasibility of such Vatican-Moscow exchanges is the fact that they have been crowned by success, Catholic hierarchs and Communist commissars nodding at one another from their key positions with mutual, even if tacit, understanding, whenever a given policy is being put forward. Only a short time past, such a pairing would have been inconceivable. Today it is a firm reality. Tomorrow, it will be the accepted, overt practice of a Catholic-Communist world.

During the pontificates of Popes John and Paul, the practice not only gained momentum, it was established as an essential part of political life, wherever the interests of the two partners meet.

Hence the promotion of certain favourite prelates of an obviously leftist bent within the Catholic Church, and the ready acceptance on the part of the Kremlin and satellite regimes of hierarchs who showed the proper understanding of the ideological importance of organised religion.

The practical results of such a policy was the curious spectacle of Catholics who were Communists, and of Communists who were Catholics, both attending church, going to mass and even taking Holy Communion, as we have already seen happening in Italy.

In the light of the new religious-political climate, the hammer and sickle has been thus blithely transformed into a symbol of the sickle and the cross. The spectacle was the more remarkable because, following as it did the Vatican revolution, it raised hardly an eyebrow either in the West or in Communist Eastern Europe.

Thus, the various Communist mayors of Italian cities and Communist members of Parliament went openly to church as practising Roman Catholics, a sight which became ever more common after the spectacular Communist triumph in the general election of 1976. The pattern was set, and subsequently became a generally accepted political practice.

Ranking political figures in the Communist regimes of Eastern Europe acted likewise. To cite one typical instance, the Premier of Communist Poland, Edward Gierek openly took his wife to Catholic mass, with the approval of Moscow, the blessing of the Primate of Poland — Stefan Wyszynski, and the hierarchy in Rome.

This prodigy, which had become a common sight by 1977-78, was in fact only the tip of the iceberg. The secret agreement between the Vatican and the Kremlin was converting the inner structure of both the administrative and ecclesiastical framework of Church and Party into a cohesive Catholic-Communist machine, aimed at transforming mutual selectivity into a common political force.

The implementation of the covert entente, besides posting the desired Catholic Communist hierarchs in vital positions, worked constantly towards a Catholic-Communist integration. This was considered a necessary step towards placing future radical prelates in positions of power.

Thanks to this kind of foresight, Communist-orientated priests became bishops; leftist bishops, in turn, became cardinals; and cardinals, primates. A common denominator, which marked most of them, was a socialist outlook. Also, many of them openly sympathised with the working class, or had vigorously supported Marxist utterances of Paul VI's encyclical, *Progressio Populorum.*

In the Communist countries of Eastern Europe, prior to the official nomination of prelates, the Catholic hierarchy of, say Poland or Hungary, had to submit the list of would-be nominees to the Communist commissars, who would either approve or veto the names. As a rule, owing to general directives from Moscow and the Vatican, the selection went smoothly, and the pro-Communist prelates were placed in their sees without any objections. When dealing with doubtful cases, the local Catholic hierarchs and Communist commissars would appeal to their respective superiors for direction.

One typical instance was that of the Primate of Poland, Cardinal Wyszynski. That country's top-ranking Communist commissar, Premier Giereck, felt that the cardinal, who was once an active anti-Communist and supporter of Pius XII, was stubbornly refusing to tow the new line. He did this by passively sabotaging the Catholic-Communist balance policy. His complaints were brought as far as Rome, and the pope intervened. The Pontiff did this not by dismissing the Cardinal, something which would have antagonised millions of his Catholic followers all over Poland, but by a subtler means. Pope Paul counter-nominated a rival — Archbishop Karol Wojtyla of Cracow — who was made cardinal with the specific aim of checking the rebel primate, Wyszynski. The Communist commissar was appeased. Shortly afterwards, in March 1977, Cardinal Wyszynski offered his resignation to Pope Paul.

Red advisors to the Pope

In Western countries, leaders of the Communist movement had similar leverage in influencing Church appointments and personnel matters. The case of Cardinal Michele Pellegrino of Turin, Italy is a fair example. The Cardinal had been one of the most activist radicals since Pope John XXIII. He was called the Red Cardinal and was best known for his energetic defense of workers' rights in the great industrial complex of Turin.

Upon reaching the age of seventy-three, Cardinal Pellegrino, in January 1977, sent his resignation to the Pope, although his retirement was not due until 1979. Thereupon, the Communist Party leaders in Italy "advised" Pope Paul to keep the cardinal on the job, or else...meaning threats of strikes.

Examples of this kind became ever more frequent in both Eastern and Western Europe. Behind the Iron Curtain, the pattern was a methodical one: various commissars would submit a list of their favourite prelates to the national hierarchs. More often than not, the lists would be approved in toto unless the prelates thus recommended were too blatantly Marxist and therefore liable to cause embarrassment to conservative Catholics at home and abroad.

This practice of mutual consultation, which was begun by Pope John, was institutionalised by Pope Paul. During his pontificate, the "consultatory list" became part of a standard procedure.

Prior to the establishment in 1959-60 of such "consultation," the Vatican had to face serious opposition from most of the hierarchies beyond the Iron Curtain. Many of their ranking prelates had been veteran anti-Communists and supporters of Pius XII. Not a few had been arrested, sent to prison or given indefinite sentences in concentration camps. The most celebrated case was that of Cardinal Beran, who spent more than eighteen years in jail for his opposition to Communism in Czechoslovakia. In that country, relations between cardinals and commissars remained difficult. This was due chiefly to the memory of Msgr. Tiso, a Catholic priest who had supported Hitler, and whom Hitler had made head of Catholic Slovakia during World War II. It was also owing in part to the refusal of the Catholic clergy to become "progressive." Many priests, and even bishops, had refused to cooperate with the Communists. Others took up manual work as a form of passive resistance, or became miners or factory labourers. One bishop, Jan Korec, S.J., who had been clandestinely ordained by Pope Pius XII, twenty years later – in 1977 – was working as a factory hand in a chemical plant in Bratislava, Slovakia "pressurised" by the combined weight of the hierachical machine.

At the same time, in nearby Hungary, Communist Commissar Miklos, Hungarian Secretary of State, became the most persistent advocate of increasing cooperation between Marxism and Catholicism. His advocacy was echoed by the Catholic press, which welcomed the Commissar's declarations as "a positive development" between Church and State.

Introducing the practice of mutual consultation had not been an easy one. Many prelates, aware of what was afoot, rebelled and protested, while others merely submitted. Pope Paul saw to it that the hierarchies of the Communist regimes of Eastern Europe followed the line. The result astounded many observers. After the vociferous clamour against Communism heard for so long from bishops and cardinals in many Communist lands, there followed an uncanny silence. This sudden silence finally, owing to direct prodding by the Vatican, was followed by cooperation with the authorities and later even support.

Thus, while the "progressive" Catholic prelates of the Western countries were selectively advanced higher up the ecclesiastical ladder, and the Communist parties of Italy, France, Belgium were cooperating with the Church, the anti-Communist hierarchs behind the Iron Curtain were being rapidly neutralised. In due course, this neutralisation was turned into conversion until, finally, most of them seemed to have understood that it was their duty, as pillars of the Catholic Church, to support the new ideological alignment, as propounded by the Vatican.

It has been a collective conversion, truly worthy of a celebration by the leftist victors and a cry of anguish from many who fought Communism for years, putting their lives and fortunes at risk.

The methodical transformation of Church leaders into willing collaborators with the Red Commissars within the Communist regimes of Eastern Europe meant the massive implementation of the Catholic-Communist pattern of a joint ideological conquest.

In practical terms, this required the active participation of both Catholics and Communists; the integration of ecclesiastical, ideological, and political matters. The top-ranking prelates of both Eastern and Western Europe acted accordingly. Many went so far as to become the effective political links uniting the Catholic Church with the Communist regimes.

The instances have been numerous. However, one typical example of such Cardinal-Commissar cooperation should suffice.

Franz Cardinal Koenig, Archbishop of Vienna, was outstanding in his vigourous pursuance of programmes being promoted by the Catholic-Communist front. From the very beginning of Pope Paul's reign, he acted as a zealous intermediary for both sides. He was in an excellent position to do so, owing to the geographical situation of Catholic Austria between East and West.

After World War II, Austria found herself surrounded by Communist countries, and the lengthening shadow of Russia across her doorstep. Because of their interjacent position, the Austrian hierarchy was made to act as a progressive implementer of the Vatican's new pro-Communist policies.

This the Austrian church did, by linking itself with the hierarchies of the Communist countries. Cardinal Koenig was charged intermittently with delicate negotiations with the red authorities of Eastern Europe. Some of these activities were preliminary to the forthcoming Vatican-Moscow alliance. Others were directed at clearing the path by the removal of misunderstandings, including the dismissal of anti-Communist prelates who obstinately refused to cooperate. The most celebrated examples of the latter were, of course, those of Cardinal Mindszenty and Cardinal Beran.

The tireless efforts of Cardinal Koenig were crowned by success on both sides of the Iron Curtain. Indeed, they were responsible for the coming together and ultimate cooperation of cardinals from the Communist countries their secular opposite numbers, the Red Commissars.

The close collaboration of these two kinds of hierarchs became so smooth and intimate as to completely baffle a Catholic or a Communist of the previous generation.

The Cardinal's activities were of a zeal and effectiveness not seen since the missionaries of old. But with one difference: now, instead of planting the seeds of traditional Christianity amongst the heathen, the Cardinal's mission was to implant a new brand of Communist Christianity into the lands where Christianity was not yet Communist.

In case this sounds too far-fetched for most readers, we had better give a concrete example:

"Shadow Kremlin" in Rome

During 1976, and again in 1977, Cardinal Koenig, prompted by Pope Paul VI and his "shadow Kremlin of Rome," began discreet negotiations with the Communist authorities of Poland with the precise objective of bringing Polish Catholic priests into Austria. The move had to be justified on the ground that there was a "scarcity of Austrian priests."

The remarkable feature of this extraordinaty export, however, was that those priests who were transferred from Poland to Austria, all had one striking thing in common: they had all been trained in leftist seminaries, where they had assimilated the ideological "truth" of Communism. The Communist Commissars in Poland had made sure that this was the case, prior to allowing them to emigrate. The expatriate priests, selected jointly by the Austrian Cardinal and the Polish Commissars of Warsaw, had to be "foolproof" in their Catholic-Communist indoctrination.

The unique union between a Cardinal and a Commissar produced a unique creature — a Catholic-Marxist priest, simultaneously testifying for Christ and Lenin. Something to marvel at, truly.

And so it soon came to pass that, thanks again to such an extraordinary marriage, the world witnessed another no less extraordinary spectacle: a Catholic Country — Austria — ailing from a "scarcity of priests," and being turned into a missionary territory which had to import priests trained in the spirit of Marx-Lenism, with the blessing of Bolshevik Russia and the tacit, but active approval of the Vatican.

The export programme became even more telling when it was revealed by an unusually candid and vocal Commissar that it had been permitted by Russia because — oh, Divine Providence! — the seminaries, all Communist-controlled, in Communist Poland, "were full to overflowing."

The operation had not been the first of its kind, nor has it been the last. But it did create a precedent of ominous significance. For it had been the first instance which received publicity both in the Communist and the non-Communist worlds.

After a few raised eyebrows, it was accepted as a natural exchange between two countries. No one pointed out that it was the logical result of the new Vatican policy of Catholic-Communist rapprochement.

But more was yet to come. The missionary territory was expanded to include traditional ones, that is, the territories where once upon a time Catholic missionaries used to operate in the name of the traditional Catholic Church, teaching traditional Christianity to the un-baptised.

In the spring of 1977, in fact, it was revealed that Communist

Poland was sending Catholic-Communist trained missionaries outside Europe as well. Polish priests and monks were at work in world missions. In 1976, for instance, ninety such Polish missionaries left for mission stations abroad, compared to sixty-eight in 1975 and fifty-four in 1972.

In 1976, missionaries, including thirty-four religious and thirteen diocesan priests; thirty-seven nuns; three brothers and three laymen went into the field. Africa received fifty-two, and the others were sent to Asia and Oceania. Libya received the largest number: twenty-three nuns and two priests.

In addition to priests and missionaries, Catholic-Communist orientated cardinals were also active, exporting the new Christian Marxism via radio and television to millions of people in nearby Communist Hungary, Poland, Czechoslovakia, and Yugoslavia. As one who understood Communism and the problems of Catholics living under Communist rule, Cardinal Koenig, for example, was listened to with eagerness everywhere.

Koenig was known as a "progressive" since the early days of Pope John, who originally sent him on a special mission to Marshal Tito back in 1960. Three years later, another of his main tasks had been to persuade anti-Communist Cardinal Wyszynski to adhere to the Vatican's new line.

This last mission, although extremely arduous, eventually was a success, to such an extent that a decade later Wyszynski was accused of having published a collection of his own sermons, which conservative Catholics considered so Marxist-inspired that they condemned them as a true and proper forgery.

Whether forgeries or not, the fact was that the Cardinal had become cooperative, thanks to the graciousness of the Communist Commissars of Poland, who bestowed favours with a generosity worthy of a clerical state. The Church received privileges undreamt of since the time of Fascist Poland under Marshal Pilsudski after World War I.

The double pressure succeeded. Cardinal Wyszynski, from an ardent anti-Communist under Pius XII, did a volte face to

Pope Paul VI dons a miner's helmet during visit to railway tunnel near Rome, where he conversed with construction workers and later celebrated Christmas Eve mass for them and their families. Event represented part of Vatican's policy of wooing working masses of the world, and co-operating with left-wing unions which the Holy See views as arbiters of the future.

In its drive to recruit the batalions of toiling workers in factories, shops, and offices of the world, the Vatican has encouraged the lower clergy and even monks and nuns to learn mechanical and trade skills with which they can penetrate the ranks of the working class in a spirit of comradeship. In photo, two English nuns are learning basic car maintenance at Hereford Technical College.

become an advocate of Catholic-Communist detente under Paul VI. After all, Poland with a Catholic population of thirty-three million, had to co-exist with a regime that was working in perfect harmony with the Vatican.

Cardinal Wyszynski's new policy paid him well. The Polish Commissars permitted special treatment to all practicing Catholics; erected schools; financed Catholic institutions (including seminaries, be it remembered); and allowed hundreds of new churches to be erected throughout Communist Poland.

The other bishops and cardinals of Eastern Europe, although less vocal, took notice and followed the example set for them. The Church had tamed the anti-Communist hierarchs, who now accepted or resigned themselves to, the new Catholic-Communist alliance as a *fait accompli.*

The more recently-created cardinals turned into new ecclesiastical commissars of the Vatican, as — on their side — the Red Commissars of the Kremlin had turned into ideological commissars of the Catholic Church.

Commissars from the Communist countries visited the Pope at the Vatican with increasing frequency. For example, Soviet Foreign Minister Gromyko was received by the Pontiff in 1964, and again in 1972. Marshal Tito was welcomed to the Holy See in 1971, and Bulgarian President Todo Zhivkov in June 1975, just to mention the most prominent visitors from the Communist Commonwealth.

In return, the Pope sent his emissaries in the persons of his own papal envoys; for example, Archbishop Agostino Casaroli, the papal troubleshooter, who was specialist in official — but more often, secret — contacts with the Communists of Eastern Europe. Msgr. Casaroli became "persona grata" to many Commissars, as when he became the "special guest" of the Marxist government of Bulgaria in 1976, following Bulgarian Commissar Zhivkov's visit to the Pope.

Archbishop Poggi, the Vatican's roving diplomat, made similar, unheralded visits to the Commissars of Poland, Hungary, and other Marxist countries, "to cement bonds" between the Vatican and the Communist regimes, and both with national hierarchies and Communist parties.

All these envoys, whether from the Vatican or from Marxist capitals, were engaged in the promotion of a common policy: the strengthening of ties between the Catholic Church and Communism; and the reinforcement of ideological and administrative bonds between Church and State.

In addition to mutually promoting the grand strategy of the Vatican-Moscow alliance in the present, they were even more active in preparing for the erection of the Catholic-Communist Europe of the future.

They did so, not only by the selection of pro-Communists as top-ranking prelates to fill key positions in Europe and elsewhere, but equally by importing and exporting Communist-trained low clergy into non-Communist lands.

The comment of a pro-Western diplomat concerning this extraordinary posting abroad of Communist-trained priests into non-Communist lands, was a cynical one:

"After thirty years of Communism, Communist Poland is importing corn from America, and exporting Catholic priests to Austria."

He could have likewise noted the exporting of radical Catholic priests to the Western world, in addition to Africa and, above all, to Latin America, where they have created political turmoil on a grand scale.

The deal between Poland and Austria, then, had been merely the prefigurement of the flood of exports to follow. A flood of "progressive" Catholic priests, bishops, and cardinals no longer preaching the traditional gospel of Christ, but a new gospel wed to and infused with, the revolutionary gospels of Marx and Lenin.

CHAPTER 27

From Christ the King to Christ the Worker

During past ages, when thrones and empires thronged the world, Christ was crowned a King. As Christianity's Divine Monarch, he dominated the world, its undisputed Sovereign. Emperors did him homage, the symbol of their own unlimited power and of the massive subservience of the societies they ruled.

Today, his crown and his sceptre have been superceded – the crown by a workman's cap, and the sceptre by a hammer and sickle, when not by a screwdriver or an automatic drill. The new image of Christ the Worker.

At present, such an image is not yet universal; but the moment is fast approaching when it will dominate a Catholic-Communist society.

For, the Catholic Church, which elevated the figure of Christ the King to its apogee in Christian and world history, when that concept served her well, now has appareled the same Christ with the blue denim of the trade unionist. This has been done the better to deal with the proletariat, through whom she intends to dominate the world.

The religious ceremony recently conducted in a Catholic Church in England, in which a bishop dressed in his episcopal vestments, received and solemnly blessed the offering of a screwdriver, a spanner, and a clamp, presented to him upon a plate by workers in their overalls, was no freak service. And even less, the ceremony of an eccentric cleric.

It was, rather, the visible formulation of a policy representing, even if in crude form, the embodiment of the spirit that now is pervading the activities of the Church. The offering was only the externalisation of something which is wholly consonant with the current Vatican-Moscow campaign of ideological togetherness.

The maintenance of Christ the King in a world which is becoming increasingly proletarianised had turned into an embarrassing anachronism. It had become a dangerous obstacle to the successful wooing of the workers, and even more, a danger to the conquest of the workers of tomorrow.

Such a Christ, therefore, had to be eliminated, since upon his disappearance there would depend the success of the new Church and, consequently, of her alliance with Communism. It was vitally necessary for her own ideological self-promotion within a society where the worker will be all-powerful.

To an ideology like Marxism, which has created the image of the dominant Marxist comrade, the Church had to conform by creating a harmonious figure of her own. This she has already done by projecting the startling new image of Christ the worker.

This emergence of a proletarian Christ is portentous, not so much because it is the parallel religious counter-image of a

To identify itself with the expanding mass movement of the Left, the Catholic Church is fostering a new image of Jesus as a white-collar office worker or factory employee. Posters like the above are currently being displayed in Italy, France, and Latin America.

Christ in coveralls is a new symbol of the Catholic Marxists, aimed at depicting Jesus as a member of the working class. It replaces the Church's traditional conception of Christ the King.

materialistic, irreligious Marxist worker, but because the new Catholic Church — "progressive" and radical — is determined to share the spoils of a crumbling capitalistic world, with its predatory partner, Russian and world communism.

The demotion of Christ the King to Christ the Worker, carried out with the utmost discretion, so far has proceeded smoothly and without embarrassment. To be sure, it has not taken place within the genteel parlours of prosperous suburban areas, nor in the board rooms of the giant, multi-national corporations of the United States and Western Europe. Yet, a most perceptive Church has already accepted the first transitional image of Jesus, that of the white-collar Christ — as an assuaging intermediary — with the still "brutish" manual workers.

The subdivision, although strictly speaking, contrary to the concept of a classless society, nevertheless is a realistic one in that the white-collar workers constitute a working class with a difference. Although, if and when they are arraigned against the capitalistic ogre, they will identify themselves with their comrades in blue overalls.

Their acceptance of Christ as a white-collar worker, therefore, is as important as the acceptance of a Christ in blue overalls. For, statistically, the first are as numerous as the latter. And as vital. Contemporary society, ever more dependent upon automation and paperwork, is dominated by their ever-multiplying legions.

Bureaucracy has turned into the *deus ex machina* of the modern world. That is why the Church has offered an up-to-date protector, saviour, and leader, i.e., Jesus Christ the Bureaucrat.

Furthermore, bureaucrats as the most parasitical and yet necessary cogs of a computerised society, could neutralise or even paralyse entire industries as easily as their fellow-workers in the factories and mills.

Hence, the necessity to give them an image all their own, with which they can identify themselves, namely, the white-collar Jesus.

Indeed, a Christ patterned in the mould of an executive, professor, draughtsman, journalist, and the like, sporting trendy, steel-rimmed spectacles.

Such an idea is not mere speculation at this point. The white-collared Christ, as well as the classy, steel-rimmed bespectacled Christ, have already appeared in Italy, where their portraits are becoming as familiar as Christ the King used to be, when Italy and the rest of Europe were dotted with monarchies.

Such portraits were displayed not long ago in the portals of more than 22,000 churches all over the country. An additional million or so copies also circulated in thousands of offices and factories.

In some of the "new-look" portraits, Christ is portrayed as being about fifty years of age, an obvious identification with the managerial class, the indispensable background of factory and office. Or indeed, with the vocal urban trade-union leaders, another rising proletarian elite of contemporary, industrialised society in which the church is now operating.

Christ the worker, whether in blue overalls, white collar, or steel-rimmed spectacles aged about 50, is already moving amongst the benches of factories and between desks of offices in Europe, Centra. and Latin America. In the not too distant future, the same figure will be circulating also, no matter how unobtrusively, through the offices and factories of Canada and the United States.

Birth of the worker image

Ironically, Christ the Worker was first launched under the pontificate of Pius XII, the most dedicated anti-Communist pope of the century.

The worker image came to the fore immediately after World War II and was soon identified with the worker priests. The worker-priest movement was initiated by a top hierarch of the French Church, Cardinal Suhard. The Cardinal's thesis was that the Church had to woo the proletariat. She could do that, not by preaching from ivory towers, but by visiting and working on the floors of the factories.

The phenomenon of the worker-priest became at once the most successful and the most explosive experiment following World War II. Worker-priests appeared in France, Italy, Belgium, Germany and other countries. They joined worker committees, worker trade unions, worker associations and worker movements of all kinds. They worked at the benches of factories, slept in worker hostels, shared the workers' tribulations, and aligned themselves against their capitalist exploiters. They took with them the traditional gospel in one hand and the banned *Das Kapital* in the other. They quoted from the exhortations of Lenin, not to mention Trotsky.

The growth of European Communism in Italy and France after World War II alarmed certain members of the Church. Others, however, tried to reassure the apprehensive faithful about worker priests, publically playing down the impertance of their role. Among the rationalisers was Msgr. Montini (now Pope Paul VI), who supported the worker priests from the start.

When, however, the progressives within the Church started to join the restless proletariat in their agitations, the Vatican, after repeated warnings, suppressed the movement. Worker priests were disciplined by their bishops. Those who did not withdraw were suspended. Some were excommunicated.

There were protests, public and private, mostly from certain French bishops who, during the war, had supported the French Communists. Not a few of them felt bitter against anti-Communist Pope Pius XII, who had used his special envoy to France — leftwing Msgr. Roncalli, the future Pope John XXIII — to convince them to wait for a more auspicious time to evangelise the proletariat.

Msgr. had promised concrete cooperation with the Christian

workers movement, and while it has never been proved, with the Communist Party of France.

Following Stalin's death, Russia had hinted in unmistakable terms that a rapprochement with organised religion of the West was possible and desirable. The ideological winds of change were already being felt in certain quarters of the Kremlin, where there had been speculation about the successors of anti-Communist Pius XII. The possibility of a drastic change of policy at the Vatican had been predicted and, indeed, expected.

The election of Pope John XXIII fulfilled the Kremlin' anticipations. Although John was more than sympathetic to the concept of worker priests, he nevertheless acted with utmost caution before reactivitating what his predecessor had so roundly condemned. His idea of a gradual but radical entente with Communism at large seemed to him to be a more feasible policy than the support of a small, pro-Communist movement like that of the worker priests.

But if the concept of the worker priest was abandoned officially, the idea of Christ the Worker soon emerged, a gradual, but highly significant figure. The campaign was conducted with carefully calculated restraint and gradualness. It was infused with ideological subtlety. Leftwing Catholic fundamentalism and low-brow Catholic literature were flooded with verbal and pictorial images of Christ the Carpenter, Christ working at the * bench with his father, a manual laborer; and of his mother, another worker, mending their clothes or preparing a meal.

Working-class clubs and associations adopted the image of Christ the Worker as being the authentic portrait of the Nazarene. More and more Catholics began to identify such a Christ with their jobs and their class. In short, with the proletariat. No Christ the King for them, since a king meant a boss, an exploiter, a capitalist; and behind it all, "dollar imperialism."

The most telling exertions of such Catholic extremism appeared in Latin America. The original figure of Christ the Worker, as it had appeared in Europe, holding in his hand the sickle

* CHRIST'S FATHER WAS GOD, NOT JOSEPH!

and the cross, so to speak, once on South American soil, exchanged both for a gun.

There, Christ the Worker became Christ the Liberator. The Liberator from political oppression, but also from industrial and agrarian exploitation. Christ the Liberator was initially inspired by the Second Vatican Council, with its concern for the "working class" and its revolutionary rhetoric. Economic and social inequalities did the rest. We have already noted the role played by Communist-trained clergy. The whole movement came to the fore in the 60s with Pope John XXIII.

The new proletarian gospel developed its own peculiar theology, known as "Liberation Theology." Priests joined not only the workers, but also the Marxist guerillas. Jesuits wrote Marxist-inspired manuals such as that of Jesuit Juan Luis Segundo of Uruguay, called *A Theology for Artisans of a New Humanity.* Others, echoing the words of Marx himself, declared that "the growth of capitalism is the same as the growth of poverty."

At the Vatican, the progress of the new proletarian Christ was in no doubt; from Christ the Worker in blue overalls, of the early sixties to Christ in white collar of the early seventies, to Christ the Liberator in the last quarter of the present century.

In those countries where the restless masses have been fired with revolutionary zeal by Marxist agitators, including priests, such a Christ has been not only acceptable, but warmly welcomed. And since the Church now was approving certain basic tenets as preached by Marx and Lenin about private property, for example; or as preached by Popes Leo XIII, John XXIII and Paul VI, why not support a Communist Party as long as such a party did not prevent them from going to church to hear mass?

It was in this way that a Communist Catholicism was brought to the fore, even before the Church had hinted at any drastic ideological rapprochement with Soviet Russia.

Jesus vs. the rich

The idea of a Catholic Communism, then, is neither an absurdity nor, even less, a theoretical speculation. It has already become part and parcel of the Vatican-Moscow sociological grand strategy. Its nature and objectives are to be found, not in any ecclesiastical interpretation, but within the context of a proletarian orientated society, where the worker will be the dominant symbol of a Communist egalitarianism which is considered to be in total harmony with the Christian Gospels.

Christ, after all (so the argument goes), had no property. His followers were workers. He never had any wealth, gold, or landed estates; and he never exploited his fellow men. He spoke against the rich. He had not even a pillow upon which to rest his head. (One might have thought such ideas would give discomfort to a privileged set of workers, sporting several cars, huge wages, the latest TV sets and other luxuries not available to the teeming millions of Africa and Asia. But the new kind of Catholicism has not yet penetrated the more affluent levels of labour's ranks).

As for the message to the less fortunate masses of workers, it goes like this: intellectual arguments about materialism or even atheism should be left to the egg-heads, since they are of little concern to the Catholic worker, whose divine Redeemer became flesh, chose to be born in a working-class family, preferred to do manual work and, therefore, is the true protector of the workers of this world.

Pope John well understood the mass subconscious acceptance by both Catholic and non-Catholic working class, of this identification of Christ the Worker. The commonalty never exalted Christ the King in the first place, except ritually and perfunctorily at that. Now the Kingdom of God had become the People's Republic of Heaven.

To make more vivid the new image of the plebeian Christ, the Vatican also began to canonise working-class saints. A typical example is the beatification and ultimate canonisation of Margaret Sinclair, a factory worker of Edinburgh, Scotland. Added to her other saintly traits of character, she was a trade unionist.

In Italy, in France, and in Belgium, Communists have made secret moves to have fellow Communists declared "servants of God," the preliminary step to beatification, and eventually to sainthood. Several Communists in Eastern Europe are also on a secret list for future canonisation, these to be announced when the moment is opportune.

A day is not far off when the world will hear a pope give his blessing — *urbis et orbis* — to the city and to the world, from the balcony of St. Peter's in Rome, in the name of a carpenter, the son of a carpenter, a member of the working class: Jesus Christ, a fellow worker, a true comrade; the protector, defender and trade union leader of all the poor, the downtrodden and exploited of the world.

* SEE p. 267.

CHAPTER 28

A Marxist Pope?

THERE WERE NO POPES IN APOSTOLIC TIMES!

Popes are a reflection of the age in which they reign. The Apostolic times turned them into saints. The turbulence of the first millenium made them turbulent. The great Moslem invasion forged them into crusaders. The Renaissance cast them as scholars; the post-Renaissance period found them acting as protectors of the humanities. Later, the dynastic intrigues of Europe forced them to become arch-intriguers. During the last century — the era of the common man — they became socially minded; throughout the first half of ours, they supported extreme right-wing movements, epitomised by fascism. Now, all the indications are that in this last, closing quarter of our century, they will expound extreme left-wing ideologies, including

Communism.

If past papal history is a reliable indication of the shape of things to come, we may expect the coming election of a Marxist pope. The radical innovations initiated by the Second Vatican Council and amplified by its post-Council policies, support this assumption. Realistic observers regard the acceptance by the Church of an ideological communion with atheistic Communism as indisputable proof of the new official line. We may not see a Marxist pope tomorrow; but there will be one in the not too distant future — say before the close of the present century.

Everything seems to be conspiring for his advent: the economic anarchy of the world, the disappearance of political stability within and among nations, the increasing ideological and racial turbulence; above all, the emergence of the cult of the worker. The latter, more than any other single factor, will induce the Church to hail him as the great leveller and therefore as the advocate of a communistic society, where religion will be tolerated only if it adapts itself to the new values preached by Marxism or its deritives.

The Vatican's political re-orientation towards Moscow, its acceptance of Communism as an ideology, its tolerance of atheism, and an un-theological interpretation of the Christian Gospels, are the best proof that today the Roman Catholic Church is preparing herself for a Communist-dominated world of the future.

The transformation is occurring on all levels of her monolithic structure, as we have detailed in the foregoing pages. The great ecclesiastical pyramid has already been cemented with the red bricks of radical Marxist priests, bishops, and even cardinals.

The process is not confined to any single continent or hemisphere, but is being applied generally throughout the world.

In Africa and Asia, for example, Paul VI saw to it that the nomination of native bishops and cardinals were first submitted to and accepted by the various native Communist dictators of those continents. Witness the elevation to the cardinalate of M.

Trin-Nhu Khue, made Cardinal in Hanoi in 1976, almost at the same time that Vietnam — North and South — were officially united to become the Socialist Republic of Vietnam. The Vatican had to consult the Communists prior to his nomination.

Many churches of Latin America became notorious because certain of their prelates, priests, and administrators, high and low, were likewise consorting with guerillas, urban or otherwise, or with left-wing movements inspired by Marx, Trotsky, or Mao Tse Tung.

Catholic priests were arrested, or wounded, or even killed when leftist guerillas were engaged by the police. Bishops and even cardinals in Bolivia, Chile, Brazil, and Argentina came into the open, propounding radical theories that were in harmony with directives of the Vatican. A typical instance was the General Conference of the Latin American Hierarchy, which met in Medellin, Colombia in 1968.

In 1972, Cuba's Communist Premier, Fidel Castro, made the realistic observation:

"The U.S. shouldn't worry about the Soviets in Latin America, because they are no longer revolutionaries. They should worry about the Catholic revolutionaries, who are." (Reported in *U.S. News,* Dec. 11, 1972).

Red Christianity in Europe

In Europe, too, the radical churchmen pressed their advantage to the full. One of the first prelates to be elevated under Paul VI was Msgr. Seper of Zagreb, Yugoslavia. This was the same episcopal see from which anti-Communist Cardinal Steinac had formerly operated. Msgr. Seper, however, was not only *persona grata* to Communist Yugoslavia, he was also *persona grata* at the Vatican, owing to his personal progressive views, and because of his experience in dealing with the Communist Commissars behind the Iron Curtain.

As a confidant of Paul VI, he became one of the most influential cardinals of the new "progressive" Curia. As the Church advanced ever more towards an organic integration with a Communist-motivated Europe, the number of such radical dignitaries increased. There was, for example, Cardinal Koenig of Vienna, who had received his *ruber galerus* from John XXIII, followed by those created Pope Paul VI on both sides of the Iron Curtain, as well as certain black and brown cardinals whose promotion had been approved beforehand by the Communist black dictatorships of the African continent.

The proportion of radical cardinals and of future members of the Sacred College whose political leanings range from light pink to scarlet red, has been mounting and will continue to increase. The inevitable result will be that, thanks to the greater number of leftist prelates, the election of a red pope is becoming ever more likely.

Two additional factors presaging such an election are of paramount importance. These are the influence which Catholic-Communist integration will exert upon the cardinal electors, and the secret influence which Soviet Russia and the Communist countries will use to have their own men nominated.

The abortive lobbying commenced by Stalin in the fifties, although a failure, nevertheless indicated the direction in which future conclaves will move.

The Soviet presence has come to stay; and it would be a serious mistake to regard it as either transitory or unreal. It will acquire more substance as the Church continues along her "progressive" path.

The rear-guard battle

Yet, after having said that, it must be remembered that not all the world's 800 million Catholics have accepted the ideological alignment of their Church with Communism. Decades will pass before the process of total acceptance is complete. Which means that opposition inside and outside the Vatican is anything but hopeless. The anti-Communist rear-guard will continue to battle on all fronts for a long time to come.

One of these counter movements is identifiable with anti-Communist forces still to be found within the religion itself, but above all, within the political and economic establishment of the world. The West, although heading with breakneck speed towards a leftist form of society, is far from becoming as yet Communist.

The greatest bastion of anti-Communism has been and remains, the North American continent. The economic and military weight of the United States is something which will be considered very carefully during all future conclaves.

The world balance of power, political and military, is something the cardinals have always weighed very carefully in times of serious crisis. It could be that the cardinals of the immediate future, even if controlled by a majority of progressives or even Marxists, will consider a tactical retreat and permit an interregnum to avoid a doubtful or risky confrontation.

Such an ideological interregnum would mean the election of a traditionally neutral pope, even a reactionary one. It was this kind of strategem that the Church has used in the past when facing the kind of possible schism she faces today.

At such times she has always managed to escape a final decision by electing a "pastoral" pope, whose single concern was religion, with politics seemingly relegated to the background.

The Church has followed this course on occasions during the past and the present centuries. When her flock is divided, as it is today, it gives her time to assess the positive as well as the negative results of her new policies.

Decisions of future conclaves with respect to the kind of supreme pontiff they elect — whether pastoral, neutral, or "progressive" — will depend not only upon such traditional tactics, but equally upon the crystalisation and polarisation of various groups within the Church.

During the conclaves which elected Pope John and Pope Paul, for instance, the group which finally prevailed upon the others was that of the leftist French cardinals. At the Conclave of 1958, they elected John, knowing him to be the radical envoy who had appeased the French Communists. His election was also a reaction against Pius XII's opposition to the French experiment of worker priests. At the Conclave of 1963, the same groups prevailed again, having concluded that Montini was sufficiently radical, without being too obviously a Russian-approved candidate.

In the future, new groups may be expected to tip the ideological balance. Left-wing cardinals, with whom Paul VI has filled the Sacred College, could take a new look at the traditional European nature of the papacy. One of these groups, for example, could come from North America where several outspoken prelates such as Archbishop Joseph Bernardin, to mention only one, were kept in cold storage because of their reputation for being too radical for the present policy of the Church. On the other hand, the Central and South American camarilla, whose radicals were notorious, could exert overwhelming pressure. South American cardinals, supported by certain cardinals from Spain (as, for example, Cardinal Enrique y Tarrancon of Madrid), or cardinals from Asia, could make permanent the new political direction taken by the Vatican.

At the same time, a vigorous reaction against the "progressive" Church is not to be discontinued. There are already signs of a serious schism. A considerable number of cardinals and high-ranking prelates have become openly critical of the Vatican's new *ostpolitik.*

Witness Archbishop Lefebvre of France, the outspoken champion of the traditionalists.

"There is a malaise in the Church," he said, referring to the changes wrought during and after Vatican II. "A new pope would, and should, change many things in the Church."

The rebellion of Archbishop Lefebvre indicated the profound uneasiness which has rent the Church from within. He symbolised the spiritual bewilderment of millions of Catholics who had followed with growing concern the radical reorientation of the Church towards Communism.

Lefebvre's call for a conservative revolt against the Holy See met with wide success. Within a year, it was estimated that one fourth of all French and Swiss Catholics were supporting his movement, and there were already 37 centres of the break-away church in Britain.

In June 1977, when the Archbishop ordained thirteen priests at Econe, Switzerland, in defiance of Pope Paul VI's attempts to thwart him, he had, as the Vatican declared, "self-excommunicated himself."

During Pope Paul's sixth secret consistory, when he named five new cardinals, the Pontiff openly condemned "all unbending traditionalists." The papal condemnation was directed not only at Archbishop Lefebvre, but at all those Catholics who could not reconcile themselves with the new ecclesiastical novelties, many of which, until yesterday, had been reckoned heretical and worse.

The left-wingers within the Vatican encouraged Pope Paul to stem the rising tide of reaction against his "progressive attitudes."

The Archbishop, as the most vocal exponent of the revolt against the red-motivated Vatican, therefore had to be silenced before the rebellion spread and surfaced in all areas of the Western world.

Lefebvre, far from being intimidated, thundered against Pope Paul and his policies.

"What is the Vatican today?" he asked during a sermon on the very day of St. Peter. "Who is Pope Paul? Who are they?" [his advisers]. The Catholic Church under Paul's guidance, he added, was being dragged "towards destruction." Indeed, the Vatican had developed "an adulterous relationship with the

Russian and European Communists."

The Vatican, said Lefebvre, had embraced heretics, Communists, Marxists. "Jesus Christ in the Gospel said that mercenaries, thieves and wolves would destroy the Church's flock. Nothing stops us from believing that these animals exist within the Church. We will not extend our hand to them."

Then he added an observation that had haunted millions of Catholics ever since the ascension of Paul VI to the throne of Peter: "Pope Paul has demonstrated himself to be a man with two faces, and I do not know which is the true face."

At Econe, the Archbishop's Swiss headquarters, there was no doubt about Pope Paul's "true face." On the walls of the seminary, Lefebvre's followers had inscribed their feelings:

"Down with *Comrade* Montini! Long live the Pope, but down with Paul VI! Down with Comrade Marty, murderer of the Faith." (Marty was the Cardinal Archbishop of Paris, whom Lefebvre accused of having joined in the signing of the Communist *Internationale* with French Communists).

These graffiti reflected the sentiments of many traditionalists. Pope Paul VI only a short time before had shocked thousands of Catholics by receiving in private audience the Hungarian Communist Party Leader, Janos Kadar. Kadar, said Archbishop Lefebvre, "has spilled the blood of Catholics in Hungary."

This was a reference to the abortive anti-Communist revolution of 1956, which we have described in the preceding pages, when hundreds of thousands of Catholics were arrested, jailed, and shot, while thousands of others were saved by the timely intervention of the United States, which airlifted them into America as political refugees.

The Econe seminary slogans were even more telling because they referred, even if indirectly, to the increasing number of left-wing cardinals in the Church, prelates who seemed to be dominating not only the Vatican, but important European capitals as well. Typical were the Cardinal Archbishop of Paris, and the

Archbishop of Madrid, both of whom were actively "accommodating the European Communist leaders," as Lefebvre declared.

The Archbishop's reprimand was fully warranted. Cardinals, archbishops, and bishops in both Europe and America had been replenishing their vacant sees with radical clergy.

Pope Paul, after condemning the traditionalists, as already mentioned, brought the number of cardinals in the Sacred College to 137. This was not only a record number, but what was more significant, most of them − 119, to be exact − could vote during the forthcoming conclaves for the election of Paul's successor.

Most of his nominees were left-wingers or had expressed pro-red sentiments in private and sometimes in public. Among the Church's top hierarchy, the traditionalists were becoming as rare as the extinct dodo. This was true not only in Europe and the Americas, but also in Africa and in Asia, where Catholic prelates were selected for their anti-white, anti-traditionalists, and revolutionary propensities.

Pope Paul's policy had been a cooly calculated one. He had been calmly packing the Sacred College with his own ideological creatures, with the specific objective of providing appropriate material for the election of his successor, that is, of another pro-Communist pope.

According to millions of traditionalists, that presaged but one thing: the sliding of the Catholic Church along the path leading to spiritual and ideological perdition.

"They excommunicate those who keep the Catholic faith," cried Archbishop Lefebvre, acting as the spokesman for millions who thought as he did; "and enter into communion with all of the Catholic Church's enemies."

The reaction of conservative Catholics was not only tinged with ideological hostility; it was one of genuine religious apprehension.

When therefore Pope Paul VI died in 1978, the College of Cardinals split into the pro- and anti-Moscow Marxists. The former, having failed to elect a full-blooded pro-Moscow pope, seconded a "neutral-non-political" man, Cardinal Luciani, Pope John Paul I.

The anti-Moscow faction however, as already seen, having become convinced that the new "naive" pontiff was nothing but a pliable puppet of the pro-Moscow faction, became determined upon his elimination. With the lay intelligence apparatus know-how of a friendly superpower behind them, and the Curia's connivance, his demise was "accelerated" after only 33 days of rule. The path for a full-fledged, anti-Moscow, Marxist pope had been cleared.

It must be remembered that the College of Cardinals, although harboring still a tiny minority of traditionalists, in reality was a hotbed of radicalism. Paul VI had filled three quarters of it with those notorious for their "progressive" tendencies. Many of them, mostly Asian, African, and Latin American, were open supporters of revolutionary Liberation Theology.

Noted for his Marxist opinions was Archibishop Wojtyla of Krakow, Poland. Pope Paul VI had made him Cardinal because of his expertise in Marxist matters, and in dealing with the communists. His cooperation with them on the local and national level had helped to smooth out problems which the Polish Primate, anti-communist Cardinal Wyszynski, had been unable to solve, as already seen in a previous chapter, "Cardinals and Commissars."

Wyszynski, who had been repeatedly approached by the U.S., although against a pro-Moscow policy, never favored a Washington-sponsored Vatican. When, however, he realised that the pro-Moscow faction in the conclave had plotted for an even more vigorous pro-Moscow cooperation via the election of a "naive" pope, John Paul I, he radically changed his mind.

After the "death" of John Paul I, he opted for the anti-Moscow faction. His personal choice: his co-regionalist Wojtyla of whose anti-Russian animosity he had ample knowledge.

Pope Paul VI's carefully prepared plan for the election of a pro-Russian pope like him failed also because many cardinals, upon reflection, became scared that too close identification between the

Church and Moscow might become irreversible. The church could not risk too prolonged an involvement with Russian ideological and territorial expansionism. Besides endangering her future, it was also turning her into an enemy of the U.S.

To avoid too close an involvement with one or the other, the church therefore had to find a solution of her own. Although that involved her abandonment of the Vatican-Moscow alliance and the acceptance of the political tutelage of Washington, the solution was possible via a compromise. The form of Catholic orientated communism which had been accepted, beginning in 1958 with John XXIII, had now become irreversible. The compromise took the form of a brand of her own type of independent Marxian-inspired Catholicism.

The ideological compromise emerged officially from the conclave of 1978 with the election of a pope, John Paul II, who, while theologically a reactionary, ideologically was a revolutionary. Indeed, he was one of the main sponsors of a new Catholic interpretion of Marxism controlled by the Church herself.

This solution presented an historical imponderable without precedent. Whereas, in political terms, it meant the substitution of Washington for Moscow and that of a pro-Moscow pope with a pro-Washington pontiff, neither pope differed in their acceptance of the Marxist philosophy and practice. The difference between them was their strategy: A radical change of lay partners.

Thus whereas Paul VI had accepted Marxism in all its crudity, Pope John Paul II had disguised it behind the screen of Catholic socialisation, tempered by the pastoral formula of Catholic progressivism.

Both popes, while following seemingly opposite tactics and seemingly contradictory approaches, in reality had adopted Marxism as the sure promoter of social unrest and economic disruption under the ideological tutelage of the Church.

In other words, Pope Paul VI, the godfather of the Vatican-Moscow alliance, although succeeded by John Paul II the sponsor of the Vatican-Washington alliance, had not preached Marxism to have a Marxist-orientated Catholicism, discarded by future popes.

On the contrary, He died confident that apart from tactical digressions necessitated by current political considerations, his papal successors would continue to sustain the disruptive ideological objectives of Marxism to bring down a society which he, as well as the church, had considered was doomed to perish.

Because of that, both popes, and indeed future popes, notwithstanding differences of policies or political alliances, had maintained, and would continue to maintain one basic objective in common: their determination to mastermind the oncoming collapse of contemporary society. Their ideological substitute would be a neo-Catholic form of Marxism whose emblem was the hammer and the sickle, crowned by the cross.

The papal banner of the future.

The successor of Pope Paul VI, Pope John Paul II had hailed from a Catholic country, whose emblem has been just that.

An omen for the rest of the Western World, including the Americas.

CHAPTER 29

Castros in Cassocks

On the twenty-second of August 1968, Pope Paul's special jet plane landed on the tarmac of El Dorado Airport in Bogota, Colombia, arriving on a direct flight from Rome.

When the Pope emerged from the aircraft, imitating the histrionics of Columbus more than four centuries earlier, he kissed the ground of the runway. Following this, he received the homage of the Colombian president, with his attendant ministers, generals, and diplomatic corps, while thousands of the faithful thundered:

"Viva el Papa!"

Innumerable statuettes of the Pontiff were sold at every street corner of the capital: on paper, glass, and cakes. Big oil firms had their signs up: "Esso greets you"; "Chrysler Imperial takes its part in the Holy Father's visit."

Paul went to stay in a palace which not so long before had been ransacked by a mob. It was situated a few streets from the home of a Colombian Catholic-Marxist guerilla priest, one Camillo Torres. Two years ealier he had died in a battle against "the forces of reaction and imperialism," that is, the Colombian anti-terrorist police.

Two days later, when Paul took off on his return flight to Rome, at the same airport soldiers stood guard around a circular hole about a metre wide. There, fervent Catholics — or, as some cynics remarked, skillfull exploiters of the faith, — had taken pieces of asphalt sanctified by the Pope's contact. Thousands of such pieces were sold at ever mounting prices to the satisfaction of the vendors and to the edification of the believers who had parted with their money.

But whatever Pope Paul had accomplished between his arrival and departure, he had certainly widened the gap between the Church activist of the left and the traditionalist Church supported by the semi-authoritarian Latin American regimes.

The Catholic Marxists had come forward to greet the Pope who, in his famous encyclical, *Progressio Popularum,* had condemned "the imperialism of money" and thus, by implication, all the anti-Marxist forces of the Southern continent.

The Latin American Confederation of Christian Workers, the CLASC; and the Latin American Peasant Federation (the FCLA) had no doubts about it. They wanted Paul to live up to their expectations. The more so, since they represented more than five million Catholic workers and peasants who had been told about the contents of his encyclical.

If the great North American oil and manufacturing companies had welcomed the Pope with their slogans, the "progressives" had also welcomed him with theirs: "The revolution is a long road, Brother Paul," warned one in an open letter, written by a Catholic Trade Union. The most telling slogan, however, was the one coined by an Argentine Catholic priest, Juan Garcia Florio: "The duty of every Christian is to be a revolutionary; the duty of every revolutionary is to make a revolution."

The previous year, Don Florio had created a stir by reading his revolutionary manifesto during a mass attended by the President of Argentina. In February 1970, he was mysteriously killed in a car crash. But if Don Florio had been liquidated, thousands of others like him were very much alive and active. They became known as the "Curas Guerilleros" (the Guerilla Priests). Many of them shouted revolutionary slogans of guerilla Catholicism from their pulpits. In one single demonstration, 140 of them urged "seizure of power by the people", leading to "national and Latin American socialism."

The Vatican became seriously embarrassed by the tactics of these radical priests, the missionaries of "Castroism in cassocks," as one senior cardinal put it to the present author.

It was not so much that these "Castros in cassocks" had been condemned by the high command of the Curia. They had been frowned upon because of their poor timing. The Vatican policy of gradualism was disregarded with tragic results.

In the grand strategy of the progressive formulators in Rome, the blatant efforts of the more undisguised radicals of the cloth were counter-productive. They were actually interfering with the Vatican's smoothly operating, even though deliberate, plan for the Catholic Marxist take-over of Latin America.

Some of the priestly revolutionaries reminded Pope Paul in a personal letter that "we are determined to trust Your Holiness to condemn outright all forms of exploitation." It added, "We trust the Pope to proclaim specifically to the agents of the international imperialism of money what he himself has declared in his encyclical, *Progressio Populorum:* 'No one is justified in keeping for his exclusive use what he does not need, when others lack necessities."

They directed their wrath also against that great bugaboo so frequently wheeled onstage by left-wing propagandists — the symbol of capitalism, the United States. "Paul VI is going to visit a continent," said *Venezuela Urgente,* "where people are being trampled underfoot by the Pharaoh of the North."

The mother of a Marxist guerilla priest, killed while fighting, wrote a personal letter to Pope Paul, reminding him that her son, Camillo, "a Catholic Marxist hero of Latin America, believed he could not fulfill his mission as a Christian and a Catholic priest without taking part in a revolution to free the poor workers and peasants.

"Camillo's thinking," said his mother, "was essentially one with what Your Holiness was later to express in the encyclical, *Progressio Populorum.*" That was why, she explained, her son, although a priest, had become a revolutionary and, in logical conclusion, had joined the armed insurrection in which he was killed.

Msgr. German Guzman Campos was no less explicit about the revolutionary duty of the Catholic Church in Latin America. In an editorial published in the August 19, 1968 issue of the newspaper, *Frente Unido,* he wrote that "Paul VI is well aware that Latin America is in a revolutionary situation; that there are guerillas already fighting or starting to fight, in several countries."

The *Venezuela Urgente* of August 1, 1968 went further: "Paul, the enemies of your people are hoping that you will come to Latin America to preach peace between cat and mouse. The cat will continue to persecute in the name of Christ. Because of this, the Latin American church is faced with three alternatives: pursue its present policy of complicity with the U.S.A.; break with the system by taking a definite stance alongside the oppressed; or adopt a centrist solution, leaning towards the U.S.A. and the oligarchs − in other words, act as mediator between Pharaoh and the oppressed people, between the workers and employers."

On August 11, 1968, a commando unit of some 250 Catholic militants, both clergy and laity, occupied the Cathedral of Santiago (Chile). At midday, two young priests, the authors of a revolutionary manifesto, accompanied by a group of Catholic priests, nuns and workers, con-celebrated "such a mass as had never before been seen in Chile."

They prayed aloud: "We implore you, O Lord, for all our brothers who have died for the liberation of Latin America; for all our exploited workers; for all the political prisoners of Brazil; for the struggle of the Uruguyan people."

After this public supplication, priests and nuns, having first received Holy Communion, raised a banner bearing the words, "Towards a Church Which is One With the Struggle of the People."

The priests were suspended for a mere two days, following a very private interview with the Cardinal Archbishop. They were then reinstated. The Apostolic Nuncio refused to see the press because "such premature manifestations have embarrassed the Church at this moment, according to the comment of a member of the diplomatic corps.

Another manifesto, also of Chilean origin, was no less explicit: "We denounce the violence perpetrated by the rich and the powerful, the exploitation of people by the iniquitous profit system of international imperialism of money."

In Brazil, a "progressive" group of Catholic prelates published *The Pastoral From the Third World,* a document which shook Catholics and non-Catholics alike for its audacity and extremism.

Its most telling feature was that it was inspired mainly by Pope Paul's *Progressio Populorum.* The *Pastoral* provoked questions in the Brazilian parliament. A member of the opposition described it as "the most important document the Church has ever produced, since the encyclicals of John and Paul."

Priests and even bishops at times quite openly praised the growing number of "Castros in cassocks." Indeed, Msgr. Fragoso of *Belo Horizonte* went so far as to eulogise "brave little Cuba."

Catholic priests of the old guard, however, opposed the "progressives." Msgr. Siguard, for instance, who penned a collective letter to the Pope, denounced "the Communist subversion at times hidden beneath clerical garb." He was unrepentant, however, declaring, "I support the courage of little Cuba, and beg God give my people the courage to imitate it, too."

The result of the widening of the gap between extreme left- and right-wing priests was that the Vatican itself more often than not had to compromise in various attempts to avoid widening the split further.

One typical example should suffice. On May 1, 1968, twenty-three priests of Sao Paolo, Brazil resigned because a conservative prelate, Msgr. Zioni, had been appointed archbishop. They could not serve under him, they said, because he was not sufficiently "progressive." The Papal Nuncio was compelled to repeal the appointment. In place of Msgr. Zioni, he named Msgr. Alberti, a member of the "progressive" wing of the Brazilian clergy, as Apostolic Administrator of the diocese.

Other Latin American hierarchies were no less "progressive." Witness the pastoral letter of the Mexican hierarchy, which condemned those Catholics who defended a situation "which is not so much order, as a social disorder born of injustice."

"We must," the bishops concluded, "remove from their pedestal of money the cult of personal success, class selfishness and property."

"The appropriate word"

The Jesuits were no less forceful about revolution: "We do not use the word revolution . . . to win sympathy for ourselves among the Marxists," they said. "We use it, and shall go on using it, because it seems to us the appropriate word to use."

Such outspoken declarations at the time alarmed even the Vatican, which sent the superior general of the Jesuit order, Fr.

Arrupe to Latin America to warn the Jesuit extremists not to go too far and too soon. The superior general, however, never condemned them. He only cautioned them by saying that they should be more moderate in their public utterances, lest they antagonise the political establishment of Latin America permanently.

The Jesuits were ordered to change their tactics. They coined slogans more appropriate to the "present conditions." The words "radical" and "revolution" were replaced with such euphemisms as "profound renewals" or "innovating changes," or "social renovation."

Parish priests were equally eager for drastic social reforms, as shown by the manifesto issued jointly by thirty-five Peruvian clerics and counter-signed by hundreds of their colleagues, including 127 English-speaking missionaries — natives of Ireland, Australia, Canada, and the United States.

In Bolivia, groups of priests demanded that the Church recognize Catholic guerrillas. In an open letter to their bishops in April 1968, eight of the fathers scolded their superiors because "the hierarchy have not taken into account the profound need for justice which underlies the very existence of the guerrillas."

In the same letter, which the Bolivian press headlined as "Eight Priests Demand Revolution in the Church," the group added:

"Nor have they provided any theological grounds for discussion of the problems of violence, which the Pope touched upon from that viewpoint in his encyclical, *Populorum Progressio.* They have been content to condemn one method without producing any other proposals for achieving the revolutionary changes . . . Bolivia needs today."

Other groups of "progressive" priests acknowledged the fact that they had been inspired to seek revolutionary changes by the words of Popes John and Paul.

The source of their initiative was, in fact, amply demonstrated by the creation of a revolutionary movement called "Populorum Progression," the very title of Paul's celebrated encyclical. In January 1968, one Father Herrera wrote:

"The present time calls for the active participation of all Christians of Latin America, who see revolution as the only effective way of expressing the love of all men. Christians must reject all those solutions called 'evolution' or 'reform.' Following the teaching of John XXIII in the encyclical, *Pacem in Terris,* Christians must be prepared to collaborate loyally with all the *genuine revolutionaries* who are now in the vanguard and are training others to promote the struggle through popular movements and armies of liberation. That must be the true purpose of the 'dialogue between Christians and Marxists,' offically approved by the Catholic Church since Vatican II.

"Summoned to meet together under the title, *Populorum Progressio,* a real revolutionary slogan for our times, we revolutionary Christians of Latin America must reflect together on the forms of our commitment and the militant action it is to take."

The most popular slogan of the Populorum Progressio movement, however, was that taken from the Gospel itself: "The Kingdom of Heaven has suffered violence and men of violence take it by force." (Matthew 11:12)

Inspired by all this, Catholic priests supported, encouraged, and joined the guerrillas. Three religious — two men and one woman — in what came to be known as "the Maryknoll affair," actually formed a Catholic guerrilla band called "The Camillo Torres Front."

The fact that Communist Fidel Castro had been in private communication with the Vatican has never been given much publicity, particularly in the United States, owing to the possibility that it would compromise the American hierarchy. Popes John and Paul saw eye to eye with "the first progressive country in the Western hemisphere," that is, Cuba, however.

As early as January 1968, at the Cultural Congress in Havana, five thousand observers from seventy countries were assembled to hear Fidel deliver the closing speech, in which he declared:

"There are some things, and one thing in particular, which have really impressed us enormously. I refer to the resolution submitted by a group of Catholic priests who have taken part in this Congress. I will not mention their names. [Their names were actually: Msgr. German Guzman Campos from Colombia; Fr. Pedro de Euzcardia from Mexico; Fr. Juan Carlos Zaffaroni, a worker priest from Uruguay; and Fr. Paul Blancquart from Belgium]. I will read out their resolution to our people:

"We, Catholic priests and delegates to the Havana Cultural Congress, are convinced that imperialism is today, especially in the Third World, a dehumanising factor. That, although Marxism and Christianity differ, it is Marxism which provides the most precise scientific analysis of imperialism... We commit ourselves to the anti-imperialist struggle. Furthermore, we condemn the economic and cultural blockade imposed on the Republic of Cuba, the first free territory in America, by North American imperialism."

The priests concluded with the following words: "The Church must act as a revolutionary force."

Castro's reading of the Catholic message at the Congress was the Cuban leader's first official recognition of the existence of genuinely revolutionary Catholic forces active within the Latin American church as well as the Church worldwide.

The recognition was the more significant because Marxist Cuba, although planted at the very doorstep of the United States, was acting as a revolutionary beacon for the whole of Central and South America, including the black islands of the Carribean, and at a later date, even of black Africa.

The acceptance of the Catholic Church as a tacit ally of such forces was the more dangerous because the "progressive" churchmen became more encouraged than ever by their awareness that now they had at their side a Communist Cuba which had become, thanks to Russian help, the largest military force in the Western hemisphere, outside North America, as assessed by no less an authority on such matters than the CIA chief in

Washington.

The most insidious feature of the Marxist-Catholic revolution, however, was not so much the open guerrilla activities, but those disguised behind the screen of agrarian reforms. This silent, but effective, revolution was widely supported by the clergy, bishops, and even primates of the Church.

A typical body, sponsoring the thinly disguised radical reforms was one called "The Popular Cultural Action." This movement was energised by Radio Butatenza in Colombia, the largest network of rural education in the whole of Latin America. It was founded by a Catholic priest and has grown into a large, well-financed organization, with its own farms covering six hundred acres; its own newspapers, and so on.

During Pope Paul's visit to the group's radio station, to celebrate the twentieth anniversary of Popular Cultural Action, the slogan written in gigantic lettering upon the building defined the true ideological tenets of the whole movement. It read: "The earth should belong to those who cultivate it."

Pope Paul made no comment concerning it. He could not since, although it was patently a Marxist slogan, it was in total harmony with his own encyclicals.

Marxist movements of this kind were dotted all over Latin America. By 1978, there were over 140 Church-backed agrarian leagues aimed at teaching peasants about "their rights." Rights which, though preached by Catholic priests, were the most orthodox of Marxist doctrine. Leading this activity were the Jesuits, as already noted. The Superior General, Pedro Arrupe, told them – quoting the Supreme Pontiff – that the revolution must be a gradual affair.

Not all Jesuits, however, followed this directive. Some of them, notably in Uruguay, disregarded the admonition. Perhaps they found themselves in a position in which it was not easy to disengage themselves from their commitments to the guerrillas, with whom they had formed a close alliance.

Such revolutionary Catholicism, with particular regard to its extreme exponents, has become a real problem not only for the various ruling Juntas of the continent, but for the Vatican itself. Revolutionary Latin American zeal, and its lack of subtlety, went against the Church's general strategy of "revolutionary gradualism."

The mounting number of priests, bishops and prelates refusing to toe the line has given sleepless nights to Paul VI and his advisers, who are dedicated to the proposition that any Catholic revolution ought to be conducted without reckless, overt acts which harm the image of the Church, or divide the faithful.

"Revolution with liberty"

Sometime in July 1965, when the present author dined with friends in Eaton Square, London, he met an eminent political figure from Chile. He had had a private audience with Pope Paul VI and leading statesmen all over Europe, where he was presented as a symbol — or so it was hoped — of a new kind of Latin American political resurgence.

He was President Eduardo Frei, who had launched his new brand of politics with a slogan which had not been heard previously — at least in South America: "Revolution with liberty."

He was supported even by the United States, despite the fact that he had nationalised the extensive, American-owned copper industry in Chile.

The importance of President Frei was that he had emerged the year before as the leader of political reform and stability, an exemplar for the whole of the southern continent. His elective majority, which he had won against a Socialist-Communist steam-roller alliance, had been the largest ever recorded in his country. He won as head of a new party, the Christian Democrats. It was one which had been modeled on the Christian Democratic parties of Europe. These, as we have seen, originally had been conceived by the Catholic political leadership in Germany and Italy.

It was the first successful attempt of the Vatican to stem the Marxist revolution by competing in the ideological field against a well-organised Communist party which had tried to go it alone.

Christian Democracy at first fared well. Then, like Christian Democracy back in Europe, it was overwhelmed by the revolutionary forces working for its disintegration, from within and without.

During the dinner, President Frei, although exuding confidence, nevertheless expressed fears that the Marxists would cause his country's political experiment to fail. According to him, the main contributory factors to such a failure would be: a) the help which the Chilean Marxists were receiving from Soviet Russia; b) intervention by foreign Communists; c) the influence of the American mining interests, hostile to his regime; and finally, d) the deviousness of the Vatican.

The Vatican, he explained, while supporting the experiment of Christian Democracy, was at the same time flirting with the "progressive" prelates of Chile. This, it appeared, was due to the fact that a good proportion of the lower clergy and part of the episcopate had definite Marxist leanings. Many were openly eager to work with the Communists.

President Frei then made a comment which shocked his Catholic hosts:

"The first Catholic Party of Latin America will be killed by the Vatican," he declared.

In 1970, the Chilean Communists put up two presidential candidates — a Communist poet named Pablo Neruda, and a crypto-Marxist, Allende. They won the election, but the neo-Communist regime which took over proved to be a disaster.

Neruda, who had won the Stalin Peace Prize in 1953 and the Nobel Prize for Literature in 1970 — the very year the Marxists chose him as their candidate — refused to take his candidacy seriously and was replaced by Allende, who formed a neo-Marxist administration which, after constant turbulence which tore the country apart, ended in tragedy when a military coup overthrew it in September 1973. Allende himself was killed during the uprising.

It was later revealed that the CIA had spent more than eight million dollars to aid the forces which planned the anti-Allende coup. On the other hand, the Communist Party of Chile, aided by special funds from the Russian KGB and another three million dollars from the Communist Party of the U.S.A., spent more than 18 million dollars in support of the Allende regime.

One of the most significant factors in the rise of the Allende regime was the failure of the Chilean Christian Democratic Party experiment. This, in its turn, was due to the fact that a large section of the Chilean Catholic clergy had supported, no matter how indirectly, the Communists. They did this with the tacit consent of the Chilean hierarchy and hence of the Vatican itself.

The implicit, even if undeclared alliance of the Chilean hierarchy with the country's Communist forces, was not a coincidence. The Christian Democratic experiment had been destroyed deliberately because the churchmen and the Communists had reached an agreement to push towards certain left-wing ideological objectives.

The entente between the two has become the standard pattern for the whole of Latin America ever since. The Vatican support for such a partnership is covert, for obvious reasons. There is too much to be lost, vis-a-vis the millions of Catholics who are still resolutely anti-Communist. Moreover, there is the reaction of the United States to be considered.

The Vatican, convinced that Marxism is the dominant political shape of the future, has in fact, already reached an accord with Latin America's Marxist leaders. The accord does not yet exist on the diplomatic level; yet in practical terms, the Church has already committed herself. The proof: her unspoken approval of the growing numbers of "Castros in cassocks" all over Latin America. If theseMarxist, priest-agitators had consistently run counter to Vatican policy and Vatican orders, they would long since have been disciplined.

In Bolivia, for example, priests were arrested for possessing guns and explosives. In Argentina, the country most noted for its urban guerrillas, within less than one year — 1975-1976 — no fewer than seven Catholic priests, plus two seminarians and three nuns, were killed while helping Marxist guerrillas and consorting with them.

In Colombia, between 1976 and 1977, three more priests and one nun were caught actively aiding Communist guerrillas.

In August 1976, Auxiliary Bishop Juan Arzube of Los Angeles, together with three other Spanish-speaking bishops from the United States, were held in Quito, Ecuador for questioning about their participation in a subversive conference held in that country. Xavier Manrique, Equadorean Minister, said the police had confiscated subversive documents and quoted one source as saying, "For Christians on the left, the option will be only between capitalism and socialism, and the ultimate project must be to unite Christians and Marxists.

In other instances, priests were tried in criminal courts and sentenced for their guerrilla activities. Witness several priests and others imprisoned in Colombia in December 1976 "for harbouring weapons and ammunition intended for use by guerrillas."

In July 1976, a guerrilla priest in Argentina was arrested and charged with the murder of an army colonel. In January 1977, in a shoot-out with Communist terrorists, Argentine police killed twenty-eight guerrillas, making a total of 1,275 persons who had died in that country as a result of political violence. Amongst these were many practising Catholics and "progressive" priests.

In Colombia, the Rev. Florentino Agudelo was shot dead by soldiers during a clash with members of the Castroite National

Liberation Party.

The foreign presence

Accounts of these "Castros in cassocks" being arrested, wounded or killed while fighting on the side of the Communist guerrillas in recent years have become a familiar feature of the political unrest in Latin America. The fact that many of them are not Latin Americans is highly significant. The large number of foreign activists is owing to the fact that the continent, perhaps more than any other Catholic area, has a scarcity of priests in ratio to the population of faithful. There is only one priest for every five thousand Catholics, as compared with one for every 370 in the United States and one for every 900 in Europe.

In 1965, out of 27,000 priests in Latin America, there were 15,000 foreign ones.

The reasons for the shortage of native clergy are many. One of the chief ones is the general disenchantment of Latin Americans with the Church and her former traditional support for semi-military regimes or juntas.

The "progressive" priests seek to justify their subversive activities on the ground that the continent is ripe for a social revolution. Also, that their Church is doing less than nothing about it.

Uruguyan Jesuit Luis Segundo, author of a book significantly entitled *A Theology of Artisans of a New Humanity,* cited in the foregoing pages, warned that the Church, if it is to have any validity or acceptance in the future, "must become a function of liberation."

The word "liberation" in this context, as in all leftist literature and slogans, is simply a euphemism for revolution.

Most of Fr. Segundo's Marxist colleagues are, like him, in dead earnest. Their reasoning is that unless the Church does something and does it quickly, the revolution will sweep over

Latin America and the Church will be left out altogether. Atheistic Marxism will take over as the traditional enemy of capitalism, which has been supported by the Church in the past. If the Church will aid the revolutionaries now, the anti-religious aspect of Marxism can be dealt with later and from within.

The Vatican is as much aware as they are that the revolution is bound to come. Not only that, but that the revolution will be Communist inspired and Communist controlled. An increasing number of the clergy, as already noted, are already an integral part of it, even while seemingly a part of traditional Catholicism in ecclesiastical matters.

The immense economic and social discrepancies of the continent appear to justify their behaviour. Communism, deceptive as always, seems to hold out a solution to the problem, even at the cost of massive upheaveals and bloodshed.

The Vatican has realistically accepted the inevitability of the catastrophic turmoils to come. But while permitting its "Castros in cassocks" to fight with guns, and her "progressives" to consort with the revolutionary forces, and its higher clergy to deal tacitly with the top echelons of organised Marxism, it has set in motion a policy of its own.

That policy is one of gradualism. While unacceptable to the left-wing extremists, eager for immediate and drastic changes, it will nevertheless be more effective when evenly pursued than all the most revolutionary activity of the present firebrand activists and their allies.

The Vatican is accustomed to think in terms not of any particular country, but of whole continents as single political units. Hence the necessity of carrying out such policies on a continental scale as part of a later strategy integrated with plans it is implementing in other parts of the world.

Central and South America, being part of the global strategy of the Vatican-Moscow alliance must therefore conform to the general pattern which the Church and the leaders of world Communism have adopted as a means of reaching their ultimate objectives.

This means the sharing of ideological condominium in the Western hemisphere as a whole, and Latin America in particular.

The somewhat contemptuous allusion to Bolivia which was once called "a beggar sitting on a gold mine" could, in fact, be applied to the whole of Central and South America when viewed in terms of potential wealth and development.

The Catholic Church is doing its best to avoid the violent explosion of a continent beneath whose surface there is burning an immense revolutionary volcano. She is watchfully biding her time to direct the coming revolution in conformity with her novel and "progressive" grand strategy, embodied in Pope Paul's encyclical, *Populorum Progressio,* and other papal documents.

Within the Church itself, meanwhile, the conservative and moderate forces with ideological and economic ties to the United States; and those of the Catholic subversives — priests mostly at the bottom of the ecclesiastical ranks, whose interpretation of the papal teachings have led them to involve themselves in Latin America's leftist political struggles, will continue their fight into the last quarter of the twentieth century, until one or the other has been destroyed.

The present progressive hierarchy of the Roman Catholic Church have no doubt who the winner will be. Hence the Vatican's discreet, and at times embarrassing, support of the Marxist Castros in cassocks.

The Church's ultimate objective is to share with the coming Communist political masters of the continent a balanced rule of more than 200 million souls — the current population of Latin America.

In her eyes, it is these millions who are the true "gold mine" of Central and South America. And if now they are the beggars of the Western hemisphere, within a few decades the new ideology conceived at the Vatican, namely, Catholic Marxism, will provide the triumphant Catholic Church of tomorrow.

CHAPTER 30

A Red Jesus For Black Africa

One sunny day in March 1977, a plain-looking man in a business suit emerged from a Russian jet in Dar es Salaam, Tanzania, Africa to be greeted by a welcoming delegation of that country's ranking government officials.

He was Nikolai Podgorny, president of the Soviet Union, and his visit represented the first time a top executive of Communist Russia had ever gone to Africa.

Comrade Podgorny's visit had been preceded by that of Cuba's Marxist leader, Fidel Castro; and the two had one well-defined common objective in mind — the implantation of a viable Communist movement on the black continent.

Speaking at a state banquet after his arrival, Podgorny left no doubt that his presence was a pledge of support for so-called liberation forces (meaning Marxists) in Africa. "We are on the side of the fighters for freedom," he declared. "Our aim is immutable."

Fidel Castro, who had travelled two days ahead of the Soviet president, announced similar "immutable" objectives: Russian and Cuban aid to all militant Marxists states of Africa.

Castro and Podgorny continued their tour with visits to various Marxist-orientated states: Zambia, Mozambique, Tanzania, Angola, Botswana, and others. Their joint task was to arm the black Marxist guerrillas.

Castro and Podgorny meant business. Prior to their arrival, the African project had been carefully thought out in both Moscow and Havana. While the preparatory steps had been taken during frequent visits of black leaders to the two capitals, the overall operation had been finalised by the Soviet ambassador to Zambia, Dr. Vassils Solodnikov.

Dr. Solodnikov was well qualified for the task. He was the KGB's leading expert on African affairs. As the formulator of the strategic policies that had culminated with Moscow's successful involvement in Angola, the former Portuguese colony, he had spearheaded the Soviet bid to secure exclusive influence over the black guerrilla armies. Angola had become Communist by the planting of a Marxist leader, helped by Russian arms, and of Marxist Cuban volunteers, supplied by Fidel Castro.

Dr. Solodnikov had been responsible for expediting arms deliveries to an increasing number of black Communist presidents, premiers, guerrilla leaders and other militants dedicated to the expulsion of the whites from Africa and to the substitution of white rule with black Marxism, from Cairo to Cape Town.

So successful was he that he was nicknamed "Mr. Kalshnikov" after the Russian automatic rifle which had become the main weapon of the black guerrillas.

The Soviet rifles were distributed just after President Podgorny's visit. Essential as they were to the black revolution, however, they were almost ancillary to the massive help in sophisticated war material and men given by Soviet Russia. This "aid" included aircraft, tanks, armoured cars, radar, anti-aircraft, and anti-tank artillery.

The military personnel assigned to the project was on a no less generous scale. Highly skilled Russian and Cuban pilots, engineers, and technical advisors were to be found in the uniformed armies of black African one-party, one-man regimes.

Their presence became the *sine qua non* of the Marxist intervention throughout the continent. It was, in fact, a follow-up of a Cuban expedition which had been sent two years before when Cuba, with the approval of Soviet Russia, had dispatched a whole army of more than 14,000 Marxist troops to overthrow right-wing guerrillas in the recently evacuated Portuguese colonies of Mozambique and Angola which, within months, were turned into Marxist dictatorships.

The Communist invasion of Africa, which was commenced about 1974-75 as the war in Vietnam was ending, was the culmination of a brassy effort on the part of Soviet Russia to transform the whole of the black continent into a Communist Africa.

The apprehensions voiced by European nations were cast aside with contempt by the reds and Marxist blacks alike in the certainty that at this juncture the United States, still half paralysed by the Vietnam fiasco and its repercussions at home, would not move.

While both Europeans and Americans watched in apparent helplessness and inertia, the Catholic Church kept well in the background, exercising the utmost caution lest she antagonise too soon and too openly the conservative white and black elements within and outside Africa.

The creation of a black Marxist hierarchy was prompted mostly by the Vatican's eagerness to exert its influence upon the emerging Marxist black Africa from the top. It was a policy also pursued with great diligence by the Church's counterpart,

Russian Communism.

Pursuit of such a policy meant the creation of a new generation of black hierarchs, who could deal on equal racial terms with the leading African politicians, military leaders and guerrilla commanders at local, tribal, or educational levels.

The policy proved even more effective than the sending of armies, technical advisors (Russian style), money, or indeed, even of guns. The Church could, at any given time, or during periods of complex political or military problems, intervene directly via her black hierarchs.

In fact, Catholic prelates, by supporting or opposing this or that white or black regime, more often than not could exert an important influence upon the affairs of any given country, quite disproportionate to their status, number, or hierarchical position.

A typical example was that of a black prelate, Cardinal Biayenda, archbishop of Brazzaville, in the former Congo. While the Soviet President and Fidel Castro were touring Africa to implement their joint Marxist grand strategy, Cardinal Biayenda was promoting that of the Church. This he did via the more subtle method of moving within the national corridors of power — that is, by attempting to exercise his ecclesiastical influence at the highest level possible, the head of the state.

In this particular instance, tribal and family rivalries intervened, aborting his attempt. The Cardinal was assassinated.

Yet, his intervention in the affairs of a large black country at a most delicate moment, with the precise objective of influencing its national ideological and military policies, was indicative of the tactic adopted by the Church.

The episode is worthy of a glance because of the significance it has in the context of an emerging Marxist Africa. Although the Vatican has been strangely silent regarding the motive of the killing — the first cardinal, as the pope sadly commented, to be murdered since the Middle Ages — the reality of the matter was that his liquidation was politically motivated. Also, that it was

The Vatican, convinced that Africa will become a Marxist or Marxist-dominated continent, where the white presence will be eliminated and with it the religion preached by white missionaries, is creating an all-black hierarchy and clergy, chosen chiefly because of their "progressive" ideas. In photo is shown Bishop Maurice Otunga of Tocape, following his enthronement as Africa's first black bishop.

intimately concerned with the Communist web of African intrigue.

The military rulers of the Congo, who had just seized power, came promptly to the fore, saying that three members of the family of former Congolese President Marian Ngouabi had been responsible for the cardinal's murder. The interesting feature of the affair, however, was that the former president had himself been assassinated a few days before the cardinal was killed.

The military council then disclosed another no less interesting item. They admitted that the cardinal had had "a very private meeting with the dead president" only thirty minutes prior to the president's death.

A few days after these events, Communist Cuban troops entered the Congolese territory of former Katanga as the spearhead of Cuban and Russian "liberation" forces. Their immediate objective was the overthrow of the pro-Western President.

From where had the Cuban and other Marxist contingent come? From neighbouring Marxist Angola, the former Portuguese colony which, three or four years previously had been invaded by Cuban troops and converted into a Communist redoubt.

The Pope expressed his sorrow "at the very bitter news" of Cardinal Biayenda's murder, and Cardinal Hume of England declared that the Church was "paying an appalling price of blood because of its stand for true freedom."

Yet the Vatican knew only too well what was going on all over Africa. The troubles there has been partially fomented by the policies the Church itself had been pursuing for years. This was clearly evident in the fact that only a few days before Cardinal Biayenda's murder, Paul VI had a private meeting with Bishop Lamont, a left-wing white prelate who had just been expelled from Rhodesia after being handed a 10-year jail sentence (commuted to exile) for helping and harbouring black African guerrillas.

Bishop Lamont had been a notorious accuser of whites in

Rhodesia, and an open supporter of the African extremists. In short, he had been a genuine exponent of the Vatican's policy of Catholic-Marxist integration with the emerging left-wing forces of Africa.

"The Holy Father was well informed of the situation," said Bishop Lamont after his meeting with the Pontiff.

Vatican ambivalence

To understand the true significance of that comment, a brief description of its background may help to elucidate the equivocal role which the Vatican has been pursuing in the subtle promotion of its anti-white, anti-Western and pro-Communist objectives in Africa.

One Sunday night — February 6, 1977 — there was a knock at the door of the Catholic mission at Musami, Rhodesia, only fifty miles away from the capital, Salisbury. A group of twelve Marxist guerrillas ordered three Jesuit priests and four nuns out of the building. They lined all seven up against a wall and fired one hundred and eleven bullets from Soviet-made machine guns, massacring the innocent victims. The guerrillas had been careful to select whites only.

That same week, despite this racially-motivated atrocity, Bishop Lamont, after having been sentenced for aiding the Marxist guerrillas, went on fulminating against the whites with a ferocity worthy of a better cause. It is not without significance that the bishop was also head of a notorious left-wing organization called "The Catholic Commission of Justice and Peace," whose booklet, *Civil War in Rhodesia,* was on sale in most Communist bookshops of England. The booklet, whose subtitle was "Abduction, torture, and death in the counter-insurgency campaign," advanced horrific proof against Rhodesia's white government.

Whether these charges were true or not, it remains that the

Catholic left-wingers who made them, by-passed in silence atrocities such as the senseless murders of the white missionaries. Indeed, the Communist sympathizers tried to turn even the massacre against the white Rhodesians, suggesting that the crime had been committed by black mercenaries hired by the white government.

This notwithstanding the fact that black Marxist terrorists went on killing white Catholics, including the former Bishop of Bulawayo, Bishop Adolf Schmidt; Father Possenti Weggatern; and a nun, Sister Maria van der Berg, murdered by a Marxist guerrilla with a Communist automatic weapon.

Despite these outrages committed against their own co-religionists, hard-core Marxist Catholic priests persisted in extending a helping hand to the Communist guerrillas. For example, Swiss Catholic priest, Fr. Paul Elgi was arrested for "aiding African Nationalist guerrillas"; and Irish-born Father Lawrence Kynh was sentenced to three years imprisonment after having been found guilty of "aiding guerrillas at his mission station on the Mozambique border." There was also the case of Father Maximus Gumbo from the Karangue Mission on Lake Kariba, who "failed to report black Marxist guerrillas in his parish."

In the eyes of black African nationalism, the Catholic Church became its most valuable ally, a most effective champion of the cause. This was true not only with respect to their national aspirations, but applied equally to their Communistic political aims. The most important feature of it all was that the black Catholic clergy, in all echelons, were acting as they did with the consent and at the instigation of the top hierarchy, black and white.

They were required to put aside their personal feelings (a minority were neutral or conservative) and made to serve as clerical purveyors of leftist theories, whose main objective was to provide assistance to any black Marxist movement. The individual and collective sentiments derived officially — even if at long distance — from the Holy See itself.

Following a mass celebrated by Pope Paul for the soul of the murdered Cardinal Biayenda, Bishop Lamont declared that "the Pope said to me before my recent trial: 'Never hesitate; I am behind you in this.' " (Meaning the bishop's giving aid to the black Marxist guerrillas.)

As if that had not been sufficient to get his point across, Bishop Lamont then stated that the moral and monetary support he received from certain American bishops during his trial was "of incalculable worth."

He added that Bishop J. Rausch, at that time general secretary of the U. S. Catholic Conference and the Conference of Catholic Bishops, sent him a cheque for five thousand dollars. Bishop Rausch told me he collected the money from the first ten U.S. bishops he discussed the matter with.

The general support for the Marxist guerrillas by bishops and missionaries first began in earnest following the Vatican-Moscow alliance. It was a logical extension of the Church's reorientation towards Marxism, following her assessment that Communism was bound to dominate a black Africa in the future.

The Vatican's ideological shift gave a new direction to the teaching of the clergy, with the result that an increasing number of schools and institutions of higher learning in Africa became centres of Marxist indoctrination.

There were seven instances in which Marxist guerrillas kidnaped entire Catholic schools. For example, in April 1977, they abducted one hundred and twenty-one school children and six staff from the Roman Catholic Mission of Manibia, Southwest Africa. At another time, when they rounded up the children and teachers at Anamulenge School in Ovamboland, near the border with Communist Angola, Catholic authorities admitted that "it is possible that some went willingly, since many pupils are politically aware, and it is believed that there is heavy support for SWAPO among them."

The Vatican also initiated the practice of planting black clergy amidst whites, to weaken the white presence in Church affairs. This policy was typified by the Church's acclerated appointment of black priests to predominantly white areas.

In South Africa where in 1920 three quarters of the Catholic population was white, in 1960 the racial make-up had changed to seventy percent black and only eighteen percent white. The policy created a rift amongst white Catholics, since more often than not, the blacks were even more racially minded than the whites.

Witness the case of Father Chickore, senior black priest in Rhodesia, when preaching at a service for the seven white missionaries who had been massacred at St. Paul's mission. Several white mourners walked out to protest the racialist overtones of the sermon.

When Archbishop Cahkaipa of Salisbury was elevated to the Rhodesian hierarchy, his advancement was explained by the Vatican on the ground that white Rhodesia would be taken over by a black majority in a few years.

The Catholic strategy in Africa is a multi-faceted plan, embracing both ecclesiastical and political activity in dealing with its current ally, militant Communism.

After Vatican II, it became an integral part of the combined strategy of the Catholic-Communist alliance, to be promoted concurrently with related programmes in the West and in America.

To accomplish its objectives in black Africa, three basic steps were necessary, namely: 1) the speedy elimination of the white missionaries; 2) the even speedier creation of a black, Marxist-orientated hierarchy; and 3) the concrete cooperation with black Marxism, bringing its activities under Church control.

The successful deployment of these fundamental policies depended, in their turn, upon the following developments; 1) a total elimination of white dominance or even of white importance in the African affairs of the Church; 2) the subtle, but complete withdrawal of the Catholic Church from involvement with the Protestant bodies in Africa, because Protestantism, with few exceptions (notably, the World Council of Churches) is still identified with caucasian cultures. Such a concept is harmful to the Vatican's aim to identify Catholicism with black nationalism; 3) the evolution of ways to collaborate with an increasingly militant black Marxism which is intolerant not only of the religious and political dominance of the white race, but even of ideological and economic assistance from white Communism; and 4) the promotion of a self-assured, self-centered black Africa no longer under the protection of either a white-sponsored religion or a white-sponsored ideology, but one which can stand on its own feet, invigorated by a totally black Catholic Church in the continent, with its own black priesthood, black hierarchy and with the possibility even of the election in the future of a black pope.

An African For the Throne of Peter?

This hope for a future black pope is not something to be dismissed as improbable. The possibility has already been envisaged in certain circles in Africa, as well as in the Vatican itself. There is certainly nothing in Catholic doctrine nor the canon law to proscribe it.

It has even been said that the usage of Latin was discarded in the curriculum of Catholic seminaries not so much because it was archaic, but also to encourage the Africans and Asians to enter the priesthood.

What will decide when and how a black cardinal is elevated to the Throne of Peter may be determined by global events outside the power of the Vatican itself. Yet one thing is certain. Black Africa, if and when it adopts a form of black Marxism, will have an influential voice in the elections of future popes.

In the make-up of the present Sacred College, the proportion on non-white cardinals, representing non-white communicants, is less than one fifth of the whole. Yet, if we consider them in relation to their flocks, it becomes clear that they have already a disproportionately high number of papal electors in ratio to the millions of faithful represented by the white cardinals.

Their number has been increasing at an ever accelerated pace since the year of the three popes.

Pope John Paul II, as already seen, owes his election also to the votes of the Third World, amongst whom were those of black cardinals who considered him a "radical" willing to reduce the church to the level of "African" traditions, without any western, European, and indeed without any white cultural back-ground. Such sentiments, although seldom expressed in public, nevertheless are powerful motivating exercises of anti-white, anti-western, and anti-American animosity.

A black cardinal who voted for Wojtyla during the Conclave of October 1978 had no ambiguity about what he wanted: "All the imperial paraphernalia of the Church," said black Cardinal J. Malula, Archibishop of Kinshana, "all the medieval remoteness and inheritance that made Europeans think that the Church is only western, all that must go. Black countries like mine, want something different. All that must change."

Cardinal Malula and his other black colleagues saw their hopes come true sooner than even they had expected.

Within less than a year from his election, their "radical" new pope set out to strengthen African Catholicism with an urgency seldom seen before. Hurried nominations and hierarchical kangaroo-jumping of black prelates became a startling phenomenon. Whites were replaced in many mission stations and dioceses. In 1982, the Pope himself, while in Nigeria for instance, pointed out this fact by remarking that, of Nigeria's 32 Bishops, 26 were Black Africans.

The most startling new reality, however, was that the Pope began to tour Africa, visiting one black country after another, from Kenya to Equatorial Guinea, from French Gabon to Upper Volta, from Ghana to the Congo, from Benin to Nigeria.

Within three years he had personal contacts with the Marxist leaders of most of them, while strengthening the black hierarchical machinery of the black church everywhere he went. The only exception in the twenty-odd countries which he visited was white

South Africa.

Wherever he went he brazenly flattered black Africa, black Christianity and encouraged, via theatrical dramatics, black African racialism, as well as black African radicalisms.

He openly fraternised with extreme Marxist blacks and semi-Marxist dictatorships to court favor for the black Catholic Church. (It has been reckoned that out of 50 black countries about 47 are one-party regimes, plain dictatorships, or Marxist-Russian sponsored administrations.)

One of these was Benin, whose official ideology is Marxism-Leninism. Its president, black Marxist Kerekou, welcomed Pope John Paul II on February 16, 1982 during his second African tour by urging the Pope to support black national liberation struggles.

"Long live His Holiness Pope John Paul II," he shouted to the airport crowds. Then pointing to the Pope standing beside him, he added, "We are now ready for the Marxist revolution. The struggle continues."

Following private meetings at the presidential palace, photos of the Pope flanked by Marx and Lenin were taken as official documents.

While encouraging African nationalism and racialism, the Pope critized the great white powers. On his second African tour, in Lagos, Nigeria, in a speech greeting President Shagani, he castigated "interference" in Africa, by "outside powers" ignoring that he represented one himself, adding that black Africa would astound the world, if allowed to develop "on its own."

The hint was directed not only to Moscow and to the U.S., but more ominously, to other religions, mainly to the evangelical and protestant churches.

Ecumenism in Africa has always been used to disguise attempts to paralyze protestant and evangelical operations. For example, the black archbishop of Lagos, Msgr. Anthony Okojie, had no doubt what the Pope had meant. "One of the biggest problems we face," he commented, "is the fundamental approach to the Bible being given by other Christians." Namely by those who are not Roman Catholics.

The Moslems of Africa also reacted dramatically. Police seized an armed man at the stadium in Lagos shortly before the Pope celebrated mass February 14, 1982. Shortly after that two men and one woman were arrested with a loaded pistol at Kaduna, when the Pope visited this Muslim stronghold.

The vigor and objectives of the Vatican in Africa can be best demonstrated by the church operation in Nigeria. Nigeria has a total population nearing the 100 millions, the largest African country. Yet, although a small minority, the Catholic Church is there running the largest training seminary, not only of Nigeria, but of all Africa. Indeed, it is the largest seminary in the whole world. The seminary, Enugu-Ikot Ekpene, during the years 1982-83, boasted more than 700 black Nigerians training for the priesthood. While there, John Paul II ordained 90 new priests, all black. Other smaller seminaries release hundreds more each year. John Paul II remarked that the church in Africa "now has become African."

He was stating a reality since these black battalions of African clergymen have already taken over most of the Catholic Church in Africa. The result is already evident. Black bishops now head most of the Catholic African Church. It has been reckoned that by 1985 white bishops will have vanished altogether. The practical and far-reaching result of this black revolution is that soon a black hierarchy will dominate black Africa, and also, that it will greatly influence the corridors of power of the Vatican itself. A fast growing African clergy will produce a fast growing number of African bishops. African bishops will generate black African cardinals. That will spell the plausibility of a black African pope.

The policy of the Vatican is not only to sponsor, even if by proxy, black racism, revolutionary revisionism, and a church inspired by a black African Liberation Theology, but also a black racial, economic, and social revolution by which the Catholic Church can become the predominant religion of Africa, independent of Moscow-Washington-Vatican alliances.

Judging by the current vigorous promotion of a highly committed black African hierarchy, the Vatican has set in motion a long-range strategy directed at insuring that the popes of the future will be identified with the steady increase of a non-white world population.

In Africa, such racial strategy has become inseparable with the neo-Marxist Catholicism, as the sponsor of black African redemption. The two are interlocked.

In this manner, the Vatican, while engaged upon the solution of the immense problems of today, is actively preparing also to open the portals of the 21st century, there to enter as the paramount religious authority in an African black society where racial barriers have been reduced to a memory of the past.

Archbishop Oscar A. Romero was assassinated by four gunmen March 24, 1980 as he said funeral mass at the Divine Providence Hospital in San Salvador. Romero was an outspoken champion of human rights and a 1979 Nobel Peace Prize nominee.

CHAPTER 31

The Cross, The Hammer And Sickle, And The Latin American Revolution

On the evening of March 24, 1980, Monsignor Romero, Archbishop of San Salvador, lifted the chalice during Mass. "In this chalice," he said, raising it high, "the wine becomes blood which was the sacrifice for the salvation of this people. May this sacrifice give us the courage to offer our own bodies for justice and peace."

At that moment a killer struck, putting a 22 calibre bullet in his heart, sending blood pouring from his mouth as he fell on his back by the altar.

Since then Archbishop Romero, one of the most vocal champions of Liberation Theology, has become a symbol of the revolutionary integration of the cross, and the hammer and the sickle, in the Western Hemisphere. Today, the radical activism of many other high prelates like him, not excluding cardinals, has become one of the most disruptive factors in contemporary Central America and beyond. It will be even more so tomorrow.

Their open advocacy of political and military commotion to come, is not only there for all to see, it is deliberately hastened by the Catholic Church herself. This was substantiated in 1982 during a massive official consensus at the annual conference in Sao Paulo, when no less than 250 Brazilian Bishops, the totality of the largest Church in Latin America, endorsed one of Archbishop Romero's most controversial tenets which questioned "the right to property."

Their unanimous acceptance of such tenets was even more revolutionary, perhaps, then the Theology of Liberation itself. It condoned not only the destruction of the economic structures of society, but supported also the justification of certain claims, some of which, although theoretically plausible, nevertheless, if enforced, would spell the collapse of all social order everywhere.

The 250 bishops blamed social unrest mostly upon the economic fabric "which forces many to work for a miserable wage, while maintaining the privileges of the few." Their assertions were crowned with a naked Marxist declaration: "The fundamental right to have a place to live," they stated, "can supersede a legitimate right to property." To the almost 2 million squatters living on the fringes of Copacabanca and other shanty towns outside the big cities, words like these spelled authorized religious justification for legislative disobedience, civil disorder and indeed open violence.

Archbishop Romero's saying that "young people seeking to be priests want to be part of a church that identifies itself with the poor," although admirable as a Christian sentiment, indicated that the Latin American Church was preparing potential revolutionary crusaders against the established order.

This is most evident in countries like El Salvador, which had one of the highest birthrates in the world and one of the lowest standard nutrition. Six of such crusaders, in fact, were killed in action fighting as Marxist guerrillas, as young priests of the poor, between 1978 and 1979, with another 7 during 1980. In addition to them, there were 167 deaths and more than 200 injured, from January 22 to 31, 1980, the worse massacre occuring January 22, when Catholic demonstrators were killed and 120 injured, many of them after listening to Archbishop Romero.

A few days later, January 27, Archbishop Romero counselled the troops themselves to revolt against the established authorities, ironically the Christian Democrats, helped into power the previous year by the Catholic Church herself. "Their duty," Romero told them, "was that of serving the people and not the privileged few."

Two months later Romero's Marxist posturing resulted in his own assassination.

The escalation continued, encouraged by active revolutionary elements of the Church. Chief among them were the Jesuits, Romero's most influential advisers. From 896 persons killed between 1978 and 1979, to several thousands in 1980, to well over 11,000 in the first eleven months of 1981, the number reached more than 22,000 in the first part of 1982, by which time the massacres became a daily occurrence, the killed and wounded at one time being counted by the hundreds, and indeed by the thousands.

The Pope, the Archbishop, and the Jesuits

This new revolutionary Marxist activism greatly embarrassed Pope John Paul II before, during, and after Romero's murder. The more so since the publicity about his death, instigated partially by the Jesuit Conference in Washington, had turned Romero into a saint and a martyr who died for the liberation of the oppressed campesinos and peones of the sub-continent. The involvement of the Catholic Church with the guerrillas fighting against Latin American regimes supported by the U.S. put in peril the spirit and the operational balance of the Vatican-Washington alliance.

Moreover, the Jesuits totally ignored the warnings from Pope John Paul II to cease their subversive activities because of their determination to pursue the policies of the old Vatican-Moscow alliance with its advocacy of direct revolutionary involvement. When finally President Reagan, and behind him the Pentagon, insisted that the Church should control the Jesuits or else, the presidential warning produced a papal hurricane against the Jesuits.

Pope John Paul II began by refusing to call Romero a saint and a martyr. By hardly mentioning his name, he paid little homage to his memory and went so far as to refuse to attend his funeral, sending in his place a Mexican Cardinal.

The Pope's behavior chagrined many catholics. An Italian judge in a letter to the press asked why a travelling pope like John Paul II, (of whom it had been said by Cardinal Hume, quoted by London Times February 17, 1982, that all you had to do was to throw a brick at the police and the pope would come to visit you) had not set off immediately for San Salvador to pick up the chalice which had dropped from Romero's hands and continued the mass. (1)

The Vatican prudently kept silence, but it quietly opened a large file in its archives. There, staring them in the face, were not only the semi-illegal and Marxist perorations of Romero, but also the collective condemnation of most Latin American prelates against Romero's revolutionary activities, and those of his sponsors.

The Jesuits' pursuance of the discarded policies of the former Vatican-Moscow alliance and their defiance against the new policies of the Vatican-Washington alliance brought the anger of Pope John Paul II upon their heads in a manner they had not experienced for centuries, as previously described in chapter seven.

Their General was made to resign. The whole Jesuit Order was put into the hands of a personal delegate of the Pope. Top Jesuits were dismissed and openly scolded, indeed "publicly humiliated," by the Pope. After having summoned 110 of their top-leaders to Rome in March, 1982, Pope John Paul II ordered them to tow his new line whether they liked it or not. Not content with that, finally he compelled them to take an oath of blind obedience, pending the election of a new General to be sponsored by the Pope himself.

It had been a rebuff comparable to the one the Jesuits had suffered during the 18th century. The popes who had done so died in suspicious circumstances, as we have already seen, while the Jesu-

(1) Corriere della Sera, Sunday Times. 1-17-82).

its, who had been commanded to stop meddling in political revolutions, emerged stronger than ever, continuing to meddle with the revolutions of Europe, even more than they had done in the past.

Violence and the Catholic giant next door

The preaching of Marxist revolutionary tenets, whether during the Vatican-Moscow alliance or the Vatican-Washington alliance, was not confined to mere theoretical sponsorship. They trespassed into the practical field in most Latin American lands. There priests, missionaries, Jesuits, even nuns, masterminded invasion by squatters on private and state owned lands, and incited peasants to acts of violence from El Salvador to the Amazonia in Brazil. Many incidents resulted in grave economic disruptions, severe physical fights, and even deaths.

Catholic lay and ecclesiastical agitators advocated violence, using even religious images as Archbishop Romero had done before them. A typical passage is found in one of Romero's pastoral letters in which he described the scene on Mount Tabor, when Jesus was transfigured. "The five people with Jesus," Romero had commented, "Moses, Elijah, Peter, James, and John, were all men of violent disposition."

These agitators, along with Romero, explained the Church as teaching that: "when there is a situation of permanent and organised injustice, then the situation itself is violence." (1)

The sponsoring of such radicalism, spelled the sure fostering of a massive social revolution, particularly in a continent where the population is composed largely of landless peasants with a rapidly escalating birth rate. In Brazil alone, for instance, they had already increased by over 30 million in the last ten years. The total population of Latin America, in fact, has been growing so fast that by the year 2000 it will harbor more than half of the total Catholic believers of the entire world, which makes of the Catholic Church the

(1)Quoted also by The Sunday Times, 1-17-82)

undisputed giant of the Continent. In numerical terms, it means that Latin America will by then have more Catholics then Africa, Asia, the whole of Europe and the U.S. put together.

The implications for Protestant U.S., of having such a Roman Catholic giant next door, are portentous.

When these hundreds of millions of desperately poor are continuing to be fed by Catholic neo-Marxism, then the portents of inevitable disasters are fearful indeed, since the Liberation Theology has become irreversible, its spirit of social disruption has come to stay, independently of the ideological advantages of the Vatican-Washington alliance. Because of its irreversibility, it will operate even more effectively in the future, independent of old or new popes.

It cannot be otherwise, since Liberation Theology has acknowledged that Marxism and the Church have a lot in common. The recent popes have all accepted this proposition that whereas Marxism says that history is a process of the massess struggling towards universal communism, Christianity likewise affirms that history is a process of the masses struggling towards the Kingdom of Heaven.

This belief carries an irresistible appeal to the starving millions of Latin America, hence their ready acceptance of neo-Marxian Catholicism; and eventually a Marxist Vatican, and finally of a Marxist-orientated pope.

Marxist cells and Catholic battalions in "the kingdom of God"

The acceptance of a neo-Marxist Catholicism spells the acceptance of a Catholic sponsored revolution. The Latin American Catholic masses will carry it out, with the blessing of their Church, by persuasion if possible, by force if necessary.

Catholic priests already committed to such proposition, have become, are, and still continue to be the spokesmen for Catholic Marxist guerrillas. Many are actively engaged in guerrilla combat themselves. When reproached for their radicalism, they reply with

Gospel quotations harmonized with Marx: " 'Woe unto ye rich,' Is not that also what Das Kapital has said?'' "He has chosen me...to set free the oppressed,'' is the reply of the committed guerrilla-priests. "He fills the hungry with good things...and leaves the rich with nothing...''.

This Neo-Catholic Marxism goes even further, however, promoting the abolition of private property, justified by the proposition that all land is owned by God. The Kingdom of God, according to this credence, is the establishment on this earth of a just society, with "all the goods in common'' like that of the early Christians.

The peril of such interpretation is portentous. It puts the Kingdom of God in the near future, just beyond the fast approaching Catholic-Marxian revolution.

The spirit of these biblical Marxist-Leninist oriented quotations has already impregnated the whole fabric of the Latin American church, from Tierra del Fuego to the borders of the U.S. Scattered all along the continent there are undetermined battalions of missionaries, priests, nuns, lay workers, preaching and practicing a combination of the tenets of Liberation Theology and the neo-Marxian Catholicism of Pope John Paul II.

Their battalions are increasing at an ever accelerated pace. Their precise number is anybody's guess, but to judge by what is already known, the portents are terrifying. By early 1982, there were already more than 53 to 54 thousand basic liberation communities in Brazil alone.

The Catholic basic communities are the equivalent of the classic Marxist cells dedicated to the overthrow of traditional society. Because they are energized by the spirit of two religions, Catholicism and Marxism, they are even more destuctive than those which created Soviet Russia. These cells, "comunidades de base'' as they are called, are formed by missionaries or priest-led peasant study groups of 10 to 12 or more families in any average size village.

They are indoctrinated by priests, local padres, ecclesiastics or religious workers from the cities. The teaching is meant to develop a political approach to economic and social problems via active disruption or even violent militancy. The "comunidades de base'' are, therefore, powerful revolutionary tools in the hands of a militant Catholic Church preparing them for use during the forthcoming commotions.

Since the advent of the Vatican-Washington alliance, they have been kept in the background not to endanger the Vatican-U.S. partnership. Yet their number is quietly multiplying everywhere, as are their activities in preparation for the DAY. They are operating, even if passively, from Argentina to Brazil, from Nicaragua to Honduras, Guatemala, Costa Rica, El Salvador, and even clandestinely, in Mexico.

Their commanders as a rule were and are the Jesuits or Jesuit-inspired priests or lay workers, something which Pope John Paul II discovered (to his astonishment) when the U.S. intelligence apparati denounced them as the main instigators of the guerrillas operating mostly against Latin American Administrations financially and militarily supported by the U.S.

Individual Jesuits at times acknowledged their involvement in the revolution. Father Luis Pellecer, for instance, when he testified in San Salvador, December 12, 1981 before an audience of diplomats and newsmen, admitted that he had served in an active guerrilla group for almost 15 years. He stated that he had joined the guerrillas in Guatemala, and from there he had helped to prepare the ground for the guerrillas in El Salvador.

"Every Jesuit in Central America," he commented, "is actively serving not God, but Marxism and the revolution."

But if Catholic priests are active in the field, some of them are active also in the higher echelons of the political-military machinery

Witness another Jesuit, Father Miguel D' Escoto, who called Liberation Theology, "a Christianisation of the Church in Latin America." Father D'Escoto, a well-educated Maryknoll priest, was a supporter of the neo-Catholic Marxist revolution, as an individual priest. He could, however, operate with the effectiveness of hundreds of priests since he was nothing less than the Foreign Minister of Nicaragua. He was helped by two other priests who were high officials of the Nicaraguan Government, as well as others in minor semi-offical jobs, sometimes not officially connected

Well armed Sandinista guerrillas parade two Nicaraguan National Guard deserters through a dirt alleyway in Leon June 18, 1979.

Spectators look at bodies of part of a group of 12 young men, their hands tied behind their backs, dumped along the road on the outskirts of Santa Ana Province in El Salvador. Their deaths pushed to 55 the number of slayings reported over the weekend in clashes between leftist guerrillas and government troops in November of 1980.

with the Nicaraguan administration.

According to President Reagan, the Nicaraguans were cooperating with other left wing, revolutionary guerrilla groups or potential Marxist administrations all over Central America by building Cuban-type garrisons, and modernising four major airfields to handle Soviet built MIG aircraft. They also had Nicaraguan pilots, trained in Communist Bulgaria, and were haboring more than 6,000 Cubans, and between 50 to 70 soviet officers to help Nicaragua with its military preparation. Nicaragua, run by Catholic priests and Marxists, had moved into the orbit of the Soviet Union and Cuba with, according to the U.S. State Department, a standing army of 25,000 to 30,000 men equipped with Soviet tanks.

The potentiality for spreading a Marxist Catholic revolution to the rest of Central America, therefore, was alarming. Its military force, including militia and guerrillas, developed to operate in nearby countries, would by 1983 reach nearly 70,000 men, by far the largest in Central America. These facts were disclosed in a briefing at the State Department in Washington, March 10, 1982, by Robert Inman, Deputy Director CIA, and J. Hughes, Deputy Director of the Defense Intelligence Agency.

The seriousness of the threat became such that the U.S. approved the setting up of special commando-operations organised by the CIA against Nicaragua, to prevent it from helping the revolutionary forces in El Salvador and other Latin American countries, and from infiltration which could help to destabilise the rest of Central America. This escalation had become a menace to the whole region.

The alarming potentiality of left-wing movements, Marxist orientated administrations, and guerrilla groups being used to establish a cluster of Marxist regimes of the Cuban type had become a positive reality.

The prospects of the future were gloomy, indeed disastrous. The establishment of a cluster of Marxist regimes in Central America, would not only menace the Panama Canal, or cause serious instability in Mexico, but would transform the whole of Central America into a Russian controlled Communist Dominion, south of the U.S.

To the Catholic Church, however, the prospect, although a dark one, was not as deadly as it was for the U.S. As one of the major forces involved in sponsoring the forthcoming revolution, she had already resolved to play the leading role throughout Latin America, with or without the U.S. But while her disruptive operations comprised the whole of South America, her ultimate objective embraced also its northern part, the U.S. itself.

CHAPTER 32

The Threat To America

The Catholic Church is convinced that whoever controls Europe will control the Western world. Napoleon, Wellington, Hitler, and Stalin all thought the same. And history has confirmed the validity of that postulate.

Military and political factors indicate that the proposition is still viable in the present era, and hence is justifiable as a world strategy. The United States, as an extension of the cultural dynamism of the old world is still umbilical to Europe; therefore, such a premise has serious implications for the whole of North America.

The radical transformation which is currently reshaping the West — politically, culturally, and spiritually — is something which ought to be scrutinised with the utmost diligence. For tomorrow, Europe will be fundamentally different from the traditional Europe with which the United States has been dealing in the past.

It will be a Europe which is solidly Marxist in economics, Catholic in religion, and Catholic-Communist in politics. As such, it will be a monolithic entity so dramatically new that it will be extremely difficult to assess it in terms of the familiar Euro-american experience.

It cannot be otherwise. Because such a Europe will be dominated by an ideology basically hostile to that of the United States. Her hostility will be hardened by the military might of her true protector, the Soviet Union, the only super-power capable of matching if not overwhelming the American thermonuclear deterrent.

Unlike the halcyon days of the Cold War, in which the United States and the Vatican were close allies, this time America will face the latter no longer as a comrade-at-arms, but as a foe. The Catholic Church will have become part and parcel of Eurocommunism and hence a political appendage of Russia.

A Catholic-Eurocommunism alliance, therefore, will confront the United States with three dangerous and experienced enemies: Marxism as a universal political doctrine; the Catholic Church as a global religion; and a functional combination of the two working together toward at least one common goal, the destruction of capitalist society.

It is this new political force which will determine the general attitude of Europe to America in the future. Continued intercourse between a Eurocommunist Europe and a capitalist America, even if tolerated, will be provisional — an expedient to outwit the opponent. This is due to the political reality that Marxism and Capitalism are, by the very nature of their respective beliefs expansionistically motivated and mutually exclusive. Coexistence and detente were political fictions accepted by both sides as a means of gaining time.

Of the two — American Capitalism and Russian Eurocommunism — the latter is the most subtly aggressive and politically experienced. Endowed as it is with the ability to infiltrate the inner structures of a capitalist society, its disintegrating power is not recognised until too late.

The insidious nature of the Marxist appeal rests upon the wholly chimerical picture it presents of economic and social egalitarianism. Americans have always chrished such an ideal, even though their prosperity and strength is based upon a denial of it. They close their eyes to the fact that implementation of such an "utopia" has always required rigid regimentation and a powerful, centralised, authoritarian government, which is historically repugnant to them.

Catholicism, a factor more imponderable than either Marxism or Capitalism, will eventually infiltrate the machineries of both. At present, having sided with Marxism, it will strengthen Eurocommunism while at the same time weakening Capitalism. As a mixture of religion and ideology, it will wield a double-pronged weapon: internal Marxism, with which to attack Capitalism from within, via the sapping of American social and political institutions; and external Marxism, in which it will associate itself with the Soviet Union and with Catholic-Eurocommunism. And it will share with its Communist partner one common goal, at least, namely the overthrow of the United States as a Capitalist military superpower.

Another and more subtle weapon will be used to attack Catholicism's religious rival, Protestantism. The first offensive along this denominational front has already been launched. It is ecumenism, which from its very beginning, coupled with Protestantism's leftist political bent, resulted in the enfeeblement of the major Protestant bodies.

The second assault will be even more insidious. It will come appareled as a pseudo-religious claim for social justice and economic equality. And it will be carried out as a programme of "progressive" Christianity, in harmony with the tenets of Marx and Lenin.

A large segment of the Protestant leadership has already embarked upon a similar programme; and it will not be difficult to enlist their support for the movement, which they will view as a common cause.

The subversion will be extended also to other levels of society, by the simultaneous use of cultural penetration, political fifth columnists, and ideological cells.

The top leaders of both Marxism and Catholicism are consummate masters in all three activities. Their success in the use of such techniques in Africa, Asia, Latin America, and Europe are impressive. In the United States, although seemingly confined to the ethnic and racial minorities, they have already achieved astonishing results.

Large sections of the press, television, radio, and the publishing medium in general, as well as the educational areas − high schools, colleges, and universities − are already thoroughly infused with disguised forms of Marxism. All these diverse "reforms," if despoiled of their American-style semantic trappings, will prove to be no different from their Russian and European counterparts. Indeed, American Marxism could prove to be even more dangerous than the others precisely because of its democratised form.

Yet, should the opportunity arise, American Marxism will prove to be as prone to violence as the traditional Communist parties in other countries. It could be even more violent, given the well-known national inclination towards violence in the United States. Workers, blacks, student minorities, and women will all be exploited as ruthlessly as have been their counterparts in Europe, Asia, and Africa, the better to undermine the democratic edifices of North America. The Catholic Church will help. Her adoption of an Americanised Marxist interpretation of certain Christian tenets and papal dicta such as those to be found in the encyclicals of Popes John and Paul and no doubt of other popes, will give religious validity to her programmes in the eyes of millions of American Catholics.

The nominal Catholic population of the United States is approaching fifty-five millions. While this is a numerical minority, fifty-five million Americans, many of them in positions of influence, could be a formidable minority if they supported Catholic Marxism. The vast network of the Catholic Church could provide a most efficient vehicle of subversion throughout the United States.

Such a network, buttressed by religious, social and cultural pressure groups, could interpenetrate the most sensitive and the most influential strata of American society. The White House, the Senate and the House of Representatives, already responsive to a Catholic lobby, are the most obvious examples.

Even left to itself, a Catholic-Marxist minority would represent a potent political force. If directed by the Catholic hierarchy, however, it would become a decisive factor in shaping the American future.

It is always possible, of course, that if an official Vatican policy of leftist politics is imposed upon the faithful in the United States, it could mean a split in the American church, from top to bottom, since a large proportion of U.S. Catholics, far from accepting the implantation of Catholic Marxism, will remain staunchly anti-Communist on patriotic, ideological, and economic grounds. The omens are already in evidence, and they should be interpreted. There are indications that the Vatican has already taken certain steps aimed at smoothing over such a division in the American church, or, indeed, of preventing it altogether.

The nomination of some bishops and even cardinals with ambivalent ideological tendencies and an unconvincing eagerness for social reforms, has already pointed the way. The traditional anti-Communist prelates are quietly being replaced by new, socially conscious ones. The latter's alertness to racial and economic injustices is the best guarantee that the Marxist reorientation of the Church will be acceptable to them. Religious and hierarchical pressure will do the rest.

Should the current Vatican strategy succeed, an even wider section of the U.S. church will be gently nudged towards the gradual acceptance of Catholic Marxism as practiced in Europe. This would mean the creation of a revolutionary minority which would carry on their subversion against American democratic institutions, disguised as a religious group exercising their rights under the First Amendment to the U.S. Constitution.

Religious fifth columnists

The dangers of religious Marxism is that, in cooperation with secular American Marxism, it could lead many believers to become, wittingly or unwittingly, fifth columnists. Thus, just as non-Catholic Marxists use their Communist Party cells as a focal point for action, the American Catholic Marxist clergy would use their pulpits for the same purpose.

To talk about Catholic fifth columnists sounds discriminatory. Yet, one generation ago, Catholic minorities helped to destroy democratic Europe. This they did by cooperating with Hitler. They helped Hitler because they were fired with ideological zeal, that is, by anti-Communism under the anti-Communist Pontiff, Pius XII. Perhaps a succinct list of concrete examples will help to prove the validity of this assertion.

Hitler came to power in 1933. In 1934, he attempts to incorporate Austria into the Third Reich and murders pocket dictator Dolfuss. Austrian Catholics and the Vatican hierarchy begin secret negotiations with the Fuehrer.

In 1935, Hitler gets the Saar with the support of Catholics. Mussolini begins the Abyssinian war, with the blessing of the Church.

In 1936, Hitler occupies the Rhineland and, again with the full support of the Catholics. Mussolini unleashes a full-scale war in Africa. A Catholic junta helps to launch the civil war in

Spain. The Vatican asks Catholics the world over to support Catholic General Franco.

In 1937, Hitler disrupts Austria with the direct help of Catholic Seyss-Inquart, the Home Secretary, and Franz von Papen, another devout Catholic; and of Cardinal Innitzer.

In 1938, Hitler annexes Austria. Cardinal Innitzer welcomes der Fuehrer to Vienna as a man of divine Providence. Hitler then turns to Czechoslovakia. Again, aiding him from within the country are Catholic supporters. The Sudeten Germans help Hitler carve his first territorial slice off the Republic.

The Munich crisis. A Catholic priest, Msgr. Tiso, in direct contact with the Vatican, cooperates with Hitler in the final disintegration of the Republic. In 1939, Hitler occupies Czechoslovakia and Msgr. Tiso becomes Chief of State of Catholic Slovakia. Albania is attacked by Mussolini. The Vatican protests because the attack is carried out on Good Friday. The Spanish Republic is overthrown; the Vatican gives solemn thanks to God. Poland is invaded. Beginning of the second World War. Cardinal Pacelli becomes Pope Pius XII.

At the bloody invasion of Poland, Holland, Belgium, and France, except for a few innocuous words of sympathy with these countries, Pius XII says nothing against the invading Nazis.

Again, who were gathered inside the Trojan horses to help Hitler topple the political and, yes, even the military structures of Belgium and France?

Once more we find individual Catholic leaders, or Catholic groups intimately connected with the hierarchies and therefore with the Vatican and Pope Pius XII. In Belgium we find Leo Degrelle, the Catholic Fascist leader; we see a cardinal counseling the Belgian King, and thus deciding the fate of the country.

In France, we meet a papal knight, Pierre Laval; a Jesuit-trained general, Weygand; and another prominent Catholic, Marshal Petain.

When finally Hitler attacked Russia, Catholic volunteers from all the Catholic countries rushed to the Russian fronts with the blessing of the Church.

If activist Catholic minorities contributed to the disintegration of European democracy, an activist Catholic minority could do the same in the United States. Instead of contributing to the establishment of a right-wing extremism, however, this time they will aid the establishment of a Catholic-Marxist America.

This speculation may be rejected as improbable, given the temperament of the majority of American Catholics. Yet the echoes of a Catholic-Fascist, anti-Communist partnership, no matter how minimal, occurred in the United States before and after World War II, as we have detailed in the foregoing pages.

In the fifties, Jesuit Father Edmund Walsh at a dinner party in Washington suggested to Senator Joseph R. McCarthy that he ought "to do something about the danger of Communism in the United States."

What followed is history. Yet, it must be borne in mind that American society still harbours within itself unlimited raw material for the recruitment of ideological intolerance and also for the enlistment of storm troopers, whether Nazi or Communist.

Extremism, under one guise or another is potentially possible in the United States, as it has been elsewhere in the world. Senator McCarthy managed to mobilise compact minorities via ideological motivation. Their activities formed an embryonic movement which, had the historical circumstances been favourable, might have led to a full-fledged programme of violence.

Unpredictable events in the near future could produce a political climate which might be conducive to implanting a so-called Christian Marxism in America. Recent developments in the social, political and religious fields all point in that direction.

To minimise the influence of the Catholic Church because of the difference between American and European Catholicism, both in numbers and in ideological outlook, is a gross error. The more so, since past history has taught us that during periods of stress or national crisis, the balance for or against a given political or social policy can be tipped by the added weight of religious or political minorities.

A precedent of the kind has already occurred in the United States during the past century. And although the alternative in that case was religious rather than ideological, it was nevertheless the equivalent of what the country might experience in decades to come.

The situation arose during the American Civil War. The Catholic Church, although then a tiny minority in the United States, supported the South against the North. The Vatican's reasons for aiding the secessionist side merit a brief examination.

The Catholic claim to America

It must never be forgotten that the Catholic Church maintains long historical vistas. One of these, so far as the Western Hemisphere is concerned, is that the whole of North America should by historical right, be Catholic. It was initially stolen from her by the heirs of the Reformation, that is, by the Protestants.

There is a firm historical foundation for such a claim. It must be remembered that the Americas originally were put on the map, not by Protestants, but by Catholic discoverers and navigators. The Americas should be under the jurisdiction of the Catholic Church for the same reason that, say, Australia, which was discovered and colonised by Protestants, has remained under the Protestant British umbrella to this day.

In 1493, only one year after the discovery of America, Pope Alexander VI, as Vicar of God, to whom belonged the entire earth, granted the New World to the Spanish Sovereigns, proclaiming that all lands discovered and to be discovered west of a line one hundred leagues beyond the Azores belonged to Catholic Spain. "We of our own motion, and by the fullness of Apostolic powers," he proclaimed, "do give, grant and assign to you, your heirs and successors . . . all the firm lands and islands found or to be found, discovered or to be discovered, towards the West and South, drawing a line from the Pole Arctic to the Pole Antarctic, that is, from the North to the South."

The Church's original programme called for Catholicizing the entire Western Hemisphere. These were not fantasies, but well-calculated plans. Most of them were promoted by nations subservient to the Catholic Church — first, by Spain, second by Portugal, and third by France.

When Protestant discoveries and explorers from countries such as England, Holland and others, landed in America, the Catholic Church set in motion a new grand strategy to prevent them from gaining a firm foothold. The Spanish Empire became the cutting edge of her plan. The commercial and colonial rivalries of England and Spain did the rest.

The inevitable decline of Spanish power in the New World prior to, during, and after the American Revolution, compelled the Vatican to adopt yet another operational design.

The birth pangs of the American Republic were watched with careful attention. These were considered at once as providing a golden opportunity for the progress of Protestant England and therefore the Protestantation of the newly-born United States of America. Once deprived of a strong protecting power like that of England, the Church reasoned that an independent America would be less antagonistic to the establishment of Catholicism.

This would be especially true if its independence had been obtained with the help of Catholic powers, like France, which indeed it had.

Hence the Catholic policy of encouraging the American colonies to free themselves from Protestant England. Franklin and the other founding fathers, therefore, once the Catholic help had been received, obliged the Vatican by permitting it to establish a Catholic hierarchy on American soil. A small payment for the effective help given by Catholic France, with the approval of the Vatican.

The establishment of a Catholic hierarchy, however, did not immediately prove strong enough to stem the tide of Protestant expansionism on the new continent. The young nation was seized with a fever for acquiring new lands. The Louisiana Purchase, if it appeared to be a bargain for Napoleon, was a veritable heaven-sent gift to the United States. With its acquisition came a taste for annexing even more non-Anglo-Saxon territory. Within one generation, the voracious appetite for more space resulted in the seizure of the Mexican territories of Texas and California. From the Vatican's point of view, these dominions, which previously had belonged by divine right to the Catholic Church, had made the United States a territorial colossus which, unless stopped, could transform the whole of the North American continent into a Protestant stronghold.

This meant that besides crippling the growth of a strong Catholic presence in the New World, that of Protestantism would be virtually unlimited. Since the American Revolution, Protestant sects had multiplied with the fertility of Biblical mushrooms.

It was clearly in the interest of the Catholic Church, then, to intervene in the American Civil War. A territorial split into two separate, sovereign nations would have likewise halved the Protestant establishment. Although the Vatican no longer had at its disposal the Catholic Spanish empire, or Catholic France to act on her behalf, she still retained one major weapon, namely her diplomatic influence in Europe.

Examined within its historical context, the Church's grand strategy will thus be seen to be quite logical. When the Spanish empire had collapsed, the ecclesiastical monopoly of the Catholic Church in those lands formerly under the rule of Spain, collapsed with it. The Church's monolithic influence, which had stretched from the tip of South America to the northernmost point of California, was fragmented. Catholic hegemony was likewise fractionised and enfeebled, both denominationally and politically.

The same formula would have applied to Protestant America, if the South were victorious in the Civil War. The diminution of U.S. stature would have spelt the automatic diminution of American Protestantism. This in its turn would have permitted the potential expansion of Catholicism in two smaller countries where Protestantism would no longer suffocate a young Catholic Church.

Publicly, the Vatican maintained a posture of neutrality. Behind the scenes, however, her activities were anything but neutral. While issuing pious words of regret the Pope and his advisers were preparing to aid the Confederacy in its fight against the North. One day, to the surprise and anger of the Union Administration, but to the jubilation of the Confederate States, Pope Pius IX addressed a letter to the President of the Confederacy:

"To Jefferson Davis, President of the Confederate States of America, Richmond:

"We have just received with suitable welcome the persons sent by you to place in our hands your letter dated 23rd Sept. last [1863]. Not slight was the pleasure we experienced when we learned from those persons and the letter with what feelings of joy and gratitude you were animated, Illustrious and Honourable President, when you were informed of our letters to our venerable brother, John, Archbishop of New Orleans; and John, Archbishop of New York, dated 18th October of last year. . . "

After expressing hopes for peace, the Pope concludes thus:

"It is particularly agreeable to us that you, Illustrious and Honourable President, and your people, are animated by the same desire for peace, etc."

"Given at Rome, St. Peter's, 3rd October 1863."

The supreme importance of the papal letter was not its message, but the fact that the Holy See had recognised Jefferson Davis as the President of an already sovereign new nation sundered from the Union. The Pope made the Church's official position clear by addressing him as "Jefferson Davis, President of the Confederacy States of America.

This meant that in the eyes of the Vatican the United States had become *two nations.* Pius IX in fact referred in his letter to the United States as "these countries," that is, the country of the North and the other country of the South — a *fait accompli.*

The Pope's avowed support for the Confederacy had widespread results both within the two warring factions and outside as well. Dudley Mann, a prominent Confederate diplomat wrote:

"The influence of that measure [the Pope's letter] on our behalf is *incalculable."* (Italics ours).

'Formal and complete" recognition

Mann, in his letter addressed to J.P. Benjamin, then Secretary of State for the Confederate States of America, described the effect of the papal recognition thus:

"In all intelligent British circles, our recognition by the Sovereign Pontiff is considered formal and complete . . . It is believed that the earnest wishes expressed by His Holiness will be regarded as little less than imperative commands by the vast portion of the human family which esteem him as the 'Vicar of Christ.' "

In another letter, dated March 11, 1864, also addressed to Benjamin, Mann declared: "To the immortal honour of the Catholic Church, it is now engaged in throwing every obstacle that it can justly create in the way of the prosecution of the war by the Yankee Guerrillas. . . "

He then goes further, referring to the direct connections which the Confederacy had with the Vatican. He reports that he had talks, not only with the Vatican Secretary of State, but also with the Holy Father himself. As a result of these colloquies he says he has entertained a confident belief that there will be a marked reduction in the number of foreign recruits for the Union armies.

To correctly evaluate the weight of the Pope's support of the South, it must be viewed in the light of the military situation of the time — the moment when the fate of both the North and the South were in balance.

During the first part of the Civil War, the forces of the Union had been tremendously hard-pressed by the Southern armies. The latter at one time appeared to be on the crest of victory that would lead to final success.

Such an ultimate victory would have spelt but one thing — the emergence of an independent second nation, the Confederate States of America.

The grave significance of the Pope's letter was also noted, with anxiety, by no less a personage than Abraham Lincoln, who commented:

"This letter of the Pope has entirely changed the nature and the ground of the war."

William Henry Seward, Lincoln's Secretary of State, spoke in a similar vein. "The design of this quasi-recognition of Mr. Davis, who is thrice addressed as 'Illustrious and Honourable President,' is manifest," he declared. "It is a last effort to get up some feeling against the North among the Catholics and to use perhaps the influence of the Holy Father to stop his Irish votaries from volunteering."

The need for volunteers was acute. The losses at the battle of Gettysburg alone, if one considers the size of both sides, were enormous. It was a disaster for North and South alike. The Union army lost more than 23,000 men; the Confederate forces even more, about 30,000.

It was at this juncture that the Pope intervened once more in an effort to tip the balance in the favour of the South. Not on the battlefield, to be sure, but in ways just as effective, even if more subtle. Moreover, it was the kind of intervention which could be repeated today or tomorrow in America.

The effectiveness of the Vatican's secret machinations is something which has escaped the notice of politicians in the past, no less than those in our own day. Yet examples of its concreteness abound everywhere, including the United States.

In another instance of the Church's effort to artfully aid the South, the hierarchy was active, *sub rosa,* in the mobilisation of American Catholics against the military machine of the North. This was done by organising the great Draft Riots in New York.

Being the master of indirect, covert manipulation, the Church employed racial and other factors to achieve its objectives. Here it promoted the real or imagined grievances of the Irish by mobilising them against conscription of men deemed necessary for the urgent strengthening of the Union forces.

It is significant that it took the Catholic Church, on the spot, only ten days after the battle of Gettysburg (from July 13 to July 17, 1863) to attempt to sabotage the North in order to help the Confederates with whom the Vatican was openly sympathising.

On the 23rd of December in that same year, and only one month after the Pope had written the letter to Jefferson Davis, General Rufus King, the new American Minister, arrived in Rome. In a letter which he wrote to State Secretary Seward, dated 15th January 1864, he related a significant remark made by Pope Pius IX.

"The Pope," wrote Gen. King, "after referring to the intervention in the Civil War, made the following comment: "As to intervening in your affairs, I have no weapon left but this pen.

"The Pope admits that his pen had the power to intervene," Gen. King continued. "It was the only weapon he had available to do so, so he himself states."

Gen. King then relates how the Pope had repeatedly stated that the Vatican would not intervene in the Civil War. "He had

had notice after notice that the United States Government could not accept intervention; and that he had, just thirty-six days before, used that pen to write to Jefferson Davis, "Illustrious and Honourable President,' which was in effect both *recognition and intervention,* and was designed *to prevent enlistment* of Roman Catholic Irishmen in the Union armies, as well as to get them to *desert.* The Vatican in fact managed to get them to do both, since many Catholics refused to fight for the North. Thousands of others deserted altogether."

The papal pen had proved more helpful to the South than if the Pope had sent whole battalions into the field.

The truth of this assertion is clearly evident in the following statistics:

Enlishment 1861-1865 in the Northern Armies

Native Americans	1,523,000	Percent:	75.48
Germans	177,800		8.76
Irish	144,200		7.14
British-American	53,500		2.60
English	45,000		2.26
Other foreigners	74,800		3.76

Desertions

Germans 16%
Native Americans 0.5%
Irish 72%
All others 0.7%

The above figures indicate that out of every 10,000 Irish enlistees — almost all Catholics — there were over 33 times as many desertions as among all the other groups put together.

The point to be made here is not only the historical one — that the Vatican intervened in the agonies of the American Civil War — but that, in a different context and in a different way, it can do the same in today's conflicts, be they military or political. And even more so in the future.

A Catholic-Marxist Trojan Horse

Catholics in the United States, as well as elsewhere in the world, can and will obey the dicta of future Pontiffs, as they have done in the past.

This observation is even truer in our time than in the past, since contemporary popes, by sponsoring doctrines which are socially subversive, but wrapped in Catholic demands for economic and social justice, are in effect fostering a form of socialism which could be a greater menace to the traditional American ideals than the Vatican's support of the South in the past century.

If, during the American Civil War, the Vatican could exercise an influence in the internal affairs of the United States, quite disproportionate to the number of Catholics in America at that time (less than 6% of the total population), what could it do now with fifty-five million faithful, or more than a quarter of the country's total population?

It is a considered question worthy of a carefully considered answer: unprejudiced, concrete, and precise. For, notwithstanding arguments and protests to the contrary, the Catholic Church is not just another American denomination, a mistaken idea most U.S. Protestants have accepted since the advent of ecumenism. The Roman Church is still as peculiarly unique to herself as ever.

Today, the Marxist-orientated encyclicals of the Supreme Pontiffs can inspire millions of American Catholics, even if reluctantly, to accept subtly subversive tenets that are anathema to traditional and cherished American polity.

Add to that the radical forces, both secular and Protestant leftist, at present working towards the same political ends, and it will be seen that capitalist America is in actual danger of real distintegration.

In the days to come, a serious dilemma will confront loyal, patriotic American Catholics — at least those who are sufficiently educated and aware of the covert political attacks being made upon their country's government and institutions under the guise of religion. They will have to re-examine their allegiance to the hierarchy of a Church which has been allied with a subversive ideology — Communism.

This could not be otherwise, because in future the teaching of their Church will no longer be inspired by a single Gospel, but by a hybrid one, consisting of the Gospel of Jesus Christ, grafted to the Gospel of Karl Marx.

The outcome hangs in doubt. Many American Catholics, if given the hard choice between the new Catholic Church (so alien to the Church of their upbringing) and allegiance to their country and the ideals it represents, might well rebel against Rome, just as Archbishop Lefebvre and his followers have done.

A too progressive Vatican, forcing the issues too fast and too soon, could thus precipitate a schism in the American Church as deep if not deeper than the political split between the country's North and South in 1860.

The Vatican is well aware of this danger and is promoting a policy of exceptional gradualism and subtle ideological circumspection.

The possibility that the "progressive" elements of the Catholic Church, acting as a colossal Trojan Horse, could be used to weaken the internal stability of America, is not a flight of alarmistic fantasy. Nor is it an unjustified political speculation. For, if and when Europe has been transformed into a solidly Marxist-Catholic orientated continent, the double pressure from a combined Euro-Soviet political system could compel the Church to overstep her original, self-imposed strategical limits vis-a-vis the United States.

That would spell open conflict.

The United States, surrounded by Marxist continents and Marxist nations, will then have to cope not only with a Communist-dominated world outside its borders, but also with the two most expansionistic doctrines of the century from within as well — Marxism and Catholicism, allied.

The signs are already there for all to see. Europe is becoming more Marxist motivated every day. Black Africa has become a boiling cauldron of Communist dictatorship in action. Asia, encompassing almost half of mankind, is already largely Marxist. Latin America is swinging from the juntas of the extreme right to the juntas of the extreme left.

The failure of several left-wing dictatorships in South America should not encourage complacency. The efforts will be repeated as they are being repeated now in Asia and Africa. And with each coup, the Communist conspiracy is gaining strength.

If the past is an indication of the future, Marxist Cuba — securely planted at the doorstep of the United States, and allowed to take firm root there — is a portent of things to come for the whole of the Western hemisphere.

Marxist Cuba was conceived and brought to birth by distant Soviet Russia, which has sustained that offspring ever since. Cuban guerrillas and military ventures directed at setting up Marxist regimes in Africa, the Middle East, and elsewhere, were but the forerunners of similar ones to be established in Latin America when the time is ripe.

It is not owing to a fortuitous whim of history that Cuba is the most militarily powerful Communist administration in the Americas, nor that she remains under the direct protection of the Russian nuclear umbrella. Neither should it ever be forgotten that it was Marxist Cuba which brought the United States and Soviet Russia to the very brink of nuclear war during the missile crisis of 1963.

Today, the outlook for America is even darker when viewed objectively and apart from the cheerful optimism with which Americans face the future, even when such optimism is least justified.

Unless events of extraordinary magnitude occur, and assuming that Europe has finally become a Catholic-Communist dominated continent; and further, that successive American administrations continue to belittle the internal danger of political and politico-religious subversion, then the approaching decades will surely witness one certain event — the steady decline and the eventual collapse of American civilization as we know it today.

CHAPTER 33

The U.S., The Vatican, The Future Wars Of Religions, And Armageddon

By the time Christ was born, the world population had reached 300 millions; by 1850, one billion; by 1925, two billions; by 1965, three billions; by 1975, four billion. Now the current increase is 200,000 a day. By the year 2000, in less than two decades, it will be between 6 and 7 billions. The population of the Americas will increase in proportion with that of the world. Latin America, however, will outgrow that of the U.S., not only in numbers, but also in that of religious affiliation. Half of the total Catholic population of the entire world will be next door to the U.S. in Central and South America.

The number of Catholics, however, will increase also inside the U.S., but disproportionally to the numerical strength of non-Catholic North Americans. Such disproportionate Catholic growth will be due, not so much to the efficient masterminding of the native Catholics via denominational education, birth control and the like, but to another no less alarming factor, immigration; by legal and illegal infiltration.

Immigration helped to build the U.S. Immigration out of control, however, might help to destroy it. This is happening now, via the lawful and surreptitious intake of more and more bands of immigrants, which the U.S. appears unable to contain. Most of these are Catholic orientated. It cannot be otherwise, since most come from Latin America. The borders of California, Arizona and Texas are violated daily by large numbers of would-be immigrants, while others enter from Cuba, Puerto Rico, Haiti, and similar areas via disembarkation from the sea.

Latin America has unlimited potentialities as a human reservoir. Its current emigratory pressure has already reached alarming proportions. In the future, unless checked, it might become unstoppable.

Mexico for instance, with a population of about 60 millions, is expected to double itself within the next 20 years. At the current level of one million per year, the general emigration to the U.S., account already for 50 percent of the annual U.S. population growth.

The significance is portentous, about 70 million more people to the U.S. population in less than 50 years.

The Catholic orientated intake within the general immigration, when added to the natural growth of U.S. born Catholics, will disrupt the whole denominational pattern of traditional North American protestantism. It will do even more, and once it has been co-ordinated with the pressure exerted from outside, that is by the Latin Catholic giant south of the border, the Catholic influence upon U.S. affairs will be irresistible.

The potentialities of such massive internal and external Catholicity are staggering, from a radical alteration of the policies of the Americas, to a general denominational de-establishment of the whole Western Hemisphere. The ultimate result of such shifting of the balance of denominational power will be that the ultimate arbitrator of the American continent will be no longer Washington, but the Vatican.

That would apply also to the U.S. itself, because a massive Catholic population within the U.S. borders would accelerate a further Catholicisation of North American society. This would spell, beside the end of a Protestant orientated culture, also the end of traditional North American liberalism. The supremacy of a Marxist orientated Catholic Church would bring with it the implantation of neo-Marxist tenets within the economic-social structures of America. Chief amongst these would be the abolition of private property in accordance with the Marxist interpretation of the Gospels and the Catholic intepretation of Marx.

The operational introduction of such neo-Marxist Catholicism would spell the total collapse of the U.S. as it is today.

If the past be an indication of the future, then the prospect is ominous for the U.S. as well as for the whole of the American hemisphere, namely the ultimate subservience of U.S. Catholicism to the Vatican.

The Vaticanisation of the U.S. would dictate also the ideological allegiance of every U.S. Catholic, and with it, that of every non-Catholic individual, by persuasion if possible, by legislative coersion if resisted. Should that ever occur, then the entire U.S. would become a Vatican domain. The warning of Abraham Lincoln: "I can see a very dark cloud on our horizon, and the cloud is coming from Rome," when assessed against the potentiality of a U.S. Catholic domination, could prove to have been a prophecy rather than a warning.

If the double-headed ideology, emblazoned by the cross, the hammer and the sickle, should ever come to control the U.S. and Latin America, the Vatican could truly mobilize the whole of the American continent for its own end. Such leverage could be beneficial to a U.S. objective, if in agreement with the Vatican; but calamitous, if in opposition. In the eyes of the Vatican, alliances are struck to benefit exclusively the Church, and not the Church's lay partners. The discarding of the Vatican-Moscow alliance and its replacement with the Vatican-Washington alliance is the most striking example of this dictum.

In a future test of strength therefore, it is possible that the U.S. would be reduced to the role of a junior partner if pressured by a Vatican with a wholly Catholicised Western Hemisphere behind it.

The Vatican, Zionism and Islam

The plausibility of future discord between the Vatican and the U.S. is more than a possibility. It is a certainty, since global forces outside their control will pull them asunder. Discord is the forger of economic, ideological, and military alliances and counter-alliances, and thus potentially the breeder of wars. In our century, wars have always fostered communism. World War I produced communist Russia. World War II produced communist China. World War III will produce a communist Africa, a Communist Europe and a Communist Latin America. So far two global wars and sundry regional wars have resulted in almost two billion human beings having found themselves under communist rule.

The Catholic Church, well aware of this fact, and even more ominously having convinced herself that the future belongs to a world dominated by left wing ideologies, has already prepared to meet the challenge. She has done so by producing her own version of Marxism under the aegis of the cross and the hammer and sickle identifiable with her new Marxist Catholicism currently seen operating in Latin America.

In the days to come, however, how will she behave vis-a-vis other global forces pulling divergently with religiously oriented movements inspired by messianic visions? The question is a factual reality which has already become an intrinsic part of the contemporary scene via Zionism and Islam, two spiritual intangibles with whom communism, the Catholic Church, and the U.S. have become deeply involved.

Unlike other global lay movements, Zionism and Islam are particularly perilous because of their peculiar claims that they are the fulfillers of some unique divine missions directly connected with territorial and political expansionism.

Zionism, the ideological face of Judaism, is the embodiment of Hebrew mysticism. It aims at the re-establishment of the ancestral home of the Jews; also at the racial, religious, and cultural cohesion of Judaism, the preliminary conditions necessary for the forthcoming advent of the Messiah.

Islam's messianism is its identification with Islamic society. Hence Islam's mission is to protect the territorial rights of the Islamic nations. Currently that includes Palestine, the historic home of the Jews, the present State of Israel.

The conflicting claims of Zionism and Islam have already provoked global commotions. These have affected Christian nations, most of whom have nothing or little to do with the messianic objectives of either. Yet these Zionistic and Islamic operations have already helped to destabilise the face of the contemporary world.

Thus, whereas Islamic influence stretches from China to India, to the Middle and Near East to Africa and beyond, that of Zionism operates mostly in the West. Its main center is the U.S. where it can exert a pressure out of all proportion to its numerical strength.

Zionism's identification with the U.S. has involved her in deadly confrontation with Islam's 750 millions, across three continents, linked, even if tangently with the U.S. enemy, Soviet Russia. The Zionism-Islam confrontation can cause the world economy to collapse, as it did in 1973 when they fought yet another Middle East war. The Arabs used the oil weapon in retaliation against American support for Zionism, exacerbated by the U.S. decision to airlift arms to Israel, and to vote her 2 billion dollars credit in the very middle of the fight. The conflict initiated a global recession.

Crises of such magnitude take mankind a step nearer to World War III.

The Vatican, seemingly above the claims of both Zionism and Islam, will side with one or with the other, as long as it can help to further the expansion of the Catholic Church in accordance with its traditional policy of political opportunism. As we have seen in the recent past, when it allied itself with Soviet Russia and then with the U.S., so in the future, it will side again with one or the other. It will do the same also with Islam or with Zionism, and indeed with any other convenient global ideology or world religion.

The involvement of three great world faiths with rival superpowers, and their identifications with the latter territorial and ideological objectives, will transform a future World War III into a sectarian global holocaust.

If to Zionism, Islam, and Christianity there be added Chinese neo-Marxist Buddism, then their conflicting messianisms will truly turn the earth into the greatest sectarian battlefield which the world has ever seen.

How involved will the Vatican become with these rival religions and their allies, each claiming it is their duty to destroy their rivals in the name of civilization, and indeed, in the name of God?

What will the popes say or do when chemical warfare will be decimating whole continents, when nuclear weapons will atomize entire nations or when orbital space complexes capable of launching laser beams will incinerate the great metropolises of the earth, beginning with Washington, Moscow, Mecca, Jerusalem and Rome?

What then will be the role of the papacy?

An ancient prophecy of St. Malachy foretold that the papacy will end for good by the end of this century. Following the present Pontiff, there will be only another two popes, after which the papacy will be no more. (1)

It will be no more, because Armageddon would truly have come, and with it perhaps the final collapse of the political and spiritual power of the Catholic Church.

(1)St. Malachy lived in the 12th Century. He identified the future popes with latin mottos. Pope Paul VI: Flos Florum (flower of flowers). He had three lilies on his coat of arms. John XXIII, the Patriarch of Venice: Pastor et Nauta (sheperd and mariner). Pope John Paul I: De Medietate Lunae (of half moon). Pope John Paul II: De Labore Solis (eclipse of the sun). After him Gloria Olivae (the glory of the olive) and Petrus Romanus (Peter the Roman). After that, says Malachy, Rome will be destroyed and the Day of Judgement will arrive.